YOU SHOULD BE
DANCING
MY LIFE WITH THE
BEE GEES

DENNIS BRYON

FOREWORDS BY

Andy Fairweather Low

AND Zoro

ecw press

"How does it feel to know the whole world was dancing to your beat?"

— Bee Gees fan to Dennis Bryon

FOREWORD by
Andy Fairweather Low

When Dennis asked me to write the foreword for his book I thought, *Well, of course he would.* Typical of me: I was the self-absorbed, self-obsessed lead singer in Amen Corner, the band we were in together all those years ago. And it's not like Dennis isn't aware of my many faults. Yet despite them, he wanted me to write this. That's Dennis.

Recently, I saw some super-8 footage of Amen Corner when we lived in London in the late sixties filmed by Neil, our guitar player. Boys-being-boys stuff. With the hindsight of more than forty years, I can see clearly that Dennis was the heart and soul of that band. I had always felt we could be a band — a *real* band — but Dennis was the one who decided it was going to be fact.

I will always remember how I first met Dennis. I was lucky enough to see him in a great band in 1965: Brother John and the Witnesses, one of *many* great Cardiff bands. When I was looking to form Amen Corner, Dennis was my first choice as drummer. It was a time when drummers were actually required to *play*. And yep — he could play. (Unfortunately, the same cannot be said of much of today's Pro Tools generation.)

As a band, we had a residency at a fantastic late-night club in London, the Speakeasy, which was the *best*. Jimi Hendrix was a frequent visitor, and one night he borrowed Neil's guitar, turned it upside down, and started playing with us — and Dennis stepped up to the plate, straight away. I know that despite my aforementioned quirks and faults, Dennis and the band tolerated me — for whatever reasons. And I am very, very grateful to them. Dennis got to deliver his dream from Cardiff, Wales, to the U.S.A. with one of the biggest-ever bands in the world. That wasn't by luck, and it wasn't an accident. You cannot survive in the music business by luck. Not as a player.

I miss Dennis (he now lives in America, and I in the U.K.), but his memory and presence stays with me. And we do get together now and then. We recently met for a band-reunion meal in Cardiff — a curry, of course.

We were boys in a man's world, a long time ago. What a joy . . . what a joy . . .

Love you, Den.

Andy Fairweather Low

Lead singer and founder of Amen Corner and Fair Weather. Session musician for Roy Wood, Leo Sayer, Gerry Rafferty, The Who, Joe Satriani, Roger Waters, Eric Clapton, Ronnie Lane, Dave Edmunds, Bill Wyman, and George Harrison.

YOU STEPPED
INTO MY LIFE
FOREWORD by
Zoro

> *"A life is not important except in*
> *the impact it has on other lives."*
> — Jackie Robinson

You should be dancing!

Why?

Because nothing brings joy to the human spirit quite like dancing. The desire to dance is written into the genetic code of every human being, and life gives us many reasons to dance.

Have you ever given thought to what prompts us to dance in the first place?

It's called rhythm. And behind all of those beautifully crafted rhythms is a drummer. The role of a drummer in all cultures is the same — to create a groove, a pulse, a special magical feel that inspires people to move their bodies and feel a passion and vibrancy for life. Drumming is a noble and culturally important calling. Without the cadence of drummers from every tribe and tongue, the world would be a terribly unexciting place.

Life has a rhythm to it, and *You Should Be Dancing* recounts the rhythmic journey of a great drummer. Since the mid-1970s, Dennis Bryon's hypnotic drum grooves have been responsible for luring much of the world's population onto the dance floor. Dennis accomplished this incredible feat by playing on one of the best-selling albums of all time — the iconic *Saturday Night Fever* soundtrack. Released in 1977, the double album received a Grammy Award for Album of the Year, and the music on it became a phenomenon that changed the cultural landscape, prompting more people to enroll in dance classes than ever before in history.

Saturday Night Fever featured some of the most memorable songs in pop music history. Bee Gees anthems such as "Stayin' Alive," "Night Fever," "Jive Talkin'," "You Should Be Dancing," "How Deep Is Your Love," and "More Than a Woman" all bore the imprint of Dennis's undeniable feel.

Equally so, the drum part he played on "Nights on Broadway," from the 1975 Bee Gees' album *Main Course*, was incredibly infectious and so "in the pocket" it felt unreal. It remains one of my all-time favorite grooves.

On top of playing such beautifully crafted drum parts as "Fanny (Be Tender With My Love)," Dennis pushed the known musical boundaries with the highly innovative 32-note hi-hat pattern he played on the bridge of "Love You Inside Out." It is one of the hippest drum parts ever created, and it really blew me away when I first heard it. The song reached number one on the Billboard charts in June 1979 and was just one of the many musical gems that sprang from the Bee Gees' *Spirits Having Flown* album.

I also have great personal reason to thank Dennis. Whereas countless drummers would cite the names of Buddy Rich, Gene Krupa, Ringo Starr, John Bonham, or Keith Moon as their greatest influences and the reason they picked up sticks in the first place, for me it was the grooves Dennis played with the Bee Gees that beckoned me down the path to becoming a drummer. His drumming made an indelible mark on my soul and set my feet dancing, which I did plenty of in those days. It also birthed within me the desire to become a professional groove drummer and play in the R&B style that Dennis had done so successfully.

When I started playing the drums back in 1977, the Bee Gees dominated the airwaves. The group penned great songs that featured catchy melodies and beautiful, warm harmonies. Intoxicating rhythm tracks were combined with crisp horn parts and lush string arrangements — all played by real musicians in real time.

This vibrant and heartfelt music was recorded prior to the technological revolution that would destroy the art of live recording and open the floodgates of mediocrity for amateurs and novices to permeate the music industry. In those golden days of recording, a drummer needed to play in real time throughout the entire track with no computer or Pro Tools software to fix mistakes. You had to *really* play!

Dennis *really* played. He served the Bee Gees well with his tasty musicianship, and he did all of this at such a young age, playing with the restraint and maturity of a much older player.

To underestimate Dennis's contribution to drumming would be a grave mistake. His renowned grooves have affected every generation since. You'd be hard pressed to find a teenager or young adult today who hasn't heard the songs Dennis played on. They've become a part of the fabric of modern pop culture. And it's important to note that Dennis is the only drummer in history, other than Ringo Starr, to have five songs on the Billboard Top 10 chart simultaneously. He played on nine number one records, plus countless hits that spent a total of 188 weeks on the Billboard Top 100.

His accomplishments are truly epic.

For years, I had wondered about Dennis and his whereabouts. Then in 2014, something came over me — I needed to meet Dennis in person. I wanted to pay homage to the man whose drumming meant so much to me.

I started my quest by replaying all the records Dennis had ever played on. I played them over and over — reliving those special moments of my youth. The effect of those grooves had in no way diminished. If anything, I came away with an even greater appreciation for that music. Dennis's drumming and the warmth of analog recordings came through clearly, infusing me with a new respect, particularly since the world is so inundated now with synthetic music and cold digital sounds.

After I'd drenched myself in the spirit of Bee Gees music and all the great grooves Dennis had played on, something welled up within me. I felt something almost spiritual drawing me to him and believed a guiding force would eventually lead me to him. I started searching the internet for anything that might help me locate this man.

As life would have it, I discovered that he lived only a few miles from me in Nashville, Tennessee. I laughed and contacted Dennis via email. He graciously responded, and we set a time to meet the following week. I purposely avoided talking with him by phone at that point, because I wanted to save any talking for when we were together in person.

I was nervous prior to meeting Dennis and wondered what this drum hero of mine would be like. But the moment I walked up to him I could sense a genuine warmth. He gave me a bear hug and we clicked instantly, as if we were long-lost twin brothers separated at birth who were finally reunited. We immediately engaged in effortless conversation and found ourselves talking like old war buddies for more than three hours.

There is an unspoken brotherhood in the world of drummers, and as a breed we bond like no other musicians I know.

At the conclusion of our time together, Dennis said meeting me was like catching up with an old friend he had known all of his life. We were kindred spirits, and I felt the same. I left that first meeting feeling much like a child who got the Christmas present he'd always wanted. I had waited a lifetime to meet Dennis, and it seemed that life had come full circle.

Prior to our meeting, Dennis had taken the time to review many of my drum performances. He told me when we met that he "absolutely loved" my drumming. To think that the drummer I emulated as a young man would one day say he loved my drumming was almost too much for me. I can't think of anything that gives a musician more satisfaction than meeting a musician who inspired and influenced him — and then having that musician pay him a big compliment.

In real life, Dennis proved to be a beautiful person with a big heart. Gracious, kind, generous, and affirming. I now understood more of why he had played so beautifully on all of those records. It was because he was truly a humble man with the heart of a servant. That's always a recipe for a great groove drummer, because it's virtually impossible to separate a person's spirit from the way he plays an instrument.

Through his musical contributions, Dennis has positively impacted the lives of millions of people and brought to them the unspeakable joy that comes from the magic of rhythm. He is one of the unsung heroes of the groove who, so far, has not received the fame due him as a drummer. I sincerely hope that will change with *You Should Be Dancing*. Time has a way of setting the historical record straight, and it's only right to honor those who have laid the foundation for so many others to build upon.

Dennis Bryon truly lived the dream! Now he comes out from behind the shadow of the drum throne to take center stage and grant us an all-access pass to his utterly fascinating adventure.

I truly hope you enjoy this book!

> *"What you leave behind is not what*
> *is engraved in stone monuments,*
> *but what is woven into the lives of others."*
> — Pericles

Zoro

Zoro is the world-renowned, award-winning drummer for Lenny Kravitz, Frankie Valli & The Four Seasons, and Bobby Brown. He is the author of *The Big Gig: Big Picture Thinking for Success* and *The Commandments of R&B Drumming* series (Alfred Publishing).

"That's when
I knew it was big."
— Dennis Bryon

I moved from the U.K. to America with the love of my life, my girlfriend Jenny, and our German shepherd, Babet, in 1978. *Saturday Night Fever* was already out in England, but it wasn't as big yet there as it was in the U.S. I had just bought a beautiful Spanish house on Miami Beach for cash. And not just any house: a house on North Bay Road, *the* place to be on Miami Beach. Biscayne Bay was in my backyard, I had my own dock for fishing, downtown Miami was four miles straight across the Bay, and . . . the Concorde flew over my house every day. We had the most amazing sunsets every single evening.

I had just bought a car back in England, prior to moving, a new BMW 320i, and it would take about six weeks to ship. One day the dock master in Miami called and said, "Mr. Bryon, your car has arrived." Thrilled, I said, "Great, I'll be right there!" Jenny didn't drive or own a car so I took a taxi the five miles or so to the docks. As we drove over the massive Julia Tuttle Causeway leading to the mainland, I took a deep breath as I tried to take in how my life was changing.

After I filled out all the paperwork and thanked the people in the office, I got in my new car and started driving back to Miami Beach. I'd been to Miami countless times recording and performing, so I knew my way around pretty well.

In the car there was a Blaupunkt radio that had five presets, three FM and two AM. The first radio station I came to was playing "Stayin' Alive" by our band, the Bee Gees. So I saved it to the first preset and kept tuning. The next station I came to was playing "Night Fever." So I saved it to preset number two and continued tuning. The next station I reached was playing "More Than a Woman." I saved it to preset three and switched over to AM. I had to go a long way down the radio but eventually I found a music station that was playing "Jive Talkin'." I saved it to preset four and kept dialing and — sure enough — I came to a station that was playing "How Deep Is Your Love" from *Saturday Night Fever*. I saved it to preset five. I remember thinking how incredible this was and I wondered if "Stayin' Alive" was still playing on preset one. I quickly hit the button and wouldn't you know it . . . they were still playing "Stayin' Alive."

Five radio stations in and around Miami . . . *all* of them playing songs by the Bee Gees from our most recent album, *all at the same time*.

That's when I knew this record was big. *Very, very big.*

This was unreal. But how had this happened? I was just an average kid from Wales who had a little luck with a boy band during my teens . . . well, *big* luck with the boy band Amen Corner in the U.K. and Europe. And suddenly it's *happening again*, but in the *United States*, the place where every British musician *dreams* of making it.

The old cliché warns: be careful what you wish for. I had no idea where this was going, only that I've always been lost in my dreams — as a child in school, throughout my early life, and when I'd played with Amen Corner. Now, suddenly, I was *in a dream again*! But sometimes dreams become nightmares . . . before turning back into dreams.

This book contains the story of my life — all of it — up to now: prior to the Bee Gees, with the Bee Gees, and beyond the Bee Gees. I've lived long enough to know what it's like to walk into a dream . . . then watch it disappear and *return* . . . over and over again.

CHAPTER 1 All Because
of Arthur

"A GUITAR PLAYER? THEY'RE TEN A PENNY!"

I was born on April 14, 1948, to Ronald William Bryon and Iris Lillian Bryon in Cardiff, South Wales. Along with my sister, Carole, I grew up in a bed and breakfast; that was all I ever knew. My father had a second job at Rhoose Airport just outside town, where he supervised the parts department.

Before he would head off to work, my father would get up and start making breakfast for the guests: sausages, bacon and eggs, and so forth. When he got halfway through preparing the food, he would hand off cooking breakfast to my mother, because he would have to leave for the airport at 7:30 a.m.

At the same time, I'd be getting ready to go to school. I would get dressed, fix my own breakfast, and slip out the front door at around 8:15 a.m., without getting in the way of my mum or the guests.

But school was hard for me; I couldn't concentrate. I was always gazing out of the window — daydreaming and looking at the slate roofs across the street — and the next thing I'd know I'd feel a piece of chalk bounce off my head: "Bryon! Pay attention!"

I often look back to a chance conversation I had with one of the boarders staying at our guest house when I was fifteen years old. It was a conversation that would change my life forever. It was 1963, and The Beatles and the Stones and all the London and Merseyside groups were never off the radio. It was a musical explosion. I spent all my time tuned to the radio. I couldn't turn it off.

We also had a few television shows dedicated to music. The biggest was called *Top of the Pops*, which came on every Thursday night. I wouldn't miss that show for anything, and as I watched the groups perform, I dreamed of playing in one. My love of music had become so deep that I was no longer satisfied just listening to it. I had to become *part* of it.

So a few school friends and I planned on starting our own group. Since Christmas was approaching, I asked my parents for a cheap guitar and a small amplifier as my main present. A couple of weeks before the holiday, my dad took me down to one of the local music stores, Barratt's of Manchester, where we dealt with one of the owners, Ray Barratt. Neither my dad nor I had the foggiest idea what we were doing, but with Ray's help we settled on a black Burns Bison guitar and a small Watkins Dominator amplifier.

Then, one morning, with only a few school days left before Christmas, I came downstairs as usual and walked through the dining room on my way to the kitchen. I saw a man sitting at the dining room table. He had his back to the wall, but his face was hidden behind a newspaper. As I walked by I politely said, "Morning . . ." It was a rule — Dad made sure I was always polite to all the guests.

From behind the newspaper the man grunted back, "Mornin'."

My mother was in the kitchen, putting away the dishes she'd just washed and dried. She pulled me aside and pointed back to the dining room. "He's a *musician*," she whispered. This was astounding, as Dad never rented out a room to the wild riffraff that he perceived all musicians to be.

On a typical day, I'd stay in the kitchen to eat my breakfast. But not this morning . . . this man was a *musician* and that changed *everything*.

I had to go talk to this guy. He was a *musician*, and *I* was going to be a musician.

After I dished up my breakfast, I went into the dining room and sat down opposite the man behind the newspaper. As I looked above the paper, I could see a plume of blue smoke going straight up and clinging to the ceiling. I took a deep breath . . .

"Mum says you're a musician."

There was a pause.

"S'right."

A longer pause.

"I'm gonna be a musician," I said.

Even longer pause.

Finally, "Oh yeah, what kind of musician you gonna be?"

"I'm gonna be a guitar player."

Short pause.

"A guitar player? They're ten a penny!" he barked from behind the newspaper. Then *thump!* Everything on the table rattled as he slammed the newspaper down.

This was the first time I got a look at the man's face. His hair was slicked back and he wore black-rimmed glasses. A cigarette hung from the corner of his mouth. I was amazed because the ash at the end of the cigarette was at least an inch long. And it didn't break off, either, as he looked me dead in the eye and forcefully said, "No, it's a *drummer* you want to be . . . *not* a guitar player!"

A drummer? I thought to myself. I never even listened to the drums. I had only paid attention to the guitars and vocals.

The man took the cigarette from his mouth and flicked the ash into an ashtray next to his empty plate and half-empty cup of tea. He didn't take his eyes off me as he placed the cigarette back in his mouth and put up the newspaper between us again.

I looked around and saw my mother appear at the kitchen door. She looked at me. I frowned at Mum and shrugged. Mum went back into the kitchen.

All of a sudden there was another *thump* as the man slammed the newspaper to the table again. He stared right into my eyes with that

*One of my earliest school photographs. Mum went crazy when she saw
I had dipped my finger into the inkwell.*

cigarette hanging from the corner of his mouth. He started to nod his head "yes."

"OK . . . who's your favorite group?" he asked.

Well, that was easy. I was convinced in my own mind — and knew for certain — that very soon I was going be the third Everly Brother. It was a no-brainer; The Beatles and most of the other groups on the radio were singing three-part harmony. Soon The Everly Brothers would be into three-part harmony, too, and I would be that third harmony.

"The Everly Brothers," I responded.

"Right," he said. "The next time you listen to your Everly Brothers, listen to the drums. You're going to be very surprised." Then, once again, he disappeared behind the paper.

I was such a huge fan of theirs. I would sing the third harmony to all their songs. I knew every single sound on their records. Everything, that is . . . except the drums.

Mum appeared in the kitchen door again and reminded me I was close to being late for school. I took my plate to the kitchen, grabbed my coat and satchel, kissed Mum goodbye, and walked back into the dining room.

The man gently lowered the newspaper and took the cigarette from his mouth. As he stubbed it out, he asked, "What's your name, son?"

"Dennis."

"Nice to meet you, Dennis," he said, holding out his right hand.

As we shook, the skin on his hand was as hard as steel.

"I'm Arthur, Arthur Dakin. And whether you're going to be a drummer or a guitar player, *heaven forbid*, just make sure you're a great one."

That day at school I was completely distracted by my conversation with Arthur. I couldn't wait to get home and play my Everly Brothers records to see what Arthur was talking about. Finally, late in the afternoon, I made it home and to our front room. It seemed to take forever for my record player to warm up, but finally I got the hum. The first single in the pile was a song called "Temptation."

Right off the bat the drums were incredible. The song started with just the drummer playing a rhythmic pattern, even before the vocals started. When the vocals came in, the drummer played beautifully to everything

The Everly Brothers sang. I'd played "Temptation" a hundred times before. How come I'd never heard the drums until now? I couldn't wait to play another song. The next record in the pile was "Cathy's Clown," another one of my favorites. I couldn't believe my ears: the drummer did it again. He started off with a really unusual pattern, but it fit perfectly with the song and the vocals. When the song got to the next section, he played another completely different part but it sounded exactly appropriate to the song.

I played "Lucille" and could not believe how powerful the drum pattern was. Then I played "Walk Right Back," "So Sad," "How Can I Meet Her," and "Crying in the Rain." I was totally blown away. I'd never been inspired like this before. I couldn't stop listening to the drums. Arthur was right. My life was changed.

Through the front window I saw my dad pull up and park his car outside the house. I was totally spellbound in that room, listening to my records. As Dad passed the front room, he opened the door a little without coming in.

"*Turn it down!*" he shouted and carried on through the dining room and into the kitchen to see Mum.

After about half an hour, my mother opened the door and told me dinner was on the table. I turned off the record player and went into the kitchen. Dad was sitting at the table and Mum was standing at the sink.

"Mum, Dad, guess what?" I said excitedly.

"Go on," Dad said in an indifferent tone.

"I don't wanna be a guitar player anymore."

"You don't . . . Why not?" Mum asked.

I looked at my dad and thought I saw a tiny smile of relief on his face.

"*I want to be a drummer!*" I proclaimed as I sat down next to my dad.

His head dropped. He closed his eyes and let out a sigh of frustration. "You've been talking to that bloody musician haven't you? I knew I shouldn't have let him stay."

Dad had only two rules that applied to the guests who stayed with us. Rule number one: only English was to be spoken at the breakfast table. Dad didn't think it was appropriate for people to speak in a language that others at the table couldn't understand.

Rule number two (which was really rule number one): *No musicians!!!*

Every time Dad let a musician stay they would always — without fail — come in drunk or stay up late drinking alcohol in their rooms, disturb the other guests, lose the front door key and get Dad up in the middle of the night to let them in, or leave in the morning without returning the front door key. They were always trouble and my dad just wouldn't put up with it. I couldn't figure out why he had let Arthur stay.

"Yeah, his name's Arthur and he straightened me right out. Guitar players are ten a penny, and playing the drums is where it's at, so I'm gonna be a drummer!"

Mum went over to the oven and opened the door. She reached in and brought out my dinner that she had been keeping warm.

"How long is Arthur staying?" I asked.

"Oh, he's not, love," Mum answered. "He's gone back to London; he was only in town for the day. He rehearsed with the orchestra at the New Theatre this afternoon. He's playing in the Christmas Pantomime on Boxing Day. He's going to be staying with us again over Christmas. Your father only let him stay because he couldn't find anywhere else."

Nearly all the B&B's in Cardiff were closed over the Christmas holiday. Most people considered Christmas a time for family, not work. This was the very first time I could remember anyone staying with us at Christmas.

The following Saturday, Dad took me back to Barratt's, where again we met with Ray.

"We've come to change the order. He's changed his mind. *Now he wants to be a drummer*," Dad said aggressively.

"We always need good drummers," Ray said with a smile. "What you need is a good starter kit."

I looked at Ray. "What's a kit?"

"That's a set of drums — that's what we call drums in the business."

Ray took us to the drum room at the back of the store.

MY VERY OWN KIT

Finally it was Christmas Eve, and late on that cold, wet afternoon there was a knock on the front door. It was Arthur.

"Hi, Arthur. You'll never guess what!" I said.

"You're gonna be a drummer."

I was stunned. "How did you know?"

"You listened to your Everly Brothers records, didn't you? You listened to the drums."

"I love the drums. Not just on The Everly Brothers records but on *all* my records."

"What kind of drums are you getting?"

"Olympic. No toms . . . I'll get them next year."

"Good. Olympic's a solid make and you don't need toms yet. They'll come when you're ready."

That's exactly what I wanted to hear. I helped Arthur carry his bags up to his room, then he went down to the pub for a drink and something to eat.

Early the next morning, Christmas Day, I got up before it was light and came downstairs. In the darkness of the hallway outside the front room stood a small table. On the table was a tray and on the tray was a single crystal sherry glass and a fancy bone china plate. Upon the plate were two small aluminum pie tins. Every year, without fail, Dad would leave a glass of sherry and two homemade mince pies for Santa. And, as usual, it was obvious that Santa had paid us a visit, because the sherry glass was empty and the mince pies were gone.

I entered the front room and stopped to look at the Christmas tree, which was set up in the middle of the bay window. The curtains were drawn and the room was very warm. Dad always left the Christmas tree lights on every Christmas Eve and Christmas night. I squinted to get the full effect of the colored lights. The room was filled with peace and warmth and the gentleness of Christmas.

As I walked farther into the room, I noticed a stack of new presents under the tree. I didn't turn on the main room light, so as not to wake anyone in the house. The smell in the room was festive: a mix of live Christmas tree, wrapping paper, and the highly polished lacquer finish of what could only be my new drums.

To the right of the fireplace and next to the tree, there was a large dark shape on the floor. I walked closer and could now see the shape was covered with a large white bed sheet. I gently pulled away the sheet and there they were in all their magnificence: my new Olympic drum set . . . my very own "kit."

I reached for the sticks, which came in a long, narrow cardboard box, as did the brushes. I opened one end of the box and slid the sticks down and out toward me. I took the sticks in my left hand and discarded the packaging. I split the sticks between my two hands. It was my first time holding a pair of drumsticks and it felt right. This was one of the many moments in my life that was *magic*. It was this moment that I became a drummer.

I quietly played the sticks on the carpet and stared at the drums in front of me. I wondered where these drums would take me . . . where they would lead me.

The next thing I knew, the door opened and the light came on in the room. The light was blinding, so I put a hand in front of my face. It was Carole. She had come down to check on her presents under the tree.

"You got them," Carole said as she approached my drums. She picked up the brushes on top of the snare drum and started to open the box. "What are these?"

I stood up and snatched the brushes away from her. "Don't touch my drums!" I shouted.

Then I heard a door open in the hall outside. My parents' bedroom was the middle room next door, between the front room and the dining room. There was my dad in his pajamas.

"Come on, you two, it's four o'clock in the bloody morning . . . you're waking the whole household. Go back to bed."

I stood up and grabbed the tuning key that was sitting on my snare drum. I made sure Carole left the room before me so she couldn't touch my drums. As I walked past Dad, he told me he had talked with Arthur, who had promised to help me set up the drums before he went to rehearsal. I went back to bed, but I couldn't sleep. I was too excited, knowing my drums were really here.

Next thing I knew I was waking up and it was nine o'clock in the morning. I hoped it hadn't all been a dream. I looked over to the nightstand and there, by my side, were my sticks, brushes, and tuning key. I jumped out of bed and went to the bathroom for a quick wash and to clean my teeth. I quickly got dressed, grabbed my sticks and brushes, and went downstairs. I entered the front room and, in the clear light of day, there they were.

DADA MAMA . . . DADA MAMA . . .

Somebody had put the white sheet back over the drums. I removed the sheet and folded it up. Then there was a knock on the door and Arthur walked in. Arthur had the ever-present cigarette in his mouth, a cup of tea in one hand, and an ashtray in the other.

"Merry Christmas, Arthur . . . I got my drums!" I shouted.

"Merry Christmas, Den . . . Oh boy, they *are* nice."

Arthur showed me all the parts of the bass drum and the bass drum pedal. He showed me how he tuned his bass drum and how to set it up properly. Then he did the same with the snare drum, hi-hat, cymbal stands, and cymbals. The last thing we set up was the stool. Finally, I was ready to sit down at my drums.

"How do I hold the sticks?"

"For right now, it doesn't matter; just hold them in the most comfortable way. Hold them between your forefinger and thumb, like this."

Arthur came over and demonstrated. He told me not to panic and to play along with my favorite records. Everything would come in time, he said — just have fun, be patient, and practice.

"Let me show you something you can practice to get started," he said, smiling.

I got off the stool, handed Arthur the sticks, and he sat down. He started playing some incredible rhythms. I didn't understand what he was playing, but it made me grin from ear to ear.

"Right, this is what I want you to practice," he said. "The proper name for this exercise is a double stroke open roll, but for simplicity and ease of memory I call it the Dada-Mama roll. It's easy to play, with practice. The right hand gets two beats and the left hand gets two beats and then you speed it up, just like this."

Arthur hit the snare drum two times with the right stick, then two times with the left. Then he started calling out the beats as he hit the drum over and over.

"Dada Mama . . . Dada Mama . . . Right Right . . . Left Left . . . Right Right . . . Left Left . . . Dada Mama . . . Dada Mama . . ."

Then he started to play it faster and faster, until his voice couldn't keep up with his hands. What I heard next was something I'll never forget. He played that roll so fast, so perfectly, and so beautifully, it sounded just like steam under pressure escaping from a locomotive train. It was pure. Then he started to slow it down, until he started to call it out again. "Dada Mama . . . Dada Mama . . . Right Right . . . Left Left . . . Right Right . . . Left Left . . ."

As he finished I said, "I can do that."

And he looked at me and said, "You can?"

He handed me the sticks, and I took his place on the stool and started shouting out, "Dada Mama . . . Dada Mama . . ." just as he had done. But of course, it sounded absolutely terrible! Arthur had made it look so easy, and I was sure I could do it the first time. I could tell by his face it wasn't a pretty thing to hear, but I was young and cocky and I didn't care.

"I'll be able to do it by the time you get in tonight," I said.

Arthur looked at me and shook his head. "Yeah, well, if you *can* do it by tonight, I'll give you a fiver."

In those days, for somebody like me, five pounds was a huge amount of money. I practiced that roll all day and learned very quickly that drums weren't the easiest things to play. But it did come to me, after a couple of hours, that this drum roll wasn't about hitting the drum; it was about letting the sticks bounce. That's how you did it. You had to control the bounce. So I practiced and practiced it — all day. I probably turned that holiday into the worst Christmas Day my parents had ever had.

Later, I saw Arthur walking past the front window. I went to the door and called out to him, "Arthur, I can do it. I can do it!"

"Do what?" He'd forgotten.

"You know — the Dada-Mama roll. I can do it!"

He mumbled something under his breath.

"Come and listen!"

I sat down on the drums and started playing and calling out "Dada Mama . . . Dada Mama . . . Dada Mama . . ."

I played faster and faster, until I got so fast I couldn't call out loud, just like Arthur had done that morning. Then came the transition from the double hits to the double bounce; that was the tricky part. My transition wasn't great, but I could tell by Arthur's expression and his half smile that I'd figured it out. My roll didn't sound like pure steam, as Arthur's did; it sounded more like frothy waves breaking on a pebbly shore. Then I started slowing down just like Arthur had done. Finally, "Dada . . . Mama . . . Dada . . . Mama"

I stopped. Arthur was shocked.

"Come on . . . pay up!" I said. I held out my hand and smiled.

"No, no, no — that's not it. That was a good start, but you've got a long way to go yet. You're going to be a good drummer, Dennis, and it's because you've got heart. Don't ever lose that."

I didn't get my fiver, but the fact that Arthur said I was going to be a good drummer was worth more to me than anything I could ever earn. I never saw Arthur again, but he'd changed my life. And today I can honestly say: *It's all because of Arthur.*

CHAPTER 2 Becoming a
Real Drummer

OUR DUSTY OLD SOFA

I loved playing drums, and I quickly became pretty good. Unfortunately, living in a bed and breakfast didn't offer a lot of opportunity for practice. The house was on Colum Road, one of the main thoroughfares leading into Cardiff's city center. It's also one of the busiest. Mum used to let me practice in the front room after school, before Dad got home from work. With the noise of the traffic outside, my drums didn't seem so loud. As soon as I saw my dad pulling up outside, I would switch from my drums to a large couch next to the sidewall. I enjoyed playing on that sofa. I could hit it really hard and make very little noise. And it gave me the ability to listen carefully to what the drummers were playing on my favorite records. I would learn the parts and practice on the sofa. Then, when I was able to use my real drums, I knew exactly what to play.

Initially the plan was to get together with three or four friends from school — my mates, as we called them in Wales — and form a band. But the band thing didn't really work out. I was keen to play and getting better at the drums, but my mates weren't doing so well with their

Prince and me. My best German shepherd friend. We went everywhere together.

guitars. They got sick of practicing and sounding awful, so one by one they gave up.

Eventually, I was left with nobody to play with.

THE STRANGERS

At that time music ruled my life. I couldn't get enough. I'd go out as often as I could to watch groups perform live at dances all over the city. I didn't go to dance; I just hung around at the side of the stage, drinking Coke and watching the drummer. But there was one band, and one drummer, in particular who moved me the most. The band was called The Strangers and the drummer was a guy named Malcolm Davies. Everybody called him Mac.

The Strangers were an extremely good four-piece band. Bilgy played lead guitar and sang, Brett played bass guitar and sang some backing vocals, Roger played excellent rhythm guitar, and Mac played drums and sang some lead vocals and harmonies. The group had a huge following in Cardiff, and no matter where they played, I'd find a way to get there, even if it meant an expensive bus ride and a very long walk home.

One day I was riding my bike to Albany Road, a popular shopping area not too far from our house. Above the bicycle shop there, on the third floor, was a dance hall called the Kennard Rooms. Inside, it smelled like a combination of mothballs and furniture polish. I had only been there a couple of times. None of the top Cardiff bands liked playing there, as the sound could be quite annoying. It was a big hall, and if there weren't many people in the audience the sound would reverberate everywhere.

As I was stopped at the traffic light I looked over toward the bicycle shop and just happened to notice a big sign outside the Kennard Rooms. It read:

UNDER NEW MANAGEMENT.
THIS FRIDAY AND EVERY FRIDAY
– THE STRANGERS.

"What?" I couldn't believe my eyes . . . The Strangers, every Friday night, and this place was within easy walking distance of my house. That Friday I got to the Kennard Rooms around seven. The doors would open a half hour later, and the band was to start playing at eight. I came around the corner from Crwys Road and was overjoyed to see The Strangers' van parked outside. A queue was already starting to form, and I joined it quickly. Seven-thirty took forever to get there.

As I stood in line, I stared at The Strangers' van, an old Ford Transit that had seen better days and was covered from bumper to bumper with messages from their fans, each written in lipstick, crayon, or paint. Over the graffiti was a thick layer of road dirt and sludge, and dents and scratches riddled the bodywork. I remember thinking the van looked so cool and I dreamed that one day I'd be in a band with a van just like it.

Suddenly, the double doors to the building burst open. Standing there was the biggest black man I'd ever seen. In an enormously deep voice he shouted, "Alright . . . we're open . . . pay at the top of the stairs . . . any fighting and you'll deal with me, and that won't be pleasant . . . *Go!*"

Everybody squeezed past him and up the stairs. I gave my money to a girl at the top landing and she gave me a ticket.

The place filled up fast, and before long the temperature in the room had risen quite substantially. At the back of the room, at the top of the stairs, there was a commotion as The Strangers came back from the pub.

As they walked down the far side of the hall, bantering back and forth, some of their fans cheered and whistled. The band took off their coats and threw them in a small room at the left-hand side of the stage.

As The Strangers took their places onstage, I felt the excitement building inside me, and I had a permanent grin on my face. Bilgy, Roger, and Brett put their guitars on and took their amps out of standby mode. Mac sat down at his drums and picked up his sticks. They checked their microphones and soon they were ready to go.

"All right!" Bilgy shouted into the mic. "Everybody all right?!"

The crowd yelled back, "Yeah, get on with it!"

"Right, we're gonna do an instrumental, just to warm things up. This is a little thing we put together. It's by a Norwegian composer named Edvard Grieg and it's called 'In the Hall of the Mountain King.'"

Mac counted the song in and the place came to life. "In the Hall of the Mountain King" was a classical piece, but The Strangers gave it a rock/pop feel. Bilgy's guitar was loud and powerful as he played the complex lead melody. Brett and Mac sounded mighty as they filled the hall with drums and bass. Center stage, Roger was strumming out an infectious rhythm guitar pattern.

At the end of the song the audience clapped and yelled and whistled. Bilgy yelled out, "Anybody like The Beatles? One . . . two . . . ah-one — *Well, she was just seventeen . . .*"

The whole room erupted. Every boy and girl got up and ran to the dance floor, and the crowd's energy was overwhelming. The hairs on my neck and arms stood at attention as I watched Mac hammer out the beat and sing in harmony with Bilgy. I couldn't ever remember feeling so happy or so inspired.

As I took in the music, for the first time in my life something touched my soul and I remember thinking, *This is what I have to do, I have to play music, I have to.* As I stood there next to that stage, I didn't realize I'd discovered a path that would guide my entire life.

"HE'S WITH THE BAND"

I went to see The Strangers play every Friday night, without fail. And every Friday night, I'd stand by the side of the stage, my eyes glued on

Mac. I watched every little thing he did, and in the week that followed, I'd practice all The Strangers' songs on my drums and on the couch. I tried to play just like Mac: strong, powerful, and loud. I even tried to make the same facial expressions. He was my hero, my inspiration.

One Friday night a couple of months later, I rounded the corner from Crwys Road and was shocked to see a line of people, but no van. The bouncer was in the street looking both ways and cursing loudly. It was about 7:45 and the band hadn't arrived.

"What's happened?" I asked.

He walked past me toward the double doors. "They're fucking late," he said. "That's what happened . . . the van broke down."

He pushed me aside and went back into the building. I'd never seen him this mad; even when he was breaking up a fight he wasn't like this. Just then I heard a van come screaming around the corner. It was The Strangers, but they weren't in their usual vehicle. This van was clean and shiny; nothing like their old one. All the doors flew open at once and the band piled out. Mac ran to the back of the van and opened the double doors. In the confusion and rush to get to the gig, the vehicle hadn't been packed properly. Mac's drums came tumbling out and down onto the road. The drums had sturdy cases so the impact wasn't too bad, but this was an emergency and I wanted to help. I ran over to Mac and picked up two cases containing his small tom and the floor tom.

"Do you want me to help you carry them in?" I asked.

"Yeah, that would be great kid, thanks."

Mac picked up his bass drum and ran through the double doors and up the stairs. I followed with the toms. When we got to the top, standing there was the bouncer. He pointed his finger at me and yelled, "Where the fuck do you think *you're* going?"

Then, out of nowhere, Mac uttered the four immortal words that I'll take to my grave. In no uncertain terms, and with great conviction, Mac looked the bouncer straight in the eye and said, "He's with the band!"

I was shocked as I raised both eyebrows and opened my mouth just a little bit. But I wasn't as shocked as the bouncer, who just stood there next to the ticket girl. Mac ran to the stage, and I hesitated a little as I looked at the bouncer for approval.

"Well, go on then, you little shit," he said.

I ran to the stage and put the drums down next to Mac, who was taking his bass drum out of the case.

"I'm gonna go down and get some more," I said as I ran toward the door. The bouncer watched me all the way across the hall. As I passed by, he mouthed, "*Little shit . . .*"

I ran down the stairs, passing other band members coming up. Everyone was in a hurry. I got to the van and saw, standing on the pavement, Mac's traps case, which held all the stands and accessories needed to set up a drum kit. I tried to pick it up, and it took all my strength just to lift it off the ground. It was on wheels so I wheeled it to the bottom of the stairs. Again, I tried to lift it. From behind me came Brett, who was wheeling his heavy bass cabinet.

"I'll help you with that. You help me with this?" Brett asked.

"Okay," I replied.

Brett got on the other side of the traps case and grabbed the metal handle, while I grabbed the one on the other side. Together, we carried the heavy case up the three flights of stairs. When we got to the top, Mac was there. He took his case and wheeled it to the stage, while I went back down with Brett to help him with his cabinet. We struggled up the stairs, then wheeled the heavy object across the dance floor to the stage.

I walked over to the drum set, put together the drum stool, and handed it to Mac. Then I started pulling other stands from the open case and setting them up.

Soon the drums were all assembled and Mac did some fine-tuning. I gathered up all the empty cases and put them in the little room at the side of the stage. It was eight-fifteen and the band was ready to play.

I went back to the entrance door to pay for my ticket. When I got my money out the ticket girl said, "Oh, you don't have to pay, luv, you're with the band." She had been there when Mac had made that monumental announcement.

"Thank you," I said, and returned to the stage. *Shit!* I thought to myself, *I really am with the band.*

After the first set, everybody went to the pub for a well-deserved pint. I didn't get a chance to talk to Mac. At the end of the night, I hung around, as usual, and this time the bouncer didn't kick me out. Mac came over to me and thanked me for my help. I asked him if he wanted me to help him pack up the drums. He accepted my offer, and I went to get his cases. I opened up all the cases and lined them up in front of the stage. Everybody was busy packing things away, but Mac was in no hurry. He was at the other side of the stage, having fun with two girls.

I walked up onstage, got behind the drums, and sat down. I was sitting behind a real set of drums that had just been played by a real drummer. I didn't dare pick up the sticks or hit any of the drums. I just let my imagination take me away and there was that smile again.

Mac wasn't paying much attention to me, so I started packing up. I broke everything down and laid it next to its case. Finally, after Mac finished chatting up the girls, he came over and showed me how each item should be put away.

We both carried everything down to the van, and Mac started loading it. I went back up and helped Brett carry his cabinet down the stairs.

When everything was packed, Mac shook my hand. "Thanks for your help, man," he said. "What's your name, anyway?"

"Dennis."

"Thanks, Den. See you next week?"

"Yes, I'll be here," I said as the van drove off into the night.

The next Friday, and every Friday after that, I got to the Kennard Rooms early. As soon as the van pulled up, I'd run over and carry most of Mac's drums up the stairs. Then I'd help him set them up and put his cases away. We didn't talk much; there was a big age difference between us. I was fifteen and Mac was about twenty-three.

After a couple of weeks, I'd help Mac carry the heavy traps case up the stairs, then he'd go straight over to the pub and leave me to set up the whole kit. At the end of the night, he'd hang with the girls while I'd pack everything up, then haul it down to the van. Mac had his little roadie and I had my drummer idol.

This Friday night routine went on for months. Then came the Friday night that would change everything forever.

It seemed like just another Friday night at the Kennard Rooms. As usual, the place was packed. The Strangers had done their first set, and had just gotten back from the pub across the street. I was sitting in my usual place at the right-hand side of the stage, sipping on a Coke. Everyone took their places for the second set. I looked around at the audience, who was on the dance floor waiting for the first song to begin.

I looked around the stage, and then at Mac. Mac was staring back at me and had a very serious look on his face. I thought something was wrong; he never looked at me. Maybe something had broken and he wanted me to fix it? I stared back with great intensity.

Then he did it.

With his left hand, in which he held both drumsticks, he pointed at me. Then he beckoned to me with his forefinger.

In an instant I knew exactly what was going on. *Oh my God,* I thought to myself. *He's calling me up . . . he's calling me up to play.*

I was having an out-of-body experience.

This isn't possible, I thought. *Mac is calling me up to play. He doesn't even know if I* can *play. We've never talked about drums or playing. He doesn't even know if I'm a drummer.*

I started to panic and, in an instant, conjured up millions of reasons why I couldn't do this . . . and only a couple why I could.

Yes, okay, I know his drums well, I thought. *I've set them up and sat behind them literally dozens of times, but I've never played them. I've never even played a tom-tom. The closest I've come to playing toms is the sofa in my front room. I can't do this . . . I just can't!*

In that very same instant, I realized if I didn't get up and play now, I would *never* get up and play. This was my chance; my one and only golden chance to prove to myself that the dreams that consumed me could come true. It was my chance to prove to Mac I was a real drummer and I could play.

But it was no good. I'd suddenly become deaf and my legs wouldn't move. I couldn't get up from the chair. Mac was still pointing at me with the sticks and calling me up. But now everything was moving in slow motion. Suddenly, from behind me, I felt two hands gently push on my shoulders. The hands pushed me out of the chair and onto the stage where Mac was waiting. I looked back to see who was doing the pushing. To my astonishment, there was no one there. The pushing stopped.

"Wanna play?" Mac grinned.

"Uhh, yeah," I said shakily.

"You okay?" he asked. "You look like you've seen a ghost." Mac got up and I sat down at his kit. He handed me his sticks. I turned the sticks around backwards so the thick end hit the drums. I'd seen Mac do this a lot; it makes the drums sound louder.

"We're gonna do a song by The Beatles. It's called 'She Loves You.' Ya know it? It starts with a fill on the floor tom after a count of . . . One – two, uh-one-two. Do the fill, then some snare hits in the intro. You got it?"

"Yeah, I got it."

"And remember, I'll be right here by your side. You're gonna kill 'em, Den. Here we go . . . one-two, uh-one-two . . ."

I hit that floor tom as hard as I could, then crashed into the downbeat of the intro.

She loves you yeah, yeah, yeah . . .

I did the snare hits, just like on the record.

She loves you yeah, yeah, yeah . . .

More snare hits.

She loves you yeah, yeah, yeah, yeahhhhhhhhhh.

I played the hi-hat cymbal as loud as I could at the end of the intro. In the verse, I came down tight on the hi-hat for the hi-hat–snare drum–bass drum groove. We were now in my territory. Kick, snare, and hat! I was used to it. It was my setup at home; that's all I had to practice on. I played Mac's drums as loud and as hard as I could. There were no neighbors or guests or parents to hold me back. This is how drums should be played . . . *all-out!*

I looked over at Mac. He was singing his heart out. I looked out front and saw the backs of Brett, Roger, and Bilgy. They were playing like never before. I looked to the audience, who were dancing wildly and singing along with every word. I was euphoric, but that would change.

I suddenly realized where I was and what I was doing. I started to panic as Mac's drums began getting bigger . . . and bigger . . . and bigger. Then, I started to get smaller . . . and smaller . . . and smaller. Soon the drumsticks I was hanging on to felt like tree trunks in my hands, and I could barely hold on to them. The sound onstage was getting louder and louder. It was echoing everywhere.

I was at the place I'd dreamed of, but I was losing it. I was having a panic attack onstage. I could feel my heart beating a million miles an hour. I had to calm myself down. I kept telling myself, *Settle down, settle down, settle down.*

I looked over at Mac. He gave me double thumbs-up, which turned everything around. I started to breathe and could feel myself coming back. The drums started to shrink and, before long, everything was back to where it should be.

My God, I'm playing drums with The Strangers, I thought. *This is beyond belief.*

We were almost at the end of the song when Bilgy turned around. He was expecting to see Mac playing, but when he saw it was me his mouth dropped. He signaled to Roger and Brett to have a look. When they saw I was playing, they both did a double-take. Everybody faced front as we finished out the song . . .

With a love like that, you know you should be glad . . .
Yeah, yeah, yeah . . .
Yeah, yeah, yeah . . .
Yeah, yeah, yeah, yeahhhhhhhhhhhhhhhh.

Bilgy gave the cue and we all hit the last note together. The audience went crazy shouting, cheering, and whistling.

When they stopped, Bilgy got on the mic and shouted, "Hey, everybody! Look who's playing the drums!"

I looked out and the entire audience was staring at me.

"What's your name, kid?"

"Dennis," I said in a shy voice.

"What?" Bilgy shouted.

"His name's Dennis!" Mac yelled into his mic.

"Let's have a big hand for Dennis on the drums!" Bilgy yelled.

The next Friday, I played two songs. As the weeks went by, it became three songs, four, and even more. It got to the point where Mac, instead of standing right next to the drum kit, moved to the front of the stage. So he was the singer, and *I* was the drummer, at least for those few songs.

The great thing about this situation was, The Strangers were such a popular group in Cardiff that all the other bands in the city would come to see them play. So when they saw The Strangers, they saw me. And that eventually led to so many other fantastic things in my career. So if it wasn't for Malcolm Davies, well, who knows? After Arthur, he was my second huge break.

CHAPTER 3 Paying
My Dues

GETTING MYSELF OUT THERE

I was getting plenty of exposure in the Cardiff music scene by working as Mac's little roadie and playing onstage with The Strangers. The band wasn't limited to the Kennard Rooms, either. They played out of town most nights, then picked up another Cardiff residency at the Capitol Theatre every Saturday night. The Capitol was a huge cinema on lower Queen Street, Cardiff's main drag. Occasionally, the cinema would be turned into a venue for live concerts; it was that big. I saw The Beatles play live at the Capitol on November 7, 1964 — the only time they came to Cardiff.

As usual, I'd set up Mac's drums while he was over at the pub, and he'd later get me up to play. I met a lot of Cardiff's musicians in the Capitol basement. It was the kind of place where bands would come and hang. Most of these guys were older than me, but when they saw me on Mac's drums I got a lot of offers to play.

At one time I must have been in six or seven different bands. It wasn't hard, because we all played the same songs: covers of The Beatles, The Hollies, The Kinks, The Who, and a lot of Chuck Berry. We played whatever was on the radio. We also covered a lot of R&B, which I loved the most. Before I knew it, I was playing almost every night. And now I was working a day job as an apprentice electrician, too. It didn't matter. I was young and serious about my music, and I had plenty of energy.

And I always had money. Before long I was making more money playing drums than I made at my day job. I'd use some of the money to spoil my mother, with whom I was always particularly close. She and I were like two peas in a pod; I'd surprise her with presents when she least expected them.

MY LUDWIG KIT

Around this time, I was starting to get some criticism from my band-mates about the loudness of my drums — or, should I say, the *lack* of loudness. I learned very quickly from some not-so-subtle suggestions that "you are what you play," and that I needed new drums. I had plenty of money for day-to-day stuff, but nowhere near what it would take to get a new drum kit.

Whenever I had a problem, I would go to my dad for advice. He was always really good to me and he was smart. But he wasn't a handout kind of guy. Dad taught me that if I wanted something, I had to earn it. I had to pay for it myself. He taught me the value of things and the value of my word.

"Dad, I need a new set of drums, and I don't have the money," I said. "If I get a set on credit, will you sign the papers?"

Dad thought for a moment, and then said, "What if you can't make the payments?"

"I will be able to make the payments. With my job and the money I make playing, I'll have more than enough."

Dad took a deep breath and screwed up his mouth. For the first time in my life *I* had to give *my dad* a good talking to.

"Dad, I just want to let you know how important it is for a musician to have good equipment. You are what you play! Did you know that? A good musician can never be a great musician unless he has great equipment. It's in all the books. I mean, how can I advance my career if I don't have good equipment?"

"What's wrong with the drums you have now?" Dad replied. "Arthur said they were good and you agreed. Can't you just go and buy some . . . what are they called . . . toms?"

"Well, it's not just not having toms," I said, "it's the drums themselves. They're just, um, ahh . . . they're just not loud enough."

"Then hit them harder!" Dad shot back. "Get bigger sticks! I've never heard of drums not being loud."

Dad wasn't getting it, and I was getting nowhere fast. He took another deep breath, and that wasn't a good sign.

"I can see what's going on here," he said. "You're getting pressured into buying new drums just because everybody else says you have to have them."

"That's not it, Dad," I replied. "They'll make me play better."

"Everybody seems to think you play pretty damn good now," he said. "I don't see how new drums can make you play any better. But I'll talk to your mother and see what she thinks. Oh, and by the way . . . you *have* a career . . . it's called an *apprenticeship!*"

The next day I worked a bit of overtime, and by the time I got home my dad was already there. I walked into the kitchen. He and Mum were sitting at the table. Before I had the chance to say anything, Dad motioned, *Okay, outside.*

When we got out there, he said, "Right, sit down. We need to talk." We both sat down at a wooden table. "I've decided to sign the papers for you, but only on one condition." Dad gave a long pause. "The condition is, you give up smoking. And you give it up now, today, this instant."

I reached into my pocket and gave him an almost-full packet of cigarettes and a box of Swan Vestas matches.

"*Now* we've got a deal," Dad said as he went back into the kitchen.

The next day, during my lunch break at work, I walked down to Barratt's. In the drum room I couldn't believe my eyes. There, in the center, was the most beautiful set of Ludwig drums. My heart skipped a beat as I took in the color: Black Oyster Pearl. They were gorgeous and included a twenty-two-by-fourteen-inch bass drum; a fourteen-by-five-and-a-half-inch snare drum; a twelve-by-fourteen-inch rack tom; a fourteen-by-fourteen-inch floor tom; and a second sixteen-by-sixteen-inch floor tom. And all-new Ludwig pedals and stands. These were a drummer's dream come true. I went back into the main shop to find Ray, the shop owner.

"I want to buy that Ludwig kit in the back," I told him.

It was tough, but I kept my promise to Dad and gave up smoking. At least, until my drums were paid off.

SLOW DOWN

Now armed with the most beautiful, killer set of Ludwig drums, I was playing every night. I said yes to everybody who asked me to play. I only had one rule: there had to be a payment, no matter how small. I saved all my money and was soon able to buy a set of sturdy cases for my drums.

One Saturday afternoon, I discovered I'd made a catastrophic error: I had double-booked myself. I had said yes to one band whose gig started at six o'clock and ended at eight, and also to another group who started playing at eight and ended at ten. The problem was, the dance halls were at opposite ends of town.

I was too young to drive, and relied on the band I was playing with to pick up me and my drums at our house on Colum Road.

I told my dad about the situation and he got really mad.

"I'll help you out, but just this once," he said.

Dad drove me to the first school hall. Luckily, we finished early, just after seven-thirty. I quickly packed up my drums and threw them in the back of the car. Dad drove like a crazy man to the second hall. We arrived just after eight, and the band wasn't too pleased. With Dad's help, though, I got through it all by the skin of my teeth. But on the way home, I got a stern lecture from him. "You can't keep doing this — playing with all these different groups at the same time. You have to settle on one."

BROTHER JOHN IN MOUNTAIN ASH

I played a lot with Jeff Harrad and his group, Brother John and the Witnesses, and that's who I settled on. In this group was a guy named Derek Weaver — everybody called him "Blue" — and he was the keyboard player. That's how Blue — who later played with me in Amen Corner, Fair Weather, and the Bee Gees — first became my friend and bandmate. The other members of Brother John were Melvyn Allsopp on bass; Jack (who, onstage, called himself "Jacques") on vocals; Laurence "Laurie" Cowley on vocals, guitar, and harmonica; and Jeff on lead guitar.

I played every Saturday night with Brother John, particularly in an area known as "the Valleys." Most of the Welsh valleys were famous for their coal mines, which were, by then, mostly closed down because of the economy and the lack of demand for coal. There were a lot of "working men's clubs," as they were called, and some of them were rough — really, *really* rough. There were *lots* of fights.

One Saturday night we were playing in a small town called Mountain Ash, in the Cynon Valley, not far from Merthyr Tydfil. The venue was an old church hall, on a street corner not far from a pub. Almost all of the other Cardiff bands stayed away from this place, as it was just too dangerous. You took your life into your own hands when you played the Valleys — the guys at the dances either loved you or hated you. They'd either help you in and out with your gear or beat the shit out of you. We'd played this place many times and had no problem with the locals.

On this particular Saturday, Jeff parked the van on the street outside the building, and we started carrying our equipment in through the double doors, around the corner, and into the hall. As we entered there was an upright piano on the right-hand side. It was completely smashed up. The local guys would break the legs off wooden chairs and smash them on the piano in time with the beat of the music. That was their "fun."

At the end of the hall was a large stage about six feet high. To get onto the stage you had to go up a set of stairs next to the wall. These stairs led the way across the right side of the stage to another set of stairs that led down to the bathrooms located behind the stage.

We set up and at eight o'clock we started to play. As usual, the crowd was sparse, but I could tell we were doing well because a crowd of boys were beating the heck out of that poor piano at the far end of the hall.

We had almost finished the first set when it happened. I popped the head of my snare drum, and the skin tore away from its hoop, rendering the drum useless. The other band members looked back at me, observing the absence of the snare drum. I played the toms in the place of the snare but they didn't have the "crack" the song needed.

At the end of the song Jeff came over and asked me if I had a spare. I

LOOK!

B.J. PROMOTIONS

INVITE YOU TO

TWIST AND SHAKE

To South Wales Leading Groups

AT THE

New Institute Ballroom, Blaina

ON

Tuesday : 7.30 to 10.30.   Admission 2/6
Thursday: 7.30 to 10.30.   Admission 2/6
Saturday: 8.00 to 11.30.   Admission 3/6

Grand Opening Dance

Saturday, September 25th.

Dancing to Cardiff's Most Outstanding Group :

THE FABULOUS

Brother John and the Witnesses

20 FREE TICKETS for Johnny Kidd and the Pirates
at Abertillery on October 8th will be given away
to patrons arriving before 9 p.m.

did, so we took a break so I could change the head. The rest of the band took advantage of the break to visit a nearby pub. While I was sitting cross-legged on the stage, changing the head, a girl came up to me with her friend. She was gorgeous and slim, with long brown hair that flowed over her bare shoulders. Her contagious smile radiated from her innocent, angelic freckled face.

That was another thing I loved about playing drums: girls! They were everywhere. They loved to dance and I loved to watch them dance. But Jeff had one simple rule about girls and band members: "Leave them the fuck alone!" *Band comes to town . . . local girls start flirting with the band . . . band starts flirting back . . . local boys don't like it . . . band gets shit kicked out of them.* So my rule was "look, but don't touch."

She peered down at me and said in the most beautiful Welsh accent, "What yu do-*in*'?"

"I broke a drum skin, so I'm changing it."

She looked at the broken drumhead. "What yu gonna do with the old one? Can I have it?"

"Yeah! You can have it."

"Will yu sign it for me?" she gushed.

I reached for my stick bag and pulled out a pen. "What's your name?"

"Alice."

"That's a beautiful name." So I wrote on the plastic head: *To Alice with love, Dennis.* I handed her the broken head.

She looked at it and showed it to her girlfriend. Then she gave me the most wonderful smile and they walked away. I was instantly in love!

As I finished changing the head and tuning the drum, I couldn't stop thinking about Alice. Soon the other band members came back from the pub and we prepared to start playing. Meanwhile, at the side of the stage that led to the bathrooms lingered a group of four or five guys. One of them stood out like a giant. Something was going on with these guys. I thought a fight was about to break out. Then I noticed the giant was crying like a baby. To my shock, he turned and pointed his finger at me.

The whole band watched this commotion. Then Jeff gave me an evil look. "What the fuck did you do?"

"I don't know," I replied. But I *did* know . . .

Band comes to town . . . local girl flirts with band member . . . band member flirts back (or in this case, gives girl souvenir and, even worse, personalizes it using the 'L' word) . . . local boys don't like it . . . band gets shit kicked out of them.

The giant came onto the stage and walked up to me. He was sobbing. "You stole my girlfriend. You gave her something and now she won't talk to me." He walked back to his mates at the side of the stage.

Jeff came over and stood next to my crash cymbal. "What the fuck did you do?"

"I don't know. A girl asked for my broken drum skin so I gave it to her." I didn't dare tell him I signed it.

Jeff closed his eyes, gritted his teeth and gave me a brutal look. "Let's do something quick . . . 'Johnny Be Good' in C! Count it in!" he barked at me.

"A one – two, a one – two – three!"

Jeff came in with the guitar intro and we all started playing. I had counted the song in way too fast but it didn't matter. Everybody in the audience started dancing and the guys at the side of the stage disappeared. We finished the song and started playing another. My heart was racing, but it seemed like things would be okay. Then the guys were back, but now there were about fifteen of them. They came thundering down the middle of the dance floor slicing through the crowd.

Everybody stopped dancing as the gang stood in front of the stage staring up at us. Jeff told us to keep playing. That was the golden rule in situations like this: "Keep playing, don't stop." Then one of them came up the stairs at the side of the stage. He was a little guy, but it was clear he was the leader. He walked right up to Laurie, who was singing, grabbed the mic and smacked Laurie in the eye. Laurie fell back, holding his face. We all stopped playing. The silence in the hall became deafening as the music echoed away.

The guy came up to my kit and kicked over one of the floor toms. Then he got right in my face. "You stole my brother's girl and now I'm gonna fucking kill you." He went to the front of the stage and yelled into the mic. "This fucking dance is over! Everybody get out now."

Apparently, everybody in the hall knew this guy, because the place emptied out like water from a bucket full of holes. As for the band, they were all older than me and a lot more experienced. They instinctively started packing their gear at breakneck speed. I was breaking down my drums as fast as I could. But the faster I went, the longer it took.

The guy who'd confronted me got down from the stage and joined the mob, then looked up at me and pointed. "Outside!" Then he and his buddies all turned around and walked out.

Everything was packed up in record time, and we piled our equipment by the double doors next to that broken-down piano. Jeff yelled that he was going to get the van and Mel went with him.

Then the two brothers came back in. The smaller came over to me and said in a threatening whisper, "You're in fucking trouble, mate!"

I was standing next to my drums, which were stacked on top of each other in their cases. Suddenly, a fist smashed into the left side of my face. It knocked the sense out of me, and I fell. Luckily my drums broke my fall and saved me from hitting the deck at full force. I lay there, arms and legs sprawled in all directions.

Everything was foggy and far away. When I finally opened my eyes, a tall man dressed in black was standing over me. He wore shiny black shoes and a white collar. I was barely conscious but could see the church vicar was trying to make peace.

"Now, boys, we don't have to fight like this. Everybody just calm down and let's try to talk things out," he said in a calm, gentle voice.

The tough guy turned to him and said, "Fuck off, vicar, or you'll be next. Get out of here!"

The vicar didn't try to argue. He turned and walked out of the hall. I began to come to my senses and slowly got up.

"Oh, I'm not finished with you!" The tough drew back his right leg and was about to "put the boot in" when, to my relief, a police officer walked in. The guy turned to the cop and said, "Fuck off, Rozzer!"

The cop drew his truncheon. He started slapping his other hand with it. "Outside. *Now!*" the officer commanded.

The younger brother turned to me and pointed. "I'm gonna remember you! Any time you show your face around here I'm gonna beat the crap out of you."

The brothers walked out into the street, passing Jeff and Mel who were coming in.

"Let's go!" Jeff ordered. We threw everything into the back of the van, piled in on top of the gear, and slammed the doors from the inside. The gang was walking on the pavement ahead. As we passed them, Jeff just couldn't help himself. He loved to spray people with water as he drove by — he always had the windshield washers aimed toward the pavement instead of the windshield. When we passed the gang, Jeff let them have it. He opened his window and yelled, "Ya bunch of wankers . . . ya fucking yobbos . . . go'n fuck yahselves, ya bunch a'dickheads!"

That did it. Most of the gang ran to two parked cars by the side of the road. One of them got on a motorbike and the chase was on. Jeff was a good driver, but not a fast driver, not unless he had to be. This was one of those times. We roared down the A4059 toward Abercynon. I was in the back of the van, being thrown around along with my drums. Cases flew everywhere as Jeff steered the van around the corners. I held on and lifted one of the curtains that covered the van's back windows.

The two cars didn't look like they were gaining on us. But the motor-bike was screaming toward us. The bike zoomed by, then braked and started zigging and zagging in front of us. He was trying to slow us down so the cars could catch us.

Jeff was having none of it. "You wanna play chicken, uhh?"

When the bike swerved left, Jeff swerved right and accelerated hard. Then, as he passed the bike, he cut to the left, forcing the bike off the road. The biker recovered, accelerated, and passed us again. This time Jeff ran him off the road to the right. Then the biker got real brave and slammed on his brakes right in front of the van.

"You little fucker!" Jeff said as he slammed his foot down on the accelerator.

I was getting scared. Jeff wouldn't back down, and somebody could get hurt or even killed. The van rammed into the back of the bike.

"Jeff!" everybody yelled in unison.

The bike jolted forward violently — how the guy didn't lose it, I don't know. The collision did some damage to the rear mudguard. It got pushed forward and was scraping on the back wheel. Sparks were flying as the biker pulled to the side of the road.

Jeff rolled down his window and slammed his hand down on the horn as we went by. "Ya fucking yob!"

I kept looking back but there was no sign of the cars. When we got to the A470 Jeff slowed down and we had a peaceful drive the rest of the way home. The van stayed pretty quiet as we passed the Cardiff city limits.

Brother John and the Witnesses. Left to right: me; Melvyn Allsopp, bass;
Jack (Jacques), vocals; Laurence Cowley, vocals, guitar; Blue Weaver, keyboards;
Jeff Harrad, lead guitar.

"You all right, Den?" Jeff finally yelled back.

"Yeah."

"That'll teach you not to fuck with the locals. How's your head?"

"Sore. I think it's starting to swell."

"How's your eye, Laurie?"

"Black."

"Who's up for a curry?" Jeff asked.

Everybody agreed so we headed for The New Karachi, one of our favorite Indian restaurants. It was good to be back on friendly ground.

I should have been kicked out of the band that night, but Jeff let me off. And I learned a painful lesson I already knew. Stay away from the locals, and if I ever have to give an autograph, just write, "Best Wishes, Dennis Bryon," and never, ever use the "L" word.

CHAPTER 4 The Birth of
Amen Corner

BE CAREFUL WHAT YOU WISH FOR

Brother John and the Witnesses was my full-time band, but on occasion I would play with other people. Dave Edmunds from Cardiff had a band called The Raiders, a loud, three-piece rock outfit with Nicky Stills on bass and Ken Collier playing drums. One time Ken couldn't make a gig with The Raiders, so Dave asked me to fill in. Even in those days, Dave Edmunds was one of the best guitarists in Wales, and The Raiders were hugely popular.

I was also going out to see a lot of other live shows. I loved many Cardiff bands, but one of my favorites, besides The Strangers, was a five-piece called The Dekkas. They featured Neil Jones on guitar, Gerald Cannon on guitar, Rob Farmer on drums, Clive Taylor on bass, and Paul Rogers was their powerful singer. I'd go and see these guys play as often as I could.

There was another band I loved, too, called The Sect Maniacs — featuring a singer by the name of Andy Fairweather Low. They were a real R&B band and I loved the songs they played.

Around that time, a rumor started circulating around town: Andy

Fairweather Low was going to steal all the best players from their various groups and put together a band that would be the best band ever to have come out of Cardiff — a "super group." Everybody laughed at this rumor; we were all sure it could never happen. We scoffed at Andy because, secretly inside, we all knew we wouldn't get picked.

On a dark, rainy Sunday night, I arrived at my home on Colum Road. It was about midnight, and I had just driven back from Merthyr after spending the evening with my girlfriend, Jenny Black. I pulled up to park, but my place had been taken. In my parking spot was a large, black Wolseley sedan. I'd seen this car before, usually parked outside one of the Indian restaurants we went to after a gig.

I parked farther down the road, on the other side. I ran across the road, past the Wolseley and onto the front porch of the house. As I did, the lights of the Wolseley came on and someone inside blasted the horn. As I turned around and looked, the door opened and somebody got out. Through the rain I could see it was Clive Taylor, the bass player with The Dekkas, and he appeared to be mad as hell.

"Where the fuck you been, man?" he bawled. "I been fucking waiting here since ten o'fucking clock in all this fucking rain!"

I don't think I'd ever heard so many "fucks" in one sentence. I was completely dumbfounded and didn't understand what he was talking about.

"What you been waiting for?" I asked.

"You, ya fucker," he replied, brandishing an empty cigarette pack. "I been sitting here for two fucking hours, my fucking car's leaking, I'm soaking fucking wet, and I'm fucking outta fucking fags!"

Hmm, I thought, *Clive just broke his own record in the "most fuckings" category.*

The front door to the house opened. It was my dad. "What's all the noise about?" he asked. "And what's with the horn? We've got guests trying to sleep!"

"Sorry, Mr. Bryon," Clive said. "I was just trying to get the attention of this fucker . . . Oh, sorry, uh . . . I mean Dennis."

"Well just keep it down, will you?"

"Sorry, Dad," I said.

Dad silently closed the door behind him, and I stood there wondering what this was all about.

"Got any fags?" Clive asked.

"Yeah."

"Oh, brilliant. Let's go and sit in my car."

Clive sat behind the wheel, then reached over and unlocked the passenger door.

"So, what's going on?" I asked, sliding in and pulling the cigarettes from my pocket.

Clive lit his cigarette and took in a deep draw. He blew the smoke out and said, "You probably heard that Andy's gonna put a band together."

"Yeah, and I've also heard it'll never happen."

"Oh, it's gonna happen, alright! It's happening right now, and I'm in it. We've already started rehearsals."

"What's this got to do with me?" I asked, crossing my fingers and holding my breath.

"We want you to be the drummer. Andy wants *you*. You up for it?"

"Are you serious?"

"I'm as serious as hell. But let me tell you one thing, Den. If you say yes, you better be ready to leave everything behind. You understand? *We're going for it* . . . So, what is it, yes or no?"

Be careful what you wish for crossed my mind. I'd never understood that saying. What did it mean? If you wish for something, you obviously want it — that's why you wished for it in the first place. Why would you have to be careful? Then it struck me: If I said yes, how would Dad take it? He'd never let me go. He was adamant that I have a trade, a future, a profession. How would I tell my boss at work and all the other apprentices that I was leaving? How would I tell Jeff? The band relied on me. How would I tell my girlfriend, Jenny?

"What's the answer, Den?"

"Yes . . . the answer's yes!"

I was in a daze as I got out of the car. I didn't feel the rain as it ran down my face. Clive roared off. I let myself in and saw Dad standing in the kitchen. He threw me a towel, and I started drying myself off.

"Who was that?"

"Oh, that was Clive. He plays in a band called The Dekkas."

"What did he want? Must have been something important. He was parked there for over two hours."

"Oh, nothing important, really," I said. "He just offered me a job in a new band someone's putting together."

"Are you going to take it?"

"I told him I'd think about it."

ONE STEP AT A TIME

When I first started playing, I had dreamed about being a famous drummer in a famous band from Cardiff. Every day I fantasized about playing on hit records and performing on radio and television. Could this dream be coming true? Andy was forming a super group to "make it big," and he wanted *me* to be the drummer. Could this really be happening? But what about my job at Page and Stibbs? My apprenticeship? Jeff and Brother John? I just had to take it slow, one step at a time.

The first thing I had to do was tell Jeff I was leaving the band. I wasn't looking forward to that. Jeff would probably rip my head off or boil me in oil.

The next gig for Brother John was a Tuesday-night dance at Caerphilly Town Hall, right over the hill from Cardiff. We did the first set and took a break. I followed Jeff to a balcony that overlooked the dance floor. We sat and looked down at the people dancing.

"Jeff, I've got something to tell you. You know that band that Andy's putting together?"

"Yeah, the one that'll never exist?"

"Yeah, that one. Well, it *is* going to exist, and, Andy's asked me to be the drummer."

"Wow! What about your job as an electrician?"

"I'm gonna have to give it up. I'm also gonna have to leave the band. We start rehearsals next week. We're rehearsing every night."

I expected Jeff to scream at me, or at least throw me off the balcony, and I wasn't ready for his response.

"That's fantastic, Den. That is *really* great. It's your chance — your chance to make it to the big time. Go for it!"

"But what about Brother John?" I asked. "I hate to let you down."

"Oh, we'll get another drummer, don't worry about that. No, Den, this is your big chance, you *have* to take it."

That was the last time I ever played with Brother John and the Witnesses. It was the last time for Blue Weaver, too. Andy had asked Blue to join the new group, as well.

Apart from Andy and Clive on bass, the new super group included Dekkas' guitarist Neil Jones; Alan Jones, who played baritone saxophone; and Mal Davis, who played tenor saxophone. Blue played a Hammond organ and Leslie. It was a big, powerful band!

We started rehearsals the following Monday night. Clive had an uncle who was the caretaker of the Cowbridge Cricket Club, in the small town of Cowbridge, about fifteen miles west of Cardiff. He had agreed to let us practice at the club, as it was closed for the winter. We kept everything about the new band and our rehearsals top secret. So rehearsing in this small nearby town was perfect.

The plan was for the band to explode onto the Welsh music scene, playing rhythm, blues, and soul music and dazzling the audience with an over-the-top visual experience. On the first night of rehearsal, we set up on a small dance floor in the middle of the club next to the bar. The bar was fully stocked, but safely protected from us behind a locked metal curtain. Nobody wanted to drink alcohol anyway; these rehearsals were too important.

The set was long and complicated, and there were a lot of background vocals for Clive and me to learn. We rehearsed every night for months. Then, when we had the music down, it was time for the sax players and the guitarists to learn their stage movements. Neil and Clive waved their guitars in a series of movements — up, down, and side to side — all in perfect time with the music. Alan and Mal did the same with their saxophones, but in a different combination of moves. It was spectacular to see, and it added another dimension to the live performance. I'd never been in a show band before, and that's what this was. Andy had a vision and everything had to be perfect.

We needed a name for the band and, as usual, Andy led the way. For inspiration, he looked to a weekly dance held at the Victoria Ballroom in Canton, Cardiff. The DJ there was a guy named Dr. Rock and he played the newest soul music from America. He called his gathering "Amen Corner." Andy loved the name, and thought it would be a good name for the band, so we borrowed it.

We brought along a guy to help us with our equipment. His name was Peter Morley, but he was better known as "Rock 'n Roll." Rock 'n Roll had two further nicknames: you called him either "Rocky" or "Rock." Most people called him Rocky, but I always called him Rock.

AMEN'S FIRST GIG

Our first real show was in a small Welsh town called Skewen, near Port Talbot, the birthplace of legendary actor Sir Anthony Hopkins. Skewen had a well-known dance hall called the Ritz, and that's where we played. The Ritz had a large single stage with two huge curtains that opened from the middle outward. We were opening for Billy J. Kramer and the Dakotas, a big act from London. The group was managed by Beatles manager Brian Epstein and produced by George Martin; they already had a number of big hits under their belt.

The large curtains in front of the stage were closed, and I could hear noise on the other side. The doors were open and people were starting to come in. I returned to the dressing room to change into my stage clothes. Before I knew it, it was almost eight o'clock and the show was about to start. Except for Andy, the whole band was onstage and ready to go.

I'd been told by one of the stagehands to wait for our introduction before counting in the first song, and not to start before I saw the huge curtains move. The noise coming from the other side of the curtain was incredible. It sounded like a thousand people shuffling around, all talking at once. Then everything got quiet as the announcer began.

"Ladies and gentlemen . . . here they are . . . the band you've all been waiting for . . . from Cardiff . . . South Wales's very own *Amen Corner*!"

I heard the crowd start to scream and watched for that curtain to move. Finally, it began to open.

"One-two, uh-one-two-three-four . . ."

We started playing the instrumental intro to "MacArthur Park," and the audience went crazy. I'll never forget the wave of heat that came from the other side, once the curtains parted. It hit me as if someone had opened a furnace door. All the nasty reverberation and the echoed delay we suffered in sound check were gone, now that the hall was full of people, and it was *packed*!

I'd never seen anything like it; the place was heaving. Wall-to-wall people; they went all the way to the back and sides of the hall. And what was most unbelievable to me . . . they were all facing the stage, they were *watching* the band. I looked out on an ocean of faces.

Alan and Mal threw their saxes back and forth and up and down in unison, while Neil and Clive soulfully danced at the front of the stage. The audience was mesmerized.

We finished the intro and flawlessly went into the first song. Andy came running in from the side of the stage, dressed in his multi-colored military jacket and pants, and the crowd went wild. All I could hear was screaming. Was this really happening? The whole audience was singing along and clapping, hands over their heads. When we went into the next song they cheered and became even more excited. They really *got it*! It was almost as if they knew what was coming next. We reached the end of the medley, finally stopping at the finale of "In the Pocket." The screaming was so loud I could barely hear Andy speak.

"Thank you, Skewen! Great to be here!" Andy called from the stage. "We're Amen Corner and we're gonna do a song by the Four Tops. It's called 'Reach Out, I'll Be There.'"

Everybody in the band looked at me for the count. The audience was so loud nobody could hear my voice, so I hit my sticks together and gestured with my head while I shouted out. It may have looked silly, but it was the only way to make sure everybody got the count. I'd never been through anything like that before, and there were no handbooks to tell me what to do. I just had to make it up as I went along. We started that famous intro to "Reach Out," and the crowd got even more fired up.

It was like this for the whole set and, by the end of the last song, I felt exhausted. Andy said goodnight and thanked everybody for being such a great audience. The band put their instruments down and we all walked off the side of the stage, while the crowd went berserk. Then out of nowhere they started chanting, "Amen, Amen, Amen, Amen, Amen!"

Andy realized what was happening and quickly led us back onstage. As we walked back under the lights, the chant turned back into screams. I was amazed; I'd never played an encore before. Opening acts never get to do encores. Was I dreaming? I looked out from my drums, with the biggest smile on my face. I was in total disbelief. We all were — except

Amen Corner. Left to right: Clive Taylor, Blue Weaver, Andy Fairweather Low, Mike Smith, Alan Jones, Neil Jones, me.

maybe Andy. He had a dream, a vision, and now we were all living it. I remembered that Christmas morning, not too long ago. I remembered sitting on the carpet in front of my kit, wondering where these drums would take me. Was I about to begin the journey of a lifetime?

Soon the word got out, and it was like that first show in Skewen wherever we went. At the time, there weren't many places in Wales big enough to accommodate the crowds we were attracting, and we started running out of places to play. It was time to move to London.

I loved my job and everybody who worked at Page and Stibbs. I attended college twice a week and went to night school three times a week. I hated school when I was a kid, but I loved going to Llandaff Technical College in Gabalfa, Cardiff. I was really starting to grasp the fundamentals of electricity: where it came from and what it did. But I couldn't be an apprentice electrician and a musician, too. I had to make a choice — but there was no choice really. I had a calling. As planned, I had been taking everything in small steps. Now all those small steps led me to a very big step. I had to give up my apprenticeship and become a full-time musician.

It was Friday evening. Mum, Dad, and I were sitting at the kitchen table. Dad had just got paid and was off work for the weekend. This would be a good time for a chat.

"Dad, can we have a talk?"

"I know what's coming next and the answer's *no!*" he said. "Just get this musician thing out of your head. You're going to be a fully qual-ified electrician; you're going to have a trade and that's the end of it. The answer's no, so there's no need to talk about it anymore. End of discussion!"

"But, Dad . . . if I don't go they'll get another drummer. Please."

"Then let them get another drummer. You're not going and that's it."

"Dad, I have to be a musician," I said.

"Your mother played piano and was a teacher when she was a girl. You don't see her wanting to be a full-time musician, do you?"

Then I said something to my mother that I don't remember, and stormed out of the house, got into my car, and drove to Merthyr to be with Jenny. I stayed at her house Friday and Saturday night, then drove home late Sunday night so as not to confront my dad. This was the first time I had ever stayed out all night without my parents' permission. I let myself into the house as quietly as I could and crept upstairs to my bedroom.

Monday morning I got up early, washed, dressed, and sneaked out of the house. I thought about not going to work and just running away. I just had to be with my band. I don't know why I didn't run. Maybe because, deep inside, I felt the responsibility my parents had instilled in me. It was a long day at work.

I knew I had to face my dad at some point, so I decided it might as well be that evening. I had hoped to talk things over with my mum before Dad got home, but I found myself pulling up behind his car. He was home really early. *Maybe,* I thought, *he's changed his mind and has come home early to tell me the good news.* I let myself in and headed for the stairs.

"You . . . in the kitchen now!" my dad bellowed.

My mother was sitting quietly at the kitchen table. As I stood facing my dad, for the first time in my life he got right in my face.

"The answer's *no,* do you get it?" he said angrily. "And . . . if you ever talk to your mother like that again, I'll come down on you like a ton of bricks. Damn those drums, damn Arthur Dakin, and damn you! Now get out of my sight! Go!"

My mother started to cry as I left the kitchen. I went into the front room and sat quietly on the couch. The couch was pretty beat up from all my practicing. I looked down at my record player and my collection of singles and albums. But the last thing I wanted to do now was to listen to music. I wondered how I was going to tell Clive and the rest of the band.

Over the next two hours I gave up on my dream and a little part of my heart died. Later, there was a quiet knock on the front room door and my mother came in with a sandwich.

"I'm not hungry, Mum. I don't want it."

"Your dad and I just want the best for you, love," she said. "We want you to have a future with a good job. We want you to have security so you can provide for your family."

Being a musician was a good job and it did have a future, but there was no point in even bringing that up.

"Mum," I said, "I don't remember what I said to you that Dad's so mad about, but if it was bad, you know I didn't mean it."

"I know, lovey; sometimes things get said in haste. I know you didn't mean it. Why don't you come in the kitchen and have a cuppa tea with us?"

"No, Mum . . . I just don't feel like anything. I think I'll go to bed early."

Mum left the sandwich on the table in the bay window and quietly closed the door behind her. After about half an hour I went to bed. I couldn't sleep, though, and my mind just wandered.

Maybe it's best for me to have a trade, I thought. *Groups are failing by the thousands, and the chances of making it big are pretty scarce. But what about what happened at The Ritz and all the other gigs?*

The next thing I knew, Dad was knocking on my bedroom door.

"Den, it's seven o'clock," he said. "Time for work."

Then the reality of what was happening came back to me and my heart sank. At that time I was working on a construction site — an unfinished house — in Tonteg, a small town between Pontypridd and Taff's Well. It was January and it was freezing. There was a layer of snow outside, covering deep mud. It looked pretty, but it was nasty when you sank in it. I got into all kinds of trouble for burning empty cardboard boxes in the fireplace of that unfinished house, trying to keep warm. The electrician under whom I was apprenticed was a guy named John Hall. He had been a technician in the Royal Air Force and was always telling me stories of his escapades.

That evening, I was sitting in the kitchen when Dad got home. He walked in and, as usual, gave Mum a big hug and kiss. He looked at me and nodded. I nodded back, then looked away.

"How was work?" he asked.

I shrugged my shoulders. "Okay."

"How was the site?"

"Cold."

We ate dinner in silence. I took my plate, knife, and fork to the sink and swilled them under the hot tap water. I set them down, excused myself, and went into the front room. I didn't come out all night and nobody came to see me. The next day I spent another freezing, depressing day on the bitter cold site. It was a real slow day so John let me go home early. I was surprised to see my dad's car parked outside the house.

What have I done now? I wondered. *Surely life couldn't get any worse than this . . .*

I walked in and headed up the stairs.

"Den, your mother and I want to talk to you," Dad called out.

I walked into the kitchen. Mum and Dad were sitting opposite each other at the table. My dad told me to sit down and I sat next to my mum.

She reached under the table and held my hand. Dad looked me dead in the eyes and stared at me for what seemed an eternity.

"Your mother and I have been doing some thinking. We know how important music is to you, and that it's your dream to move to London with your group. We both decided you should follow that dream and see where it takes you. But we'll only let you go if you promise us one thing."

I couldn't believe what I was hearing. I kept perfectly quiet and Dad carried on.

"You have to promise us that if everything doesn't work out the way you want it to . . . and if that dream doesn't come true . . . and the band thing turns into a failure . . . you have to promise us that you'll never be afraid to come home."

"Dad, it's gonna work out," I said. Mum squeezed my hand underneath the table.

"Promise us."

"I promise, Dad. I promise, Mum."

Mum started crying and so did I. She put both arms around me and held me tight. "I don't want you to go, lovey, but you must."

"Come on, you two," Dad said, "less of the slop." He got up and filled the kettle with water, put it on the stove, and lit the gas under it.

"Right, that's done," Dad said. "Now let's get down to business. What about your job?"

"I'm gonna have to give it up."

"I know that. Do they know down at the firm? Have you told them?"

"No, I had to get it right with you and Mum first."

"Well, you have to tell your boss, and you have to tell him personally. Not through the foreman or one of your mates; you have to go in there and tell him face-to-face, man-to-man. Do you know how much that firm has invested in you? You've been there for almost a year, and they've been training you every single day. They're putting you through college and night school, and now you're just gonna walk away. You owe that company more than just a 'sorry, I'm leaving.'"

"Why do I have to tell him personally, Dad?"

"Because you made a decision, and a big one. Making a decision always has consequences. Making a decision on its own never hurt anybody. It's only when you act on that decision that the fun begins. Den, let me explain something to you, love. Your mother and I made a decision. Probably the hardest decision of our lives. We decided to let you go. We acted on that decision when we told you you could go. And now, your mother's heart is broken and I'm scared to death. But we made a decision and we're sticking to it. If you decide to leave your boss, you have to tell him. If you change your mind and make the decision not to go to London, then nothing's changed."

Dad was giving me a way out.

"This is a huge decision, Den. The biggest one you've ever made. Maybe the biggest you'll *ever* make. It's what we call in the grown-up world 'a life changer.' You have to be one hundred percent certain this is really what you want to do."

The kettle started to boil and Dad made a pot of tea.

"Your life is going to be full of decisions. When you act on one of those decisions, there will always be consequences. Sometimes good, sometimes bad, but you can be sure of one thing: your actions will always yield results. Be careful! And you have to know one last thing . . . No matter what happens out there, good or bad, your mother and I will always be here for you. We'll be right here." He sat back down. "Right, lecture over, let's have some tea."

The next morning, instead of driving to Tonteg as usual, I went into the office. Before clocking in I asked the foreman if I could see my boss, Mr. Christmas Page. I was led into his office and I told Mr. Page my plans. He wasn't pleased, but he didn't try to stop me. He asked me if I could work until the end of the month. I agreed. Mr. Page shook my hand and wished me all the luck in the world.

Now I had to tell Jenny I was leaving for London. After some intense words she told me I had to make a choice: "It's either me or the band," she said.

Sadly, a few weeks later we broke up.

On the last Friday I worked for Page and Stibbs, I was still on the building site in Tonteg. The day was warmer and sunny. John Hall wasn't happy I was leaving; I think he was a bit envious. At four-thirty in the afternoon, I gathered all my tools and put them in the boot of my car. I walked over to John to say goodbye. He reluctantly shook my hand, and then said, "You'll be back!"

CHAPTER 5 Amen Corner — The Big Years

THE MADISON

On a damp, misty, gray Monday morning in February 1967, Clive picked me up at my house on Colum Road. Two other band members were already in the van: Neil and Mal. I kissed my mum goodbye and gave her a big hug. She did a good job of holding back tears, wiping only one lone drop from her face. "See you soon, Mum," I said, as I walked off with my suitcase in hand. I didn't know exactly when I'd see her again; I was heading into the great unknown. It could be months. I threw my suitcase in the back of the van, climbed over the front seats, and found a spot on one of the purposefully packed speakers. There were no seats in the back of the van, so if you didn't score one of the two passenger seats up front, you were in for a hard ride.

Clive headed for Ely, a district in west Cardiff where we picked up Rocky. Then we drove on to Llanrumney to Blue's house, then Andy's. Finally, we headed out of town toward Newport. Once Alan was onboard we drove east to our destination: London.

Somebody had recommended a rock 'n' roll dive called the Madison

Hotel. Lots of bands stayed there. Supposedly it was "cheap and nasty," which wasn't a problem. Especially the "cheap" part.

We'd saved the proceeds from most of our shows in Wales, and that's how we financed everything. But that money would soon run out. Andy chose to be in charge of the cash flow. I brought a little money from home, but I had to make it last.

The drive seemed to take forever as we negotiated the boroughs and districts of London. This place was big! Finally, with the help of *London A–Z (Geographers' A–Z Street Atlas)*, Clive found the Madison.

After a couple of weeks, both money and gigs were scarce. We had become friends with some of the other bands staying at the Madison — they stepped up and recommended some agents and managers. We found an agent who was willing to work with us, and some small gigs started to come in. We'd accept anything; we needed the money to eat and pay for the hotel. We even played some weddings — the money wasn't great, but the food was. These weddings were always catered and, after the show, we'd get as much food as we wanted. That was just as well, because we were only guaranteed one meal per day and that was breakfast at the Madison.

AMEN — ICING ON THE CAKE

We started playing out of town, landing some gigs on the south coast of England. We played Portsmouth and Bournemouth and began to form a fan base. One of the bands at the Madison had a manager named Ron King; they suggested we call him. Ron ran a music company called Galaxy Entertainment, with an office on Denmark Street in the west end of London. His partner was a guy named Tony Burfield. Ron sent Tony to see us play and scope us out.

We had a return gig at the Pavilion in Bournemouth, where we'd played about a month earlier. We'd gone down so well the promoter had called our agent and re-booked us. Before the show, we were sitting in the dressing room and there was a knock on the door. Tony Burfield walked in and introduced himself.

"I've been hearing a lot about you guys," Tony said, "so I thought I'd come down to catch the show."

Tony was slim and good-looking. He was not very tall and had a permanent smile on his face. He was full of life and talked with a slight cockney accent.

We all spoke at once. "Nice to meet you, Tony."

"Yeah, and oh, by the way, nobody calls me Tony. Call me Burf."

The audience was growing impatient, and from the dressing room we could hear them chanting: "*Amen, Amen, Amen, Amen!*"

Everybody introduced themselves and we shook Burf's hand as we headed for the backstage area. We had to put on a good show — Burf had driven all this way to see us. We did our regular set, which ended, as usual, with a soulful rendition of "Gin House." We had also just learned a new song called "Amen," written by Curtis Mayfield and Johnny Pate, and tonight we planned to play it for the first time.

After the last song we walked off stage and the audience went crazy — screaming and begging for more. We came back after a minute or two and did a two-song encore. Then Andy set up the finale.

"Thank you, Bournemouth! We love you, we love your town . . . We're gonna do one more song. It's by The Impressions. It's called 'Amen.' And I want everybody to sing along with us. Here we go!"

I counted the song in and Andy, Clive, and I started to sing a cappella, "Amen . . . Amen . . . A – A – men . . . Amen, Amen."

"Come on, everybody, sing along with us!"

The band started singing the second verse, clapping along, and then the audience joined in. The whole place was singing in unison. "Amen . . . Amen . . . A – A – men . . . Amen, Amen!"

"Everybody sing it now!"

After four times around, Andy gave us a sign and the entire band came in. We kept playing the groove until Andy gave us another cue. As he did, we modulated a whole step up to another key. The audience knew what to do and it was magic. We played "Amen" for at least five minutes and the audience never stopped. Even when we finished the song and walked off the stage, they kept on singing.

After we finished changing and drying ourselves off, Burf came back into the dressing room, smiling.

"Guys, that was amazing," he said. "I've never seen anything like it. Tell you what I'm going to do." He reached down into his inside jacket pocket, pulled out a business card, and handed it to Andy. "I'm gonna talk to my partner tonight and have you guys come in for a meeting," Burf said. "Andy, call me tomorrow at two o'clock and we'll set it up."

Things couldn't have gone better. The band was tight, the show was great, and the audience was totally into it. But the new song, "Amen" (which would go on to become our signature chant), was the icing on the cake.

GALAXY ENTERTAINMENT

Andy called Burf the next day and arranged a meeting. We were to meet at the Galaxy Entertainment offices on Denmark Street in London's west-end Soho district. Denmark Street was a busy place, bustling with activity. It had lots of small shops and plenty of places to eat. There was even a music store. We found the address indicated on the business card — number seven — and went inside. It was an old three-story building with a narrow staircase on the left leading up. There were offices on the ground floor and a hallway leading to a backyard. The walls were made of paneled wood and the place reeked of furniture polish. We climbed the stairs to the first floor and went through a door marked Galaxy Entertainment.

The room was huge. The walls were covered with posters, flyers, and pictures of the many artists Galaxy represented. To the right was a large bay window that overlooked Denmark Street. In front of the window was a large desk full of papers and clutter. On the back wall was another desk, this one neat and tidy. Behind the desk was a beautiful girl with long, dark hair.

Tony Burfield came out of another office, located to the left. This office was higher up than the one we were in and had two steps leading down from it.

"Hey, guys, thanks for coming," Burf said, skipping down the two steps. He shook everybody's hand and sat down at the desk in the bay window. There was a huge commotion going on outside on Denmark Street — shouting and the blare of a car's horn.

"Oh-oh," Burf said as he got up, turned around, and looked down onto the street. "Look, there's gonna be a fucking punch-up."

We all went over to the window and looked down. Two men were fighting over a parking space on the other side of the street. One of the men was big and tall, dressed immaculately in a light tan suit and tie. He was driving a Rolls-Royce Silver Cloud. The other guy wore jeans and a light jacket. The front end of the Rolls was pointing into the single parking spot, while the other car was trying to back in. The cars were actually touching each other as they blocked the street. Things were at a stalemate. It looked to me as if the small car had been there first and the guy in the Rolls was just muscling in on the space.

Both men stood in the street yelling at each other, neither ready to give in. Then the man in the suit got back in the Rolls-Royce. I thought he'd had enough and conceded to the other guy. But no — he started the engine and began nudging forward.

"Oh, this is gonna be fucking good," Burf said, staring down.

The girl behind the desk made her way to the window, and Neil moved aside, making room next to him. They gave each other shy smiles. Back in the street, the guy in the jacket watched in horror as the heavy Rolls-Royce pushed the smaller car along the road. The sound of screeching tires filled Denmark Street, grabbing the attention of pedestrians on both sides of the road. Once parked, the guy in the suit got out of his car and approached the other guy. He got right in his face and started talking to him very calmly. The man in the light jacket stepped back and slowly turned around. He got into his damaged car and drove off.

The man in the suit went back to the Rolls, opened the back door, and pulled out a briefcase. He locked the car and made his way across the street, toward our building. Just before stepping onto the pavement, he looked up at us staring down. He mouthed "fucking wanker" and flashed the V, which, in Britain, has the same meaning as the American one-finger bird.

From outside the door I heard the sound of someone running up the stairs. The loud footsteps suggested that the person was heavy. The door burst open and the man in the suit stood there. He was a big man: tall, wide, and very clean. His powerful cologne instantly filled the air.

"Did you see that fucking guy, trying to take my fucking parking place? The nerve of some fucking people . . . Oh, sorry, love," he said, trying to mind his manners for the girl with the long hair. "Fuckin' 'ell, oo's this lot then?"

We all tried to step aside as he walked through us toward his office. He took the two steps up in one go, slipped off his jacket, and hung it on a coat rack at the end of the room. He came back and stood in the doorway, looking down on us. He was wearing a white silk shirt with big gold cufflinks. The initials RK were sewn into his shirt pocket. I couldn't help but notice how big his hands were. He wore an assortment of large gold rings on his fingers.

"This is the band I was telling you about," Burf said. "Guys, this is my partner, Ron King."

"And I'm Pauline," the girl with the black hair said as she sat down at her desk.

"Fuck me, there's *enough* of you. What — they never 'eard of fucking Durex in Wales? Shit, I'm gonna have ta order some more fucking sheep." Durex was a British brand of condom, and sheep jokes were a worn-out put-down of the Welsh people.

"Sorry, love," Ron said as he looked at Pauline. "S'all I ever do is say 'I'm fucking sorry' . . . Sorry, love," he said, looking around at us. He then stared down and looked at us individually. "What was the name of the band again? Something about a church?"

"Amen Corner," a few of us muttered in unison.

"That's it, Amen Corner from Wales. If you guys are half as good as Burf says you are, then we're gonna make some decent fucking money. Oo's in charge?"

Andy raised his hand. I was glad he was in charge and not me. Ron was intimidating.

"What's your name, mate?"

"Andy Fairweather Low."

"Fuck me, that's a mouthful. Okay, tell me who you are, one at a time, starting with you."

One by one everyone introduced themselves. When it came to Neil, he looked at Pauline and smiled. "I'm Neil Jones from Cardiff."

Pauline smiled back.

"Fuck me, love is in the fucking air. I can see I'm gonna have to keep my fucking eye on you two," Ron said. "Come on, let's go into my office and you can tell me what you've got going on."

The meeting lasted about two hours, and by the end of it, Ron desperately wanted to see us play. He told us if he liked what he saw and heard, he'd introduce us to a friend of his who worked for the William Morris Booking Agency on Oxford Street. William Morris was the biggest agency in the world, so we really started to get excited. Ron told us he ran some dance halls around London and some others farther out of town. He said if we could fill them up he'd give us a percentage of the door.

"Where are you guys living?" he asked.

"The Madison."

"Fuck me, that's a fucking hole. I have a guy that works for me. He's a paddy; his name is Danny. Lovely man. He has a house in Brixton. Let's see if we can get you guys some decent fucking digs."

Ron had us audition for him in a dance hall in Romford, a town in northeast London. It wasn't that big, but he told us he always had a good crowd. We put on our usual show, finishing with "Gin House" and "Amen." We brought the house down. Ron loved the show so much he told us afterwards he wanted to sign us to King, Burfield Management, or, as it was known, KB Management.

We were all so young, and as green as the hills we came from in Wales. We didn't know anything about the music business. It turned out we couldn't actually sign the contract with KB and have it be legally binding, because we were all too young. After some expensive contractual advice from a music attorney, we learned the only way the contract could become legal was if a parent of each member signed it. They did, and on June 29, 1967 — for the first time — Amen Corner had management representation.

The signing of the contract was a new beginning. We moved out of the Madison and into a three-story house at 70 Helix Road, Brixton South West Two. This was our first band home, and I loved living there. Brixton was a rough area, crime-ridden and full of street gangs, but there were lots of great, hard-working families there, too. The people on our street left us alone, and we became known as "those white guys down the road."

It was while I was living on Helix Road that I had a "realization moment" that will stay with me forever. I was in our local grocery store on Brixton High Street trying to find something to drink when it hit me: here I was, living in London with my band. We had a management contract, and now everybody was talking about a record deal. I couldn't believe my luck; I couldn't believe this was happening to me.

I looked around and settled on a bottle of fizzy orange pop. I paid for it and walked out onto the street. It was noisy, lots of traffic and people everywhere. I opened the bottle and took a swig. No orange pop before or after that moment ever tasted so good.

OUR FIRST RECORDING SESSION

We had a PR person who got us into all of the major pop magazines: *Mirabelle, Melody Maker, New Musical Express, Jackie, Top Pops, Record Retailer, Disc, Fab 208,* and *Record Mirror.* Our faces were everywhere, and thanks to the success of our fan club and the enormous amount of publicity we were receiving, our fan base became huge.

In 1967, the Decca Record Company launched a new subsidiary label, Deram. Ron and Tony had meetings with the heads of Decca, and we became the first act to sign with Deram. Deram assigned a record producer to us by the name of Noel Walker, and we went into the studio to record our first album.

The recording went really well. We got most of the songs in two or three takes. I always try to remember what Noel told me: it's up to the drummer to add life, personality, and especially *dynamics* to a recording.

In a relatively short time, our first album, *'Round Amen Corner,* was complete. Now it was time to promote it.

Our live performance of "Gin House" was always the song that brought the house down, so it made total sense to include it on our first album. The recording turned out so well it was decided "Gin House" would be our first single on the new Deram label. The release was heavily publicized and, because of our enormous fan base, to our delight the song made the *Melody Maker* Top 50. It entered at number forty-eight, which was huge.

One of the things you never forget is the first time you hear yourself on the radio. During the time of the release of "Gin House," we were committed to an eight-week stint at a playhouse in Great Yarmouth, booked to play there every Sunday night. Great Yarmouth is a seaside town on the east coast of England. It's only 112 miles from London, but it was a pain to get to. The road was narrow and congested and it took forever to get there.

At that time, *Pick of the Pops* was a radio show based on the current top twenty singles in the U.K. It had a huge audience. I'd listened to the broadcast every Sunday since I was a kid. Not only did the DJ play the entire top twenty — counting down from number twenty to number one — but he also played new artists who had a buzz going on. "Gin House" had just entered the top fifty, and that constituted a buzz. The record company told us the song would be featured that Sunday on *Pick of the Pops.*

That Sunday afternoon we were on that agonizing drive from London to Great Yarmouth. We were in "Proud Mary," our name for our Ford Transit van, and I was driving. The reception on the van's radio wasn't great, and we had a hard time finding the BBC show. Andy sat in the middle passenger seat, turning the dial, looking for the broadcast. With his ear to the single speaker in the center of the dashboard he finally tuned in the station.

The show had already started, but the sound was awful. It kept fading in and out and we could hardly hear it. I had to find a place to stop, but we were behind a slow driver on a two-lane road and there was no way to pass. Then I saw a break in the oncoming traffic. I dropped Mary down to second gear and pulled out. The Transit didn't handle well, especially when it was full of gear and bodies; none of us ever pushed her to the limit.

I got on the outside of the annoyingly slow Sunday driver, shifted up to third, and floored it. We were driving on the wrong side of the road, and I could see another car coming toward us in the same lane. The slow car wasn't letting me back in and the oncoming car was quickly approaching. At the last moment — when I wasn't really sure I was fully past the slow driver — I swerved Proud Mary to the left. The car ahead let me have it with his horn, and so did the car I had just passed.

In the distance I saw a road on the left-hand side. There were some trees there, and behind the trees I could see a large grassy area. I slowed down and made a left-hand turn. The radio continued to fade in and out as I pulled onto the flat grassy common.

My beautiful Ludwig drums.

I did some fancy maneuvering until I found *the* spot where the radio came in at full strength. We all piled out of the van and everybody lit up. Andy turned up the volume on the radio and the DJ said, "When we come back I'm gonna play a new release by a group that's gonna be huge. First time in at number forty-eight; this band is on a journey straight to the top. And I can say a big *Amen* to that! Stay tuned!"

"That's us, that's us, that's us!" we all yelled. "We're on next!"

We opened the doors to the van and ran around it, screaming like a pack of out-of-control children. Then the DJ was back. The iconic theme song of *Pick of the Pops* blasted through the little speaker in the dash of Proud Mary.

"Ladies and gentlemen, boys and girls, here they are . . . seven Welsh boys with a massive future . . . doing one of my all-time favorite songs . . . their brand-new single 'Gin House Blues' . . . Here comes . . . Amen Corner!"

The song started to play and we all lost it. We were lying on the grass, screaming and kicking our feet in the air like a bunch of kids who had just got the best Christmas present ever. After the initial excitement wore off, we got up and stood in two groups of four, next to the open doors in the front of the van. You couldn't wipe the smiles off our faces as we put our arms around each other's shoulders. Amen Corner was on the radio!

I'll never forget that afternoon — hearing myself on the radio for the very first time. It just doesn't get any better than that. "Gin House Blues" was going up the U.K. singles chart. Another dream was coming true.

RECORDING FOR THE BBC

"Gin House" was getting some serious airplay and we were promoting it every night with our live gigs. The record was selling like wildfire, and before we knew it the song entered the U.K. Top 20.

Top of the Pops was an iconic BBC television music show at that time, airing every Thursday night at seven-thirty. The thirty-minute show was massive and featured live performances by various artists on the Top 20 chart. The producers of the show contacted Ron King, and we were booked to perform "Gin House." This was another first for Amen Corner: *television and the BBC!*

The next day we were told to report to the BBC Television Centre on Wood Lane in Shepherd's Bush. Be there at eight o'clock in the morning, they told us, *and don't be late.*

After our rehearsal we went back to our dressing room. We had to wait a couple of hours before makeup. Finally, a producer knocked on our open door. "Are you girls ready to get *all tarted up*? I can take you down to makeup two at a time. Who's first?" Clive and I volunteered.

This was my very first visit to the makeup department, and it all felt very unnatural. When I looked in the mirror, I had a hard time recognizing the guy looking back at me. When we were done, Terry, the producer who had taken us down, led the way back to the dressing room.

Clive and I walked in together. We took some stick from the rest of the band, but we didn't get teased too badly. Terry took Blue, Neil, and Andy to makeup. It was their turn.

I decided to call home in the meantime, and I made my way to the pay telephones Terry had pointed out to me on a wall outside the dressing room. I thought I'd get some strange looks on the way, or that I might be stared at, but the people at the BBC were used to seeing others in makeup, so I just blended in. The phones had small wooden privacy screens between them, and there was a large telephone directory attached to a chain and hanging from the wall next to the phones. I picked up the receiver on a phone at the end of the row and dialed zero.

Click! "Hello, this is the operator speaking. How may I help you?"

"Hi, I'd like to make a reverse-charge call, please."

I dropped a six-penny-bit into the slot on the phone. The coin triggered a switch that activated the dial tone.

"What is your name, the name of the city, and the telephone number you are calling, please sir?"

"My name is Dennis and the number is Cardiff 26277, please."

"Please wait while I connect the call. Thank you."

Dad answered the phone. "Cardiff 26277."

"Good afternoon, sir, this is the operator. I have a reverse-charge call from Dennis in Shepherd's Bush, London. Will you pay for the call?"

Soon I was speaking to my dad. "Hi, luv," he said. "What's going on? Are you at the show?"

"Yeah, Dad, it's fantastic. It's just like it is on television. But it's a lot smaller than it looks on TV. We've done one rehearsal, and we have to do one more before the show. It's going to be on live at seven-thirty. And Dad, guess what?"

"What?"

"I'm wearing makeup."

I could hear my dad laughing. *"He's wearing bloody makeup."* Then I heard my mum and sister laughing out loud.

"Dad, how's everything at home?"

"Everything's good here, Den. Don't you worry about a thing, luv. Just concentrate on your performance and do the best you can. Carole's having some friends over tonight, and we'll all be watching. I don't know what it means, but one of the blokes at work said, 'Tell him to break a leg.' Have a good show, Den. Break a leg."

"Thanks, Dad. I have to go now; we have a rehearsal. I'll call again after the show."

I hung up, went back to the dressing room, and changed into my stage clothes. By this time everybody had their makeup on and we were all ready to go. Terry knocked on the door and led us back for the dress rehearsal. I was nervous, but the practice went well. All the shots worked and everything went without a hitch.

By the time it got to be seven-fifteen, everybody was edgy. Finally, Terry was at the dressing-room door again.

"Okay, guys. This is it . . . let's go."

Alan and Mike picked up their saxes, and Neil and Clive strapped on their guitars. Along with Burf we all followed Terry down the corridor and around the corner to the set. The studio was now jam-packed. Girls and boys filled every space between the cameras. Men in suits lingered in the darkness behind the cameras, and flashes popped as people took pictures with their instant cameras.

We huddled together in a small group, waiting for instructions. The makeup ladies came over and put some finishing touches to our makeup. My heart started to race as the big moment grew nearer.

Soon one of the floor producers came over and waved for us to follow him. "Come on, boys," he said, "time to walk out of the shadows and into the headlines."

We sliced our way through the packed audience. I walked up onstage, past the footlights, and over to my drum riser. I stepped up to my drums and sat down.

The colored lights above seemed to shine brighter and more intensely than before. I picked up my sticks and put a spare pair on top of my bass drum, just in case. Camera one was in place just to my right. The cameraman looked up from his monitor and toward me. We made eye contact, and he gave me a long wink. I nervously nodded back. Then the magic moment was at hand as the voice of producer Johnnie Stewart came through the studio monitors.

"Here we go, everybody . . . Have a great show . . . And we're live in five – four – three – two – one." The iconic theme song for *Top of the Pops* started to play and the crowd cheered. After the opening credits, the music faded. From a stage behind Blue, Alan Freeman introduced the show.

We were the second act, following a collage of still images of Stevie Wonder. I'll never forget how the audience danced while "I Was Made to Love Her" pounded through the speakers. The music came to an end, and I could barely hear Alan Freeman introducing us.

Neil's guitar started to play, and the red light on camera one came on. It slowly moved by me. I looked right into the camera, but I was nervous and shy, and it was all I could do to smile. Camera two lit up as Andy started to sing. Girls in the audience reached out, trying to touch him. Andy reached back, making contact with his fingertips.

Camera one turned, made its way back, and parked in front of Alan and Mike. The red light came on as it focused in on Clive's and Neil's guitars. The camera moved toward my hands, getting a close-up as I played. The light went out when the camera lifted up as it passed me by. The cameraman looked directly at me. This time he gave me double thumbs up.

The song played on as I looked out over the audience. I was up high on my riser, but I was feeling even higher. I was performing live on *Top of the Pops* with my band and it felt like I was on top of the world. *If it never gets any better than this,* I thought, *this is enough!*

Before I knew it, camera one was looking down at me again. The red light came on, and I pounded out the drum fill that took "Gin House" into the final bars.

Then it was over and *Top of the Pops* moved on to the next act. We went back to the dressing room to change out of our stage clothes. Everyone from Galaxy was there, along with friends just waiting to congratulate us on a great performance. Champagne flowed as we all heaved a big sigh of relief; we had successfully got through our first *Top of the Pops* experience.

After I changed, I went to the pay telephone and called home. "Did you see it? What was it like?" I asked my dad. I could hear lots of people laughing and talking in the background. It sounded like there was a party going on.

"Den, it was fantastic. You were great, luv . . . and you *all* were great. There was a good shot of you right at the beginning of the song. Your mother started crying, she was so happy."

My dad told me how proud of me he was. I'd never heard him this emotional. I stayed on the phone for about half an hour, talking to everybody, trying to find out what it was like being on the other side of the camera. But they all wanted to know what it was like on *this* side of the camera.

Amen Corner was featured many times on *Top of the Pops* over the years. But for me, none of the performances was ever as special as that first show.

FIRST TIMERS

We were gigging at least five times a week to build our fan base and make enough money to live, but there's no exposure quite like television. After our first *Top of the Pops* appearance, Galaxy booked us on a talent show based out of Manchester, England. It aired live every Wednesday night at eight o'clock. *First Timers* was produced by Johnny Hamp for Granada Television. It took the form of a contest that was divided into various categories; Amen Corner was in the "group" category. There was also "singer/songwriter," and in that group was a young guy from London named Elton John. The show was popular, and past winners included Herman's Hermits and The Beatles.

Every Wednesday we'd board a train to Manchester, and that night we'd perform on the show. Week after week we kept on winning our category, and at the end of the season, Amen Corner won the whole thing.

A couple of weeks later we received a telegram. It was addressed to: THE AMEN CORNER C/O JOHNNY HAMP GRANADA TELEVISION MANCHESTER 3. It read: FROM ONE FIRST TO ANOTHER CONGRATULATIONS AND GREAT SUCCESS IN THE FUTURE = JOHN GEORGE PAUL AND RINGO.

None of us could believe it, but it was no joke. Every year after The Beatles won the very first *First Timers* contest, they sent a congratulatory telegram to subsequent winners in the "group" category. Even now when I look at that framed telegram on my wall, I still can't believe I received a telegram from The Beatles.

CHAPTER 6 Swinging London
. . . and Touring
with Hendrix

THE GIBSON FLYING V

With a hit record under our belts and a massive fan club, we started playing some pretty big gigs. At that time, in the late 1960s, it became fashionable for promoters to stage "package tours," bringing together many top acts. One such tour featured The Jimi Hendrix Experience, Amen Corner, The Nice, The Move, Pink Floyd, Eire Apparent, and The Outer Limits.

The tour was massive, and we played to sold-out audiences every night. Being on the same bill with all those acts was such an inspiration for me. And knowing we were second on the bill to Jimi Hendrix was just unbelievable. I watched all the bands play every night, but seeing Hendrix from the side of the stage was an experience unto itself. Apart from being an amazing guitar player and singer, he was a real showman.

At that time there were no pyrotechnics or special effects in concerts, but that didn't stop Jimi — he made his own. He'd take a can of lighter fluid and, while he was playing, he'd pour it on the fingerboard and frets of his guitar. Then he'd pull out a Zippo lighter and set the whole neck of his guitar on fire. He'd play through the flames at a dazzling speed. The lights onstage were dimmed and the audience went crazy.

I never missed a single show. Back then, in rock 'n' roll, things were much simpler and more primitive. For instance, a Marshall Stack was not what it is today. It consisted of one amplifier sitting on top of another and that was it.

Jimi had just such a stack. He'd turn up the volume on his guitar and amp until it produced loud feedback. Then he'd start bashing his guitar against the top Marshall. The wailing feedback, the impact of the guitar against the amplifier, and the mastery of his technique produced sounds none of us had ever heard before. Jimi had a roadie kneeling behind the stack, holding on to the top Marshall. His job was to prevent the stack from crashing to the stage.

Jimi had a white Gibson Flying V guitar that he'd switch to at a certain place in his set. He always had trouble tuning this particular guitar, and one night the feisty guitar stretched Jimi's patience past its limit. He was standing in the middle of the stage, trying to get the Gibson in tune. It was taking longer than usual and the crowd was growing impatient. He kept tuning and tuning, but that guitar would not cooperate. The audience started a slow handclap. Everybody backstage felt for Jimi as he became more and more frustrated. Finally, somebody in the front row started singing, *Why are we waiting?* Then the whole audience joined in.

Jimi had had enough! He took the strap off, turned around, and aimed the Flying V at the Marshall stack. The audience immediately stopped clapping and silence filled the huge concert hall. The guitar was still plugged in and at full volume. I watched in horror as the instrument sailed through the air in slow motion, producing a dark, ghostly tone. It was right on target, heading toward the Marshall stack and the roadie crouching behind it. I gasped as it made contact with the top speaker and, like an arrow, pierced the amplifier. It missed the roadie's head by inches, but the effect from the audience's point of view was spectacular. Everyone thought it was part of the show and started cheering louder than ever.

Jimi walked over to the guitar, which was embedded in the top Marshall. The feedback was violent as the Gibson sang back at him, as if in defiance. He ordered the roadie to get out of the way and kicked the

Jimi's Gang. The Jimi Hendrix Experience, Amen Corner, The Move, Pink Floyd, The Nice, The Eire Apparent, and The Outer Limits. PICTORIAL PRESS LTD / ALAMY

whole stack over in one go. The sound was deafening as the rig crashed down onto the wooden stage. The audience went nuts and started chanting *Jimi . . . Jimi . . . Jimi . . . Jimi!*

The roadie scurried to get the stack up and running. The wrecked Marshall was lying on its back, lifeless, the Flying V pointing straight up in a salute to the magic of its master. The roadie brought in a new Marshall to replace the top one, and Jimi grabbed one of his guitars lined up on the side of the stage, then casually walked over to the new stack. He plugged in like nothing had happened and went right into "Purple Haze."

THE SPEAKEASY

One of the coolest places to play in London was the legendary, members-only club The Speakeasy, or "The Speak," as we called it. This was the time of Swinging London — the late sixties — and anybody who was anybody felt the calling of The Speak.

"The beautiful people" frequented the club, and it was almost impossible to get in. All the top bands and musicians had memberships, and it was always filled with famous models and acclaimed actors and actresses. This was the one place in London where important people could go, knowing they wouldn't get hassled.

Amen Corner had a residency at The Speakeasy; we played there every Tuesday night. It was a hard gig — load-in was at eight o'clock at night and we didn't start playing until one o'clock in the morning. But it was worth it; everybody was there. The space had a cool, showbiz family atmosphere, as if everybody knew each other. Everybody was always buying somebody else a drink. I don't know how the wait staff kept up.

It didn't matter how big a star or celebrity you were, nobody at The Speakeasy gave you a second look . . . that is, until a certain someone walked in.

It was about two-thirty in the morning and the place was packed. There was a large dance area in front of the stage, generally filled with models and celebrities. The guys were handsome and wearing brightly colored silk shirts, or no shirts at all, while the girls were gorgeous and had on tight blouses, miniskirts, and boots, which were all the rage. I think some of the girls were competing to see who could wear the mini-est of miniskirts. Some of the skirts were so short they left nothing to the imagination (which was okay with me).

We were in the middle of a song called "I Can't Turn You Loose" by Otis Redding. It's a high-intensity number, and the dance floor was boiling. Everybody was dancing like their lives depended on it. As I looked out and over the crowd, I saw something I'll never forget. From the back of the room people stopped dancing and looked behind them toward the entrance. The effect spread through the crowd like wildfire until it reached the front of the stage. Suddenly nobody was dancing, as they looked back in blind expectation. This *never* happened at The Speakeasy.

From the back of the room I could see the people making way for a tall man with a wide-brimmed hat. As he walked toward the stage, the space behind him filled in. He walked right up and stood there, looking up at the band.

It was Jimi Hendrix. He'd heard we were playing and had come down to The Speak for a jam. After we finished the song, Andy bent down and asked him if he wanted to play. Andy yelled to us, "Jimi's getting up!"

Neil took off his Stratocaster and handed it to Jimi, who started scratching out a rhythm and playing some licks. He played the guitar upside-down . . . I kicked in with just my bass drum . . . Blue delicately Leslie'd in on his bright red Hammond B-3 organ . . . Alan and Mike started playing a riff they made up on the spot . . . and, finally, Clive boomed in on the bass guitar . . . The jam was on! About fifteen minutes in, Andy took over on bass guitar while Clive picked up a tambourine.

The audience couldn't believe their luck as they watched Jimi Hendrix, this iconic superstar of the sixties, jam out. They had come to party and dance, but their night out had turned into a free concert by one of the most — if not *the* most — influential guitarists of all time.

We jammed for about forty-five minutes, and during that time Jimi looked back at me a lot. He always gave me a smile and a nod of approval. I was onstage at The Speakeasy jamming with Jimi Hendrix — *how cool is that?!*

Many years later, while I was living in Tennessee, the phone rang. It was Andy.

"Den, how ya doing? I'm in Atlanta playing with Eric Clapton and I thought about you. How far is Nashville from Atlanta?"

"About a four-hour drive."

"You wanna come down and see the show? It's a pretty good band! I'll take care of everything. Just tell me how many tickets you need."

The next day, five of my Nashville friends and I piled into my 4Runner and we left for Atlanta. Andy's and Eric's whole entourage were staying at the Ritz Hotel, so we did the same thing. The show was polished and professional. Eric was incredible and the band was exceptional.

After the show, everybody went back to the hotel; we gathered in the penthouse bar on the top floor. As we sat at a table overlooking the city, Andy poured me a glass of wine and we reminisced about the old Amen Corner days.

"Den . . . Do you remember the time we played with Hendrix at The Speakeasy?"

Like I could have forgotten that. "Yeah," I answered.

"I was onstage with Jimi Hendrix. I was onstage with one of my biggest heroes. Then I did a real selfish thing . . . I just couldn't help myself . . . I *had* to play with Jimi. So I asked Clive for his bass and he gave it to me."

Andy went silent for a few moments.

"Anyway," Andy said, "there I was, playing up a storm, and I'm smiling and Jimi is smiling right back at me . . . and then he pointed at my hand on the guitar. And I'm thinking to myself, *God, I'm playing with Jimi Hendrix, and Jimi's digging it! Jimi's loving it! He's pointing at my hands! I'm smiling, and he's smiling!* And then Jimi moved in closer and yelled right in my face, 'You're in the wrong fucking key!'"

JENNY, JENNY

Things were looking good for Amen Corner. Our second single was called "World of Broken Hearts," and it reached number twenty-two on the U.K. charts. The next release, "Bend Me, Shape Me," was a cover of a hit song by a U.S. group known as the American Breed. It was slightly more pop and made it all the way to number three. After the Hendrix tour, we went back to playing our own gigs, and some of them were massive.

The band was doing so well financially we were able to move out of the house in Brixton and into a mansion in Harrow on the Hill, an affluent area in northwest London. The house was large enough for each band member to have his own room, and there was also a big lounge and a sizable kitchen.

Outside, a circular driveway led up to the house, and a large metal gate secured the entrance from the street. The band was so hot, there was always a group of girls outside waiting for an autograph or a photo.

Because our income was steady, each member was able to take a wage of fifty pounds a week. This doesn't sound like much money, but in those days it was. And the revenue from the band paid for many perks, including the rented house, a cleaning woman who came twice a week, all groceries at the house, all the utilities and telephone bill, a van, two roadies, and a Daimler limousine for us to get around in. We were doing well.

Our latest single was called "High in the Sky," and it was sitting at number six on the U.K. Top 100 singles chart. We'd done all the press and television shows to promote the song, including another appearance on

Top of the Pops. The band was popular all over the country, but for some reason we were particularly well liked up north.

During this period, we had a gig in the small northern town of Redcar, about ten miles from the large industrial city of Middlesbrough. That part of the country is located in north Yorkshire, and the people who live in this area are known as "Yorkies" or "Geordies." We'd played this place a few times before. The club was not huge, but it was always packed. And this Tuesday night was no different. As we went through the set, I noticed a girl in the audience looking right at me. She had long hair and was wearing a headband; she looked beautiful. Every now and again we'd make eye contact and she'd smile at me. We had a fantastic show and had to fight with the audience to finish the second set. When it was over, I sorted out the money with the promoter and went back into the almost-empty club for a beer.

I was sitting by myself at a table at the back of the room, trying to come down from all the excitement of the show. Rocky was onstage packing up the equipment and I could see Clive and Neil talking to a couple of girls in front of the stage. Alan and Andy were at the bar, going over things with the promoter.

I looked around and focused in on a girl down by the left-hand side of the stage. I squinted and leaned forward in my chair, not believing what I was seeing. There she was . . . the girl I had seen while we were playing . . . probably the most beautiful girl I had ever seen in my life. She left all the models at The Speakeasy standing in the dust. She was slim, with light auburn hair that glistened as it fell all the way down to her bare waist. She was wearing a light brown suede miniskirt, a short silk blouse, tall brown boots with platform heels, and an Indian-style headband that made her look like she belonged on the cover of a magazine. My mouth was open as I felt myself drooling.

There was just one problem: she was talking to Mike Smith. Mike was the new tenor sax player who had replaced Mal Davis. When you're in a band, like it or not, the other members become your brothers. And, as in any family, there are certain rules you have to abide by. In this case, it was the "she's mine, fuck off" rule. If one of the other guys is chatting up a girl, the unwritten law states that you never-never-ever try to pull that girl away from the other guy.

I couldn't take my eyes off this *vision* as Clive and Neil sat down at the table. "Will, look at that girl talking to Mike," I said. "I think I'm in love. Clive, look at her, man, she's gorgeous."

"Yeah, she's nice . . . That fucking Mike Smith!" Clive said as he looked down.

We all had various nicknames for each other; mine was Plentis, a name Neil had conjured up, because I used to be an apprentice — and Plentis or Plent was morphed from that word. Clive's nickname was Will, because one of his middle names is William. We called Mike by many names, some too crude to share. Sometimes he was known as Paddy, but usually it was Badeye, because he wore wide-rimmed glasses with thick opaque lenses.

"Hey, Badeye, get the fuck over here!" Clive yelled.

Mike looked up to our table. He lifted his hands and shrugged his shoulders.

"Get the fuck over here now, ya prick!"

Mike walked up to the table and Clive continued.

"What the fuck are you doing, man?"

"What?" Mike answered.

"That girl, what the fuck are you doing?"

"What about her?" Mike replied.

Then Clive turned everything around. "Plentis was chatting her up before he went for the money. You know the rules, Paddy. Fucking back off, man."

Mike looked at me. "I didn't know."

"Well, you know now, asshole. Leave her the fuck alone," Clive continued.

His tail between his legs, Mike went back to the girl who was talking to her friend. He said something to them and disappeared backstage.

"Go on, then," Clive said, motioning to the girls. "Go on, Plent. Off the fuck you go."

I got up and started walking across the room. The closer I got, the more beautiful she became, until finally I found myself standing next to a dream.

"You're the drummer, aren't you?" she said in the loveliest Geordie accent.

"Yes, I'm Dennis. What's your name?"

"Jenny . . . and this is my friend Jackie."

I seemed to have a thing for Jennys. We shook hands. Even Jenny's hands were beautiful, with long fingers and immaculately painted fingernails.

"I liked watching you play the drums," Jenny said. "You hit them so hard."

"Well, you have to . . . you have to show those drums who's boss . . . who's in charge . . . You gots ta slap 'em about a bit, as Popeye would say. A-gah-gah-gah-gah-gah-gah."

"You're silly," she said. Then, "Can I have a go?"

I looked up onstage, where Rocky was just starting to break down my drums.

"Hang on a minute, Rock," I shouted up. "Give me a minute to show somebody my drums."

I helped Jenny up onstage — her hand was so warm — and walked her over to my Ludwig kit. "This is Rocky. He's my slave."

"Yeah," Rocky said, "for the money you pay me I might as well be. Nice to meet you, luv."

"This is Jenny," I said.

I didn't know it then, but I'd be introducing Jenny for the next forty-something years. She sat down on my stool, and I handed her two drumsticks. Rocky gave me a look and rolled his eyes.

"What do I do now?" Jenny asked.

"Just hit them, make some noise."

Jenny started hitting the drums wildly. She thrashed about in a concerto of chaos. Andy walked past the front of the stage.

"Den?" Andy said.

I looked down at Andy. He looked at me and shook his head *no*. I held up my hands and signaled for Jenny to stop. I reached out and she handed me the sticks.

"Let me guess . . . Keith Moon," I quipped.

"How did you know?" Jenny replied.

"I know all his solos," I joked back.

"Was I good?" Jenny asked.

"No!" I said sternly.

Jenny laughed and for the very first time I saw that smile up close. I helped her down from the stage and we made our way to the bar. As we walked together hand in hand everything seemed to fit. There was no awkwardness, no shyness, and any silence between the talk was just beautiful.

I managed to buy Jenny a drink from a bar that had been closed for at least half an hour. She was impressed.

As we sat at the bar I took a deep breath. "Do you want to come back to the hotel?"

After a long pause, she replied, "I don't think so."

"You can trust me."

At exactly the same time we both leaned in and in unison said, "Never trust a man who says 'You can trust me.'"

We laughed.

"No, I mean it . . . you *can* trust me."

"I know I can," Jenny said softly as she looked into my eyes. "I have to be at work tomorrow."

"I can get you home. I'm driving the car. All I want to do is just sit with you for a while."

"I have to find Jackie and make sure it's okay." Jenny headed outside looking for her friend.

A moment later, Clive came up and sat on the stool next to mine.

"Plentis, Wentis . . . the things I do for you, mate. You owe me big time."

"Aw, Clive, she's amazing."

Jenny came back and I got down from my stool. "Jenny, this is Clive. Clive, this is Jenny." They shook hands.

"Nice to meet you, luv," Clive said. "He's handsome, our Den, isn't he? Sometimes I even fancy him myself."

"Clive, give it a rest."

Jenny laughed and told me Jackie was riding home with her sister and she could come back to the hotel for a little while.

I took Jenny to the dressing room and picked up the suit bag containing my stage clothes, then we walked outside and blended into a crowd of people from the audience. All the other band members were there, signing autographs and talking to the fans. The Daimler limo pulled up with Clive at the wheel. I opened up the huge boot and threw my suit bag in, then opened the back door on the pavement side and helped Jenny get into the backseat. The limo was fairly new and still had that leather smell. I sat down next to her and put my arm around her shoulders.

"This is posh," Jenny said.

"Only the best for you, Jen," I replied.

Andy got into the front seat, next to Clive. Alan, Mike, and Blue sat in the fold-down jump seats in front of us, and Neil slid in on the other side of Jenny.

"Den, how'd we do?" Andy shouted from the front.

"Twelve hundred and fifty-two," I shouted back.

"Alright!" Everybody gave a little cheer.

"That's how much we made tonight," I whispered in Jenny's ear.

"Twelve hundred pounds?" she asked in amazement.

Clive pulled out and within a few minutes we were at the hotel. This was a small place, not much bigger than a bed and breakfast, but it did have a small bar that stayed open until the last guest went to bed. Everybody headed for the bar.

I got the keys for the Daimler from Clive, and Jenny and I walked through the small lobby on our way to the stairs. Usually girls were not allowed to go up to the rooms, for obvious reasons. The man behind the reception desk gave us a serious look and was about to say something, but as we passed the desk, I managed to get in first.

"Uh, this is our fan club secretary. She's gonna do a quick interview for the next newsletter. We'll only be a few minutes."

Jenny opened her eyes wide and nodded yes at the man. He gave her a very suspicious look.

"Alright, but I'll be waiting here. Don't be long."

We started up the stairs. When we reached the second floor, I took Jenny's hand.

"You're a good liar," she said.

"So are you," I said back.

"But I didn't say anything."

"I saw that look . . . you don't always need words to tell a lie. I see I'm gonna have to keep my eye on you."

"I hope so," Jenny replied.

When we got to the room, I unlocked the door and we went inside. It was tiny, not much bigger than the single bed inside. There was no bathroom, but at least it had a small sink. Jenny sat down on a chair next to a mini desk. I threw my suit bag on the bed and took off my jacket. I pulled my shirt from out of my jeans and began to unbutton it from the bottom. Jenny watched in horror.

"What are you doing?" she asked with concern.

"Not what you think . . . I'm just taking off my corset."

She believed me, and the look of horror turned to one of *I have to get out of here.* I reached inside my shirt and undid the fasteners on a wide money belt that held the cash from the show. I threw it down on my suit bag and reached down under the bed, pulled out my British European Airways travel bag, unzipped it, and slid the money belt inside. Then I put the bag back under my bed.

Once I'd buttoned up my shirt and tucked it back into my jeans, I looked back at Jenny. Her face started to change as she turned a deathly shade of white.

"Are you alright?" I asked. "You look like you've seen a . . ."

"I think I'm gonna be . . ."

"Do it in the sink!" I shouted, and she barely made it. She threw up all over the porcelain and the taps. Her long hair didn't escape the mess. I grabbed a towel next to the sink and pulled her hair back as she continued to heave for a minute or so. After she stopped, I turned on the water and washed everything down the drain, then put her soiled hair under the tap and rinsed it clean.

I reached for a second towel and began to dry her hair, but she was upset and flustered and started to cry.

"I feel embarrassed . . . I wanted to be so perfect for you."

"You are perfect." I lifted up Jenny's head with my fingers. She was beautiful, even through the tears. I wiped them away. "This is excellent," I added. "Look on the bright side . . . now we've got something to talk about. Wait till I tell Clive you threw up all over me."

"I didn't throw up on you. You won't tell anyone, will you?"

"No, this is our secret."

"I have to go, Den. I've got work tomorrow."

Jenny and Denny. NEIL JONES

Jenny put herself back together, and I grabbed my jacket from the bed. Luckily enough, the man at the front desk wasn't there. As we passed the bar, I saw Clive and Alan talking to some girls.

In the car, Jenny was upset and hardly said anything on the way, except for directions to her home in Middlesbrough. We reached the house on Hoylake Road and parked outside. The front seat of the limo was a huge leather bench-type seat. I pulled Jenny over and put my arm around her.

"I think my breath smells," she said hesitantly.

"I can fix that," I quickly replied.

I reached down into my jeans' pocket and pulled out half a packet of Polos. I tore back the silver paper and handed Jenny a mint.

"You're a big spender," she said sarcastically. Then she gave me a huge smile.

"Yeah, I take care of my girls."

"Girls! How many girls do you have?" She was feeling better.

"Just one, she's a Geordie."

"A Geordie? Where does she live?"

"Right there." I pointed to her house.

We both moved in and our lips met.

"Will I see you again?" she asked.

"When I was growing up, my mother taught me all the basic things. She taught me how to sew, she taught me how to knit, she taught me the right way to wash my own clothes, and even how to iron them. I think she thought I'd never find a girlfriend. Then one day she gave me a piece of advice I'll never forget: she said, *If you ever come across the girl of your dreams . . . make sure you never let her go, no matter what happens.*"

"Am I the girl of your dreams?" Jenny asked.

"I've been dreaming about you for a long time . . . You're the one."

I made that long journey from London to Middlesbrough many times before Jenny moved to London and joined me in the rock 'n' roll mansion on the Hill.

THE END

Amen Corner lasted almost four years. We had a good run, releasing six singles and two albums. All of our records charted, and in 1969, our fifth single "(If Paradise Is) Half as Nice" reached the coveted number one spot.

Over the years, our music changed. It went from tight R&B to more of a commercial pop feel. After a while, Andy decided it was time for a more radical change. It was time to make the music a little more progressive or *edgy*. We had a serious band meeting and decided to carry on without the saxophones.

So at the end of 1969, Amen Corner disbanded and a new group called Fair Weather was born. Amen Corner's breakup drew national attention; the announcement even went live on the BBC six o'clock nightly news.

We had heard about the TV announcement in advance, so we all gathered around the television set in our house waiting for the nationwide newscast to air. It was an achievement indeed for any group to be mentioned on the weighty BBC television news program, but it was bittersweet knowing that *that* report meant the end of something great, the end of an era.

As we sat waiting for the news, it brought to mind the day we heard "Gin House" on the radio for the very first time. This newscast was another first, but sadly, this first would be our last. During the announcement, I couldn't help but think the story was about another group. It was as if the news announcer was talking about somebody else. He listed all our hits and said we were the biggest group ever to have come from Wales. Then he said we'd be missed by all our fans.

After it was over, there were no handshakes or pats on the back. Everybody quietly walked out of the lounge and to their rooms. As we went our separate ways, I knew this was the end of an important part of my life. Four years ago I had given up my apprenticeship as an electrician to follow my dream. Now it became very clear that today was the last day of my apprenticeship into the music business.

CHAPTER 7 Fair
Weather

BEGINNING FROM AN END

The first thing we did as Fair Weather was move out of our house in Harrow. It was too expensive and now too big for the new band. We found an old Norwegian barn for rent in the picturesque village of Elstree, near Borehamwood in Hertfordshire, about fifteen miles northwest of London. The village is also home to the famous Elstree Film Studios.

The Norwegian barn was the real thing. Originally built in Norway, the wooden structure was disassembled, shipped to England, and reassembled on the grounds of the Edgwarebury Country Club. It was huge, with a large room in the center that would become our gathering place. The room had two big horse stalls, one on either side of the great room, that became Neil's and Blue's bedrooms. Jenny and I had a room in the middle of the house. Our room had a door that entered the kitchen and another that opened onto the hallway that led upstairs, where Andy and Clive had bedrooms.

Neil's girlfriend, Lesley, moved in and so did Blue's girlfriend, Anne. Andy had a serious relationship with Neil's sister Barbara, who was a model in Cardiff and came up most weekends if we weren't playing. The house was full and there was plenty of girl power.

Fair Weather was nowhere near as popular as Amen Corner, and the band's income definitely reflected the difference. I was still doing the books and it was always a struggle to survive. Sometimes when we didn't have any gigs, there was no money to pay the bills. Of course, that meant there were no wages for us.

Fair Weather signed with RCA Records, and in 1970 we had a number six hit with a song called "Natural Sinner." With a hit record, things picked up and we started playing more and making good money again.

Because Fair Weather was not in the same league as Amen Corner, we had to scale everything down. We sold the luxurious Daimler limousine and bought a brand-new, more practical Ford Transit van. The van was custom; apart from the driver's seat, it had four leather airplane-style reclining seats, and an incredible built-in stereo sound system. It also had a metal bulkhead behind the back three seats that separated the front cab area from the cargo space. It was nice.

Living in the Norwegian barn with Jenny was fantastic. The building itself was located right next to a thick wooded area. In front of the house was a flat grassy meadow and behind the house a huge apple orchard. We were surrounded by the English countryside; the location, peacefulness, and serenity were enchanting.

One Sunday evening, after a weekend visit to Cardiff, Andy arrived back at the barn, hauling in a large cardboard box from the back of his car. He brought the box into the kitchen, put it on the floor, and opened it up. Inside, on a small blanket, was a tiny five-week-old German shepherd.

The poor dog was covered in feces and vomit from the journey. It didn't matter; Jenny reached in and gently lifted out the puppy. Andy went up to his room and left the dog with us. We took it into the bathroom, bathed it in warm water, and washed it with soap. We dried the dog off and took it into our bedroom.

The puppy calmed down and settled on our bed. Andy came in and sat down beside it. "I got her from my cousin, who's a breeder," he said. "The paperwork on this dog is ridiculous. She's a full-blooded German thoroughbred; her pedigree's immaculate."

"What's her name?" Jenny asked.

"Babet."

"She's lovely . . . yes, you are . . . you're lovely," Jenny said as she scratched Babet under her chin.

Andy took the puppy up to his bedroom. An hour later, he came down to the kitchen. "Jen, you got anything to clean up puppy pee?"

Jenny went to the cupboard and pulled out a roll of paper towels and a plastic bottle of glass cleaner.

An hour later Andy came back down again. "What's good for cleaning up poop? Do we have any fresh-air spray?"

It didn't take long before Andy got fed up cleaning up after the puppy. Over the next few months, Babet spent more and more time with us. Then one night Andy came into our bedroom and said, "Why don't you let her sleep with you tonight?" From that point on, Babet bonded with us.

The months turned into almost two years and, although Fair Weather was popular and the gigs plentiful, we weren't moving ahead. After "Natural Sinner," none of our singles charted, and our album *Beginning from an End* did nothing.

One day, after we had just returned from a small tour of Scotland and were on our way to the barn, we drove Andy to Paddington rail station. He was going home to Cardiff. Before he got out of the van, Andy turned to us and made an announcement:

"Listen, guys, I have something to say . . . It's been a good ride, but the band's over . . . Fair Weather is no more!"

And with that, Andy climbed out of the van, grabbed his guitar and suitcase from the back, and he was off.

We all saw it coming; it was just a question of when. Now we knew, and for me, in a strange way, it was a relief. We got back to the barn and I told Jenny, who started to cry. She wasn't upset that the band was breaking up so much as she was about the possibility of losing Babet. Babet lived in our bedroom, sleeping on our bed every night. Wherever Jenny and I went, Babet went with us. She was our shadow, but technically she belonged to Andy.

A few days later, Andy came back to gather up his things. I was sitting on my bed with Jenny and Babet when I saw Andy in the hall outside. I opened the door and walked out.

"Andy, can we talk?" I was deadly serious, which was not like me.

Andy stopped in the hallway. "Yeah, man."

"It's about Babet. Jenny and I want to keep her. We've taken care of her ever since she was a puppy, but you brought her here and she's your dog. Can we take her?"

Andy thought about it for what seemed like forever and finally answered, "Yeah, you and Jen did a good job of training her and bringing her up . . . It seems only fair that you keep her." He started to walk away.

"Andy, just one thing more," I said. "If we take her, she's our dog. You can't come back in a year or two with her papers and claim her back. If we take her, she's ours forever."

Andy looked at me dead in the eye. "Den, she's your dog, yours and Jenny's. She's yours forever. I'll even give you her papers."

"Let's shake on it, Andy."

Andy stuck out his hand and we shook. To this day, I've never given a handshake that was more resolute. As our hands locked, Andy sealed his word and Babet became our dog.

Back in the bedroom, Jenny was sitting on the bed with Babet. She was crying. I was going to do my usual thing and make a joke that it had all gone terribly wrong, but this was too serious. "Andy said yes, she's ours."

Jenny started crying even more then, hugging and kissing Babet. I'd never seen her so happy.

Over the next month or so, we wound up the finances and affairs of Fair Weather, working closely with our accountant. There was just enough money in the band account to pay our taxes and all outstanding bills.

I didn't know what I was going to do next, but I did know I would need transportation for my drums. I wanted to buy the Ford Transit from the group but didn't have enough money. Luckily, I had a really great relationship with my bank manager at Barclays, who arranged for a loan to buy the van. I also borrowed enough money for Jenny, Babet, and me to live on for the next six months.

It was sad as we all finally said our goodbyes at the Norwegian barn. There were a lot of hugs and tears as everybody went their separate ways. I'd come a long way since that cold winter's morning in 1967 when I left home with my band. Bound for London, I had been armed only with a handful of luck and a pocketful of dreams. Now I could look back on almost five years chock-full of unbelievable happenings, experiences, and memories.

I'd fulfilled my dreams of becoming the drummer in the most famous band to ever come out of Wales; to play on hit records, even a number one on the charts; to appear on television shows like *Top of the Pops* and radio shows like *Pick of the Pops*; to be in the headline band at Sophia Gardens, the biggest venue in my hometown of Cardiff; to be in a group with a fan club that numbered thousands. I'd jammed with Jimi Hendrix, met the girl of my dreams, and found a dog that *just maybe* comes along once in a lifetime. Did all this really happen to *me*?

DON'T EVER BE AFRAID TO COME HOME

I wasn't scared of going home. Why should I be? It's not like I hadn't achieved anything; I hadn't failed at anything. Why would I be scared to go home? But strangely enough, I was! Now I understood what my dad meant when he said, so long ago, "Don't ever be afraid to come home."

I talked to my dad at least once a week on the telephone, and he encouraged me to return. My parents had bought the house next door to their house on Colum Road. Carole and her husband were living on the ground floor, and Dad said I could move in upstairs with Jenny and Babet.

I was tired and needed some time to get my thoughts together, to make plans and conjure up some more dreams. The thought of living in Cardiff after the hustle-bustle of London was very appealing, and after a long conversation with Jenny, we decided to move home.

Everything was great there for a while, but after six months I was growing restless. It seemed to me time was wasting; I had to get back into music. Jenny could feel my frustration and was sympathetic but, more importantly, she was supportive on every level. I had to move back to London and find a band. The problem was, I didn't have enough money to support Jenny and Babet. There was no way Jenny would be separated from Babet, so she suggested going back to her home in Middlesbrough for a while.

I started calling my friends in London, and put out the word that I was looking for work playing drums. I also needed a place to stay, so I put that out there, too. One day the phone rang next door at the B&B. It was my friend Claudia, a French girl who worked as secretary to a successful manager in the music business in London. We were old friends from the Amen Corner days. Our mutual friend Judy — who worked for a music rental agency called The Cabin in Shepherd's Bush, West London — had told Claudia of my plans. Claudia offered me the couch in her flat, as long as I didn't stay forever. I immediately jumped at it.

It was an emotional day as Jenny, Babet, and I left Cardiff for Middlesbrough. Saying goodbye to Mum and Dad was much harder this time. Leaving Jenny and Babet in Middlesbrough was even more difficult, but this was something I had to do. I had to find work.

That Monday evening, at exactly six o'clock, I rang the bell on Claudia's door.

CHAPTER 8
Supertramp

TOUR MANAGER?

Claudia was the most amazing person. The first thing she did was give me a big hug and welcome me back home to London. She opened a bottle of wine, sat me down, and asked me all about Jenny, Babet, and everything in Cardiff. She was very encouraging; she told me I'd find some work in no time. I could use the phone in the flat as much as I wanted, she said, but if I was going to call Jenny in Middlesbrough, make it quick!

The next morning, after Claudia left for work, I made myself a cup of coffee and started reading the morning paper. Suddenly, the phone in the flat started to ring. I felt awkward about answering somebody else's phone, but Claudia had told me to make myself at home, so I picked it up.

"Hello, this is Dennis."

"Hi, Dennis. This is Judy. Welcome back."

"Hi, Jude. Yes, I got in last night."

"Den, let me ask you a question . . . Do you still have that beautiful van with the airplane seats?"

"Yes."

"There *are* four passenger seats, right?"

"Yeah."

"Let me ask you another question: Do you have your passport with you, and is it current?"

"Yes, I do and yes, it is." I always made sure my passport was up to date because you never know . . .

"*Hmmmmm*," Judy said. "Dennis, I have to be very tactful about what I'm about to say, because I don't want to insult you in any way. I know you're looking for a gig playing drums and you probably don't want to be a driver, but I have a problem . . . a problem that could work out to be very good for you."

"Okay," I replied.

"We're working with a band who's doing a short tour in Europe. They're playing all over the place, and yesterday their van blew up! They need reliable transportation and a good driver, and I thought about you. It's only for two weeks and the money's good . . . *very* good."

"What's *very* good?"

"Hotel, all expenses including food, *and* two hundred pounds a week — *cash*! There's no equipment to haul or set up, all you have to do is drive," Judy said.

I wasn't insulted, and I didn't have to think about it; I was broke. "Count me in, Jude. Thank you. Who's the band?"

"It's a group called Supertramp. They're opening for Ten Years After. Den, these guys are great. You're going to have so much fun. Come into the office this morning and we'll get everything sorted. Bring your passport and driver's license. We have to get you on their insurance. Oh, and by the way . . . The Cabin takes ten percent of your wages as a commission for getting you the gig. Is that cool?"

"Not a problem."

"One more thing, Den. You leave London tomorrow morning at eight o'clock sharp."

"I'm ready to go. I'll be in the office in about an hour."

I became very excited, thinking about the 400 pounds. This meant I could start looking for a place of my own straight away.

At The Cabin agency in Shepherd's Bush, I found Judy's office and knocked on the slightly open door. Judy came out from behind her desk and we hugged like old friends. We took care of all the paperwork and caught up on our lives, and before I left, Judy gave me 500 pounds in cash for expenses. She showed me the way she wanted me to keep track of my spending. *Make sure you write everything down,* she insisted. Then she gave me detailed maps of the various countries we'd be visiting. She provided me with an itinerary listing all the cities, venues, show times, and hotels for the next two weeks. This was going to be work!

Judy arranged for me to meet the band the next morning outside The Cabin. On the way in, I stopped at a brand-new American donut shop — the first one in London — that had just opened nearby. I bought a dozen assorted donuts that had just been made and five large cups of coffee with cream and sugar on the side. I showed up at The Cabin five minutes early, but the band was already there.

I shook hands with everybody, and we put the guitars and suitcases in the back of the van. The guys said goodbye to their girlfriends, wives, and the people who had dropped them off, and we all got in the van. Before we pulled away, I handed out the coffee and donuts. The donuts were warm and the coffee was steaming hot. Judging by the silence and the *Oh my God*s, I think I scored a home run.

The first show was in Cologne, which was a bit of a drive. We took the ferry from Dover to Calais, then started the long trek through France and Belgium. Once we crossed the German border, it was an easy drive to Cologne. Roger Hodgson sat in the front seat next to me. He knew his way around Europe pretty well and, with the help of the maps Judy had provided, he got us to the hotel.

Supertramp wasn't playing that night, which was just as well; everybody was exhausted from the long journey. The hotel was nice; brand new and very modern. Everybody unloaded their suitcases and guitars from the back of the van and made a pile in the lobby. I looked across and, at the other side of the lobby, noticed a nice bar.

"Why don't you guys have a beer and I'll check us in," I said.

I went over to the front desk with my list of band members. All the hotels on the tour had been booked for weeks in advance and were paid in full. All I had to do was check us in and check us out. I asked the girl behind the desk if she wouldn't mind typing me a list, including all five of our names, with the room number next to each name. She was more than happy to help me.

As I checked in, I kept one eye on the guitars and suitcases sitting unattended in the lobby, and after the receptionist gave me the keys and the lists, I went into the bar. The band was sitting at a round table next to a roaring fire. There was a beer in front of an empty chair with my name on it.

"Come on, mate," Roger said. "Sit down and have a beer. You deserve it after that drive."

I lowered myself into the chair and blew out a big sigh. The cold beer definitely hit the spot. The fire was warm and hypnotizing, but not enough to keep my attention from the guitars and bags in the lobby. I handed out the room keys and the lists with the room numbers. It was good I'd made a list; we were all on different floors.

According to the itinerary, Supertramp's rehearsals would be at 2 p.m. the next day at the gig. I suggested we meet in the lobby at one o'clock, which would give us plenty of time to find the stadium.

The next day, everyone got to the lobby on time. Roger directed us to the stadium with no problem, and we drove to the back of the building for load-in. There were two huge tractor-trailers there, covered with the Ten Years After logo and artwork. Another tractor-trailer owned by the sound and lighting company was also parked there. All three trucks were from England, with the steering on the right — in mainland Europe, as in America, everybody drives on the right-hand side of the road. I parked the van and we unloaded the guitars from the back. We carried them up a long, sloping ramp that led to a set of double doors entering the building at the back of the stage. As we walked in, I could see members of the sound crew setting up a huge PA system. There were lighting technicians and stagehands on ladders putting together a very complicated lighting rig that hung over the whole stage.

As I looked around, I noticed a lot of the crew looked very familiar. I peered out into the huge, empty space. Sitting in the middle of the arena was a large mixing console that controlled the sound. There were three sound engineers sitting behind the desk.

"Aww, fuck me, I don't believe it! Mister fucking pop star himself!" came

blasting through the huge side speakers. Everybody looked at me and began to hoot and jeer. I'd been *made*. Some members of the sound crew had been on the Hendrix tour and remembered me from Amen Corner.

One of the sound mixers at the console pressed the talk-back button and started to sing through the main PA speakers, "Bend me, shape me, anyway way you want me, long as you love me . . ."

Then everybody onstage joined in with "*It's all right!*"

"Bend me, shape me . . ."

Everybody was having a good old laugh at my expense. I was praying a hole would open up in the ground and swallow me whole, but it didn't. This was *road humor* at its best, and all I could do was go along with it. I'd be working with these guys for the next two weeks and I *had* to take it. I put down the guitar I was carrying and walked to the front of the stage. I looked out at the three guys behind the desk and started to bow as if I'd won an Oscar. Then I turned to the lighting crew and did the same thing. I couldn't show that I was embarrassed.

I walked back to the side of the stage, where the band was standing, enjoying the schtick. "Let's find the dressing room!" I said, and asked one of the lighting guys for directions. He pointed to a tall man talking to one of the stagehands on the other side of the stage. 'That's the promoter, he'll know," he said.

We walked across the stage.

"Hi, we're Supertramp, and we're looking for our dressing room?"

The promoter gave us a confused look. "Who you say you are?" he replied in a thick German accent.

"Supertramp . . . We're the opening act. Where's our dressing room?"

"Aww, Supertramp, ziss vay."

We followed him down a long corridor. We passed a door on the right marked TYA 1, then another that said TYA 2, then a third door that read TYA 3, then, finally, a fourth door with a sign TYA 4.

The last door had an empty space where a sign once had been. He opened the door and walked in. We all followed and became very confused. We were in a men's toilet. There were six urinals in a row, with four stalls on the back wall and two sinks on the side wall.

"Ziss is it . . . here vee are."

I looked around at the guys; we stood there in disbelief.

"This is a toilet," I said. "Where's our dressing room?"

"Here . . . ziss is it . . . Supertramp, dressing room!"

"No, no, no, this is a toilet! Where's our dressing room?"

He waved his finger at me. "Understand . . . ziss . . . iss . . . Supertramp dressing room!"

"*No*, you understand *this*! If we don't get a dressing room, we're going back to London right now!" I said firmly.

I suddenly had the terrible feeling that I'd overstepped my bounds. I had no right making a statement like that without consulting the band. I looked around for support. To my relief, everybody gave me a nod of approval.

"Ziss iss your dressing room!" Then he began a long rant in German that I was glad I didn't understand.

"Come on, guys," I said. "Let's go." We all turned and marched out of the toilet. My heart started to race as we began the walk down the long corridor. Suddenly I felt a hand on my shoulder.

"Vait, I see vot I can do. Vait in here."

The promoter opened the door marked TYA 4, then led us in. He told us he'd be back soon.

The room was big and smelled like it had just been painted. It had thick wall-to-wall carpet. A false ceiling made out of square mahogany tiles hung elegantly above. There were plenty of comfortable leather chairs and soft sofas all around. The walls were covered with loud abstract paintings and murals of modern art. Impressionist paintings dotted the room in no particular pattern. This place was classy.

After several minutes, the promoter walked back into the room. "Come wiz me, I szink you will enjoy ziss."

He led us back up the corridor and across the stage. We went down a corridor identical to the first one. When we came to the first door on the right he stopped, pulled out a key, and unlocked it. He led the way.

"Ziss is zee office of zer manager of zer whole stadium," he said, motioning for us to come in. We followed. "And ziss . . ." he said as he proudly produced another key to unlock a door on the back wall, "ziss is his private guest suite."

We followed him into the dark room. He hit the light switch and the whole room lit up tastefully. It had the same feel as the TYA guest room we'd been in, but this room was subtler. The ceiling lights were built into the white plaster above and faintly rained down light into the room. Each painting had a brushed chrome light above it that gently illuminated the work. There were small tables throughout the room, with matching lamps sitting on top of each one.

At one end of the room was a glass dining table with eight chairs surrounding it. At the opposite end of the room stood a long wooden sideboard that stretched almost the entire width of the room. On the sideboard sat a beautiful thirty-two-inch Bang & Olufsen television set with a matching stereo system with a turntable and speakers. Sitting opposite each other, next to the sideboard, was a pair of overstuffed leather sofas, and between the sofas, a modern chrome table with a thick glass top. A door on the side wall led to a private bathroom with a chic commode and a white ceramic contemporary sink.

"Yeah, man. This is more like it!" we said as we walked in.

The promoter handed me the two keys and told me to make sure both rooms were locked whenever nobody was inside.

"What about food and drinks?" I asked.

"I vill see to everything. You vill get it all. Zest gives me some time."

"And, we want a dressing room with food and drinks at every show!" I insisted.

"Yes, yes, I vill take care of it. Don't vurry . . ."

With that, he turned and walked through the manager's office and out into the hall, cursing in German all the way. We were pretty stoked as we put down the guitars and settled into the luxurious suite. But before we'd had a chance to really kick back, there was a knock on the door. It was one of the stagehands; it was time for a sound check.

The TYA crew was handling all of Supertramp's equipment; all the band had to do was plug in, tune up, and make some final adjustments to the drums. The rehearsal went well, and when they were done we all returned to the dressing room. An hour or so went by, then we felt the whole building shake as Ten Years After did their sound check.

At about five o'clock there was another knock on the door. A procession of waiters dressed in white chef-type jackets and white gloves filed in toward the large glass table. There they unloaded their large, heavy, silver trays.

The fare was as good as, if not better than, the food in room number four on the other side of the stage. The promoter had made good on his word.

Soon it was show time. Every seat in the giant stadium was filled, and as Supertramp opened up for Ten Years After, they had no way of knowing that they were on the brink of achieving their first commercial success with *Crime of the Century* a year later. Then, in 1978, their sixth album, *Breakfast in America*, would go quadruple platinum, winning them two Grammys and launching them to superstardom.

I stood by the side of the stage, watching the band play. They were excellent. As I observed Keith Baker on drums, I realized I had to find another band; I needed to get back in the seat.

The next two weeks were grueling, with just a couple of days off. Sometimes we'd drive all night to reach the next city. Although it was arduous, the tour was a huge success. Every show was sold out, and every night Supertramp performed brilliantly in front of thousands and thousands of fans.

The promoter stood by his promise, and every night there were five dressing rooms backstage: one for each member of TYA, one for their guests, and one for Supertramp, with food and drinks.

"WHERE DO YOU GO TO (MY LOVELY)?"

The day after we got home, I went into The Cabin to present my receipts and leftover cash from the float. I brought in two large coffees and a few hot donuts to share with Judy. I went into her office and set the refreshments on her desk.

"You'd better sit down," Judy said.

"Why? What's going on?" I asked.

"You'll never guess what," Judy replied. "This morning at nine o'clock, I had a phone call from Supertramp's manager. They want you to be their permanent tour manager, starting right now."

"What!?"

"I'm not kidding. He told me you did so well that they want to put you on the payroll."

"Oh, my God . . . that's great Jude, but I can't! I want to play drums again, and if I take on a permanent job like that I'll never find my band. I love those guys and I'd love to work with them again, anytime, but I can't take on a full-time job like that."

From behind me, I heard a very quiet knock on Judy's door. A tall man dressed in a dark suit walked in and stood beside me.

"Dennis," said Judy, "this is Ray, he's my boss. He owns The Cabin."

I stood up and we shook. "Nice to meet you, Ray."

"I hear you had a very successful tour with Supertramp."

"Yeah, man. Great band and great people."

"Judy tells me they offered you a permanent job. Wow, are you going to take it?"

"I'd love to work with the band again, but I can't commit to something like that. I want to play drums again."

"Oh, I completely understand," he said. "Listen . . . I'm always looking for good people. I can keep you working as much as you want, and for good money, too. Can you handle a PA system?"

"I've never tried, but I'm sure I could figure it out."

"We're working with a guy you probably know. He had a big hit with a song called 'Where Do You Go To (My Lovely).'"

"Peter Sarstedt?" I answered.

"Yes, that's him. And he's looking for someone just like you. The only thing is . . . this time there's a small PA system involved. It's a real easy setup. The line-up is just two acoustic guitars, bass, and three vocal mics, nothing to it. He plays a lot; he'll keep you busy. I can show you how to set up the PA in five minutes. It's dead easy."

I looked at Judy and nodded. "Okay, let's do it."

"Great, after you settle up the accounts with Judy, I'll show you around. Oh, and speaking of money, I'm going to waive my commission on the Supertramp tour. One, because it's your first time working for me, and two, because you did so well. Welcome to The Cabin!"

While employed at The Cabin, I worked a lot with Peter Sarstedt and his brother Clive. They had a bass player named Paul, who also sang backing vocals. Peter's audience was a bit more mature than I was used to, but they were just as enthusiastic as a younger crowd. He was a storyteller and captivated his fans every night. He was extremely intelligent and astute, deeply committed to world politics and current affairs. Peter had the gift of communication without intimidation; he never made me feel uneasy. He also had a razor-sharp sense of humor. As we traveled in the Ford Transit, we'd blast the stereo as loud as it would go, all four of us singing along at the top of our voices. The miles flew by as we sang and laughed our way home.

One day we were driving to a gig in Marlborough, about sixty miles from London. Peter suddenly turned to me as I was driving, gave me a look of revelation, and pointed his finger at me.

"Of course! That's who you are!" he said. "How could I have been so blind for so long? You're 'Captain Cardiff,' superhero of South Wales . . . armed with just a leek and shadow and a sword made from daffodils, defending the rights (and wrongs) of Taffs all over the world!" (A "Taff" is somebody from South Wales. The river Taff rises in the Brecon Beacons, then runs south through Merthyr Tydfil, Pontypridd, Taff's Well and Cardiff City Center, and empties into Cardiff Bay.)

From that point on, I became known as "The Captain" or "Captain Cardiff" or simply "CC."

Peter offered me a permanent job, but he understood when I told him I couldn't take it. However, I worked with him as often as I could.

LES AND ANNIE

Neil's ex-girlfriend Les and her friend Annie knew I was anxious to give Claudia her space back. They shared an apartment in the Maida Vale district of London and asked if I wanted to join them there: "You can stay with us 'til you find your own place." Having my own bed would be nice after spending so much time on Claudia's sofa.

Les and Annie took me to their home on Fernhead Road. It was a large terraced house, joined on both sides to the neighboring homes. It consisted of three floors, with different tenants on each. Les and Annie lived on the top floor, a woman we never saw lived on the middle floor, and a guitar player who came from northern England lived on the ground floor with his wife and their little girl. His name was Alan Kendall and he was the latest guitar player for the Bee Gees, who had reunited in 1970 after briefly breaking up, just after Amen Corner disbanded.

We carried my things upstairs; the two-room apartment was nice.

Then Annie led the way to her room and put my things on the bare mattress next to her bed.

"Am I sleeping in here with you?" I asked.

"Don't worry, Den. Annie's seen it all!" Les replied.

"Not like *this*!" I bragged and winked at Annie. We all laughed.

"Dennis, I used to go out with the bass player from the Four Tops. Trust me, *I've seen it all!*" Annie joked.

The three of us cracked up. I had a feeling my stay with Les and Annie was going to be, let's say . . . *unique.*

I worked solidly for The Cabin and had plenty of cash. I was able to pay my third of the rent and take Les and Annie out whenever we all had a free night. The three of us did everything together. We became inseparable. We went to see bands play all the time . . . we tore up the town. Although I felt guilty about Jenny and Babet being so far away while I was having so much fun, something inside told me this wasn't the time to go get them; I needed a permanent job!

Meanwhile, I kept on answering ads in the "Musicians Wanted" section of *Melody Maker* and went to plenty of auditions. Most of the bands were "heavy metal," and I just didn't fit in. At the end of each audition, I had to say no, which made me uncomfortable.

I was making so much money working for The Cabin I was able to sell my Ford Transit van and buy a brand-new white Mercedes Benz L408 van. The 408 was a status symbol in the music community in the early seventies. If you had a 408, you were doing really well. All the top bands had to have one *and so did I.*

I customized it, putting in a metal bulkhead halfway down to separate the passengers from the equipment. In front of the bulkhead, I installed eight leather airplane seats that fully reclined: one in the front, three in the middle, and four at the back. The floor and the walls were carpeted. I had new windows put in on both sides, reaching back to the bulkhead. I'd never forgotten the claustrophobic feeling one experienced while trapped in the back of the old Amen Corner van. Of course, I had a state-of-the-art stereo system installed, with speakers built in. This van was ultra cool.

One day, Ray, the owner of The Cabin, called me aside and told me he wanted to take me out for lunch. At the table, he became serious and businesslike. He said he wanted to grow the company and offered me a fifty percent partnership. I was really flattered, but I told him I couldn't do it — all I wanted was to find the right band and play drums again. He was disappointed, but he understood and let me keep my job working for him.

Meanwhile, back at the apartment, I never saw much of Alan Kendall. He was always off in some other country, playing guitar with the Bee Gees. Whenever he'd come home, he'd show up at our apartment with a huge bottle of duty-free Johnnie Walker Black or the like.

One afternoon I was at home, soaking in the bath — I had bottles of Badedas bubble bath left over from my trips to Europe. I was lathered up pretty good, with just my head showing, when I heard somebody coming up the stairs. Les and Annie were out; I was home alone.

I heard the footsteps stop at the top of the stairs, then the strong northern accent of Alan, back from another stint with the Bee Gees. "Knock, knock, is anybody there?"

"Yeah, Al. I'm in the bath. Come on in."

The door was to my left and behind me, so I couldn't see Alan. It was slightly ajar, then I heard it squeak open.

"Bloody hell, what the . . . ?" Alan said, looking down.

"Bubble bath, man. You never had one?"

"Certainly not, old chap. You'd never catch me in such a preposterous position," Alan said in his fake aristocratic accent.

"Come on, man. It's just bubbles," I answered back.

Then Alan came back to his real voice. "Hey, Dennis. The boys are looking for a drummer and I mentioned you. Are you interested?"

CHAPTER 9 Auditioning for
the Bee Gees

WELCOME TO THE FAMILY, MATE

The first thing I did was to go to The Cabin and get my drums out of storage. I dusted them off, polished up my cymbals, and made sure everything was still in good working order. It was now the winter of 1972, and I hadn't touched the kit in almost two years. I packed the drums in their hard shell cases and tied them down in the back of my Mercedes.

At the time, the Bee Gees had just released *Life in a Tin Can*, their first album on RSO — Robert Stigwood Organization. Both the label and the Bee Gees were counting on this album to revive their careers.

The day after Alan told me the Bee Gees were looking for a drummer, he had called the band's personal manager, Dick Ashby at RSO. He told Dick I was interested in the job, and Dick had set up an audition at Barry Gibb's house, just outside of London.

Barry's place was only about an hour drive from the heart of London. I arrived on time at 1 p.m. and parked my van in front of the house. It was huge: a mansion with an enormous driveway. I must say, that white Mercedes 408 did look good in front of Barry's house. Alan told me I didn't need to lock it up, then led me to the side door, which entered into the kitchen.

As soon as the door opened, the smell of bacon came wafting through the air. Barry's wife, Linda, was standing at the stove, frying pan in one hand, spatula in the other. Linda was a gorgeous woman, with long, shiny black hair and a perfect, slim figure.

"I'm not good at introductions," Alan said. "So you're gonna have to do it yourselves."

Linda turned to me and waved the hot spatula through the air like a sword. "En garde!" she said with a welcoming smile. "Hi, I'm Linda. You must be Dennis."

"Yes, nice to meet you," I teased as I challenged her back with my invisible sword.

"Aye, laddie, and I'm George, Linda's dad." George smiled at me, his medium-built frame standing over the kitchen counter. "Can I get ye sum tea?" he said in a thick Scottish accent. He was filling an oversized teapot with boiling water.

"Hi, George. Nice to meet you . . . Yes, a cup of tea would be great."

George introduced me to his wife, May, who was standing at the sink drying dishes.

"Can I get ye a biscuit, bairn?" May said. (She pronounced "bairn" *burrn*, Scottish slang for "baby.")

"Yeah. Thanks, May."

May put down the tea towel and reached up into the cupboard above, where she pulled out a new packet of Rich Tea biscuits. She opened the packet and dumped half the contents onto a china display plate on the counter.

In the corner of the room and below the window was a large built-in kitchen table. Sitting at the table was a guy reading the local morning paper.

"And that's Tom Kennedy, laddie," George said as he handed me a cup of tea. "An din ye listen tu a ward he says. Aye, he's fulla shite that one," he said with a smile.

Tom laughed as he looked back at George. I reached over, and we shook hands. Tom was a big guy, but not heavy, and was grinning like a butcher's dog. The vibe in the kitchen was beautiful; fun and affection were everywhere. From behind me I heard somebody else approach the room.

"Hmm, something smells good," Barry Gibb said as he entered the kitchen.

"Barry, this is Dennis," Alan said.

Barry walked over. "Aw, yeah, Amen Corner . . . 'Gin House.' Hello, mate," he said as we shook hands. "Now I remember."

Barry went to the kitchen table and shunted Tom along the bench seat into the corner. As he did, Linda put his breakfast plate down in front of him. Then George slid over a large mug of steaming hot tea.

"Oh yeah," Barry said as he looked at the bacon and eggs on the plate. Tom picked up the newspaper and started reading aloud. He was complaining about something Prime Minister George Heath had said the day before. George joined in with his own opinion, and soon a heated debate was under way.

Barry was tucking into his breakfast right in the middle of the discussion, but his appetite wouldn't be lessened by the politics. He was enjoying every bite as he looked at me, shrugged his shoulders, and smiled.

George looked down the hallway beyond the kitchen. "Oh, shite. Here he comes, the noo. Ya best hush up."

Robin Gibb walked into the kitchen. He wasn't as tall as Barry; Robin had long brown hair and wore a white polo-neck sweater and brown pants. This was the guy with the beautiful voice. "Allo, allo, allo," he said as he looked around the room. "Any tea on the go?"

He didn't have to ask twice; in an instant George handed Robin a mug of hot tea, with just the right amount of milk and sugar. George was on tea duty, and he took his job *very seriously*. He had a state-of-the-art Russell Hobbs kettle, and before the teapot had the slightest chance to cool off, George had the old tea bags out and fresh ones in, all the time topping it up with boiling water. I knew exactly what George was doing. That had been one of my jobs in the bed and breakfast when I was a kid.

Robin joined in the political conversation, but soon it went from raw politics to raw humor. We started reminiscing about the old days of *Top of the Pops*, *Beat Club*, and all the odd television shows Amen Corner and the Bee Gees did together. In the late sixties, both bands were on the

Maurice and me looking at Polaroids outside Criteria Studios in Miami.

charts at the same time, so we often did the same TV shows. And we were always bumping into each other, especially at Heathrow Airport. We'd be coming in, and they'd be going out, or vice versa. But it was always Maurice (pronounced "Morris" and nicknamed "Mo") who would come over and bust us.

"You know what?" Maurice would say. "You guys suck . . . You can't play, and your songs are lousy . . . I don't know why you even bother!" Then he'd flash that big "Mo smile," wink, shake everybody's hand, and wish us well. "Good luck," he'd say. "You guys have a great show. You deserve it."

Suddenly, from Barry's kitchen, I heard a low, growling rumble outside. It was Maurice Gibb, arriving in his brand-new Aston Martin sports car. When the rumbling stopped, the kitchen fell silent. A moment later the kitchen door burst open, and Maurice made his entrance. Maurice was handsome in pressed white pants and a western embroidered shirt underneath a black leather waistcoat.

"Is that our *Merc* out there? . . . Did we have a hit record or something? . . . Nobody told me! . . . I thought we were broke!"

"No, that's Dennis's Mercedes," somebody said.

"The new guy, huh? Holy shit, can we afford him?"

Everybody laughed as Maurice stared me down. "I *know* you," he said, as he pointed his finger and moved in. I smiled back and stuck out my hand for a shake. He knocked my hand aside and gave me the biggest bear hug ever.

"Now I remember you." He stared me in the eye and stood back. "Amen Corner, now I remember. Welcome to the family, mate."

"Woah! Hang on a minute, Mo. You're a bit premature; we haven't heard him play yet," Barry said.

"Yeah," Robin said. "He may play like a girl."

And without even thinking, I shot back, "Well, at least I don't sing like one."

I heard Barry gasp as he laughed and almost choked on his tea.

Oh my God, what have I just said?

Everybody in the kitchen let out a "Whooooa" and hushed sniggers followed. Then came a silence I never want to hear again.

In a real serious voice, Maurice suddenly broke in. "Ya know . . . come to think of it . . . he *does* sing like a girl." And everybody, including Robin, laughed out loud. Maurice looked at me and, without anybody else seeing, gave me a knowing wink. *I think Maurice just saved my life,* I thought. *No, I know Maurice just saved my life.*

Barry grinned, and in a few seconds everything was back to the way it had been — except now Maurice was in the room. Whenever Maurice was there, everything always went to another comedic level. All the Bee Gees had a great sense of humor, but Maurice was way out there. He was zany. He was onstage all the time.

I immediately noticed how close the brothers were. They seemed to read each other's minds, finishing off each other's sentences. All they had to do was look at each other and they knew exactly what the others were thinking.

About a half hour or so of conversation and joking went by, and then

Barry called out, "Okay, let's go and have a knock." I started to go get my drums from the van, but Tom Kennedy turned to me and said, "No need, squire, I've already got your drums set up in Barry's studio."

What!?!? This was a level of pampering I could get used to. *Hm-mm. This is a good thing.*

We walked through Barry's house, past a full-sized snooker table, and I noticed all the walls were blanketed with gold records and awards the Bee Gees had won. Every flat surface had a prize or a trophy on it. There was gold and platinum everywhere.

When we reached the recording studio, I saw Barry had two Studer ReVox tape recorders just like mine. True to his word, Tom had already set up my drums. I adjusted them to my liking and sat down in great anticipation. This was so exciting — aside from a few television appearances together, I'd mostly seen these guys from in front of a TV screen, and here I was sitting on my drums in the same room as Barry, Robin, and Maurice Gibb, about to play some of their greatest hits. I didn't know what to think.

Barry got out his acoustic-electric guitar, Maurice strapped on his bass, and Alan plugged in his electric guitar.

"Okay, what should we do?" Barry asked as he tuned.

"Let's do 'Bend Me, Shape Me,'" Maurice said. "I love that song!"

Alan burst out laughing.

"Maurice, *please* be serious. This is important," Barry shot back.

Maurice looked at me and behind Barry's back pulled an absurd face and mouthed *Maurice, please be serious.* Without even looking up, Barry smiled and scolded his younger brother, "M-a-u-r-i-c-e."

I was trying not to laugh as Barry finished tuning. "Right, let's do . . . What about 'To Love Somebody'? Do you know that one?" Barry asked.

"Yeah, I've heard it," I answered, trying not to sound facetious. *I've heard it all right — along with virtually everyone else on the planet*, I thought.

"Okay," Barry said. "You want to count it in, or do you want me to?"

"You can do it," I said, and Barry began to scratch out the rhythm of the song on his guitar strings. After the count, we all came in. We were only two guitars, bass, and drums, but the Bee Gees had a way of making it sound like a full orchestra. All the humor instantly disappeared as Maurice guided me through the intro and into the first verse. Then Barry's powerful voice came through the PA system.

I had goosebumps as I became part of that incredible song. Robin was sitting down on a chair next to Barry, scribbling on a small piece of paper. As the chorus approached, he got up and stood in front of his mic. Maurice took a step forward toward his own mic. All three brothers were in each other's face as the chorus hit in beautiful three-part harmony. Again Maurice guided me through the diamond — that moment in a song where all the musicians stop at the same time, then carry on playing — and onto the chorus tag.

My goosebumps produced their very own goosebumps as we started into the second verse. Then something very strange happened. Barry stopped singing and started scratching his guitar strings for no apparent reason. Everybody stopped playing.

"Okay . . . let's do something else," Barry said as he continued to tune.

Maurice again looked at me and began mouthing *Bend Me, Shape Me*.

Again, I tried my hardest not to laugh, but Barry knew exactly what was going on. This time, though, he didn't say anything to Maurice. "Okay . . . how about . . . um . . . 'I've Got to Get a Message to You.' Do you know that one? Have you heard it?" Barry asked.

"Yeah, I know it."

"The intro's a bit tricky; there's a couple of pushes in it," Barry warned.

"Just follow me," Maurice said.

Barry scratched out the tempo and counted it in. Maurice guided me through the intro, then for the first time I heard Robin's beautiful solo voice.

Was this really happening to me? Was I actually in Barry Gibb's home studio, playing drums with the Bee Gees? Bloody hell, I was!

I didn't think my goosebumps could take any more as Barry and Maurice joined Robin for the chorus.

We went into the second verse and the same thing happened as had in "To Love Somebody." Barry stopped playing, and then we *all* stopped. "Okay, that's enough of that," Barry said. "Why don't we do one of Rob's songs? How about 'Massachusetts'?" Barry asked.

"I can play it, but I can't spell it," I replied with a smile.

Maurice shot me a dirty look and pointed his finger. "Hey, I'll do the jokes 'round here, mate. Just cool it with the humor." Then he flashed that smile again. "Play it, but can't spell it? Hmm, nice one, Den Den." I laughed, because no one had ever called me Den Den before.

We sailed through "Massachusetts" without a problem, and this time we played the whole song.

"Do you know a song called 'Words'?" Barry asked, and I nodded.

Maurice took off his bass guitar and handed it to Alan. Then he sat down at an upright grand piano against the side wall. I couldn't see Maurice's face, as he was sitting on the piano stool with his back to me. "Come in on the second verse, Den Den," Maurice instructed from over his shoulder.

"Hey, Tom," Barry called to their roadie, who was almost lost in a large white beanbag chair at the back of the room. "Can you ask George to put the kettle on, mate?"

"Not a problem," Tom said. He got up and headed out toward the kitchen. I'd only just met George, but I was willing to bet that Russell Hobbs was already filled with boiling water and ready to go. George was a pro!

"Okay, 'Words.'" Barry nodded to Maurice, and Maurice began the intro.

Maurice threw his head back, and I came in on the downbeat of the second verse. Maurice lifted up his left arm as if to salute, and, without looking back, gave me a one-handed thumbs up.

This was unbelievable. I had become lost in the beauty of the song. I felt like I was inside a deep secret; it was magical. The hair on the back of my neck stood up. I'd always loved this song, and here I was, playing it with the Bee Gees themselves. Even if I didn't get the job, this moment was enough . . . *No, I want the job!*

We got about halfway through the song and again Barry wrapped things up.

"Right," he said. "Let's go and have a cuppa tea."

I thought this was a bit strange, because we'd only been playing for about a half hour. And most of that time was spent tuning and watching Maurice do his routine.

We all followed Barry back into the kitchen, where Robin pulled out a large bottle of Southern Comfort.

"Not for me thanks," I said. "I can't drink when I'm playing."

"Oh, you can have a drink, mate," Barry said. "We're done. But don't rush off. Stick around for a while, have a drink."

I looked to Alan for the lead. "I'm game," Alan said, and Robin began to pour.

I was a bit concerned; we'd only played parts of three songs, and once through "Massachusetts." Was that it? Was that my audition? *Maybe I played so bad that everybody just wanted to get rid of me. Maybe they were just too polite to say, "Piss off."*

"Have you had this before?" Robin asked, as he handed me a large glass of Southern Comfort.

"No, never."

"It's an American liqueur. It's good."

Alan knocked his back in one go. "That it is, old chap. Would there be any . . . *m-o-r-e*?" Alan's fake aristocratic accent was back.

Robin refilled Alan's glass and started telling us about the history of Southern Comfort. "It was created in the middle of the last century by a drunken barman in Louisiana. He couldn't get any women, so he came up with this."

"Then he got all the *Southern comfort* he needed," Barry said from the kitchen table.

"Exactly!" Robin replied.

"That's not true," Alan said, as he laughed out loud.

"It *is* true," Robin replied. "But the strange thing is, originally it wasn't called Southern Comfort."

"Go on," Maurice said with a yawn.

"Originally it was called 'Cuffs and Buttons.'"

"Ooooo, never get any action with a name like that . . . Better come up with a new name quick!" Barry replied, fast as lightning.

"That's right," Robin continued. "He changed the name to Southern Comfort, and the rest is, you know, history."

"Yeah, and I bet he died with a *big* smile on his face," Maurice said.

I looked over at George and May, who were standing near the sink. They were both laughing and enjoying the banter. This was a close family.

"I'm outta here . . . Good luck, guys," Maurice said, as he gave Robin a look of disbelief.

"It's true," Robin insisted, shrugging his shoulders. Then after about thirty minutes of hilarity between Barry and Robin, Robin left, too.

Alan told me he had to get back to London to meet his wife, Lissie, and their little girl Heidi.

"Well, I guess I'll go pack up my drums," I said.

"I've already done it," Tom said. "They're in the van. You're ready to go."

Now I was *really* starting to feel uneasy. Nobody mentioned the audition and everybody had gone home. I said goodbye to Barry and George and hugged May and Linda. Tom walked Alan and me out to the van. Then Alan and I started the journey home.

It was all over in a flash and I was confused. "Al, what just *happened*?" I asked.

"Oh, don't worry about it," Alan said. "That's just the way they are."

"But I didn't finish the audition," I said. "I did half of three songs and 'Massachusetts.'"

"Just call Dick at the office tomorrow," Alan said.

So the next day I called Dick Ashby at RSO. "Hi, Dick, this is Dennis Bryon. I auditioned for the Bee Gees yesterday . . . drums . . . and I was wondering if I got the job."

There was a slight pause. "Do you *want* the job?"

"Yeah, I do. I want the job," I said.

"Then you got it," Dick said.

I was, of course, elated by that news. But the irony was that I took a big pay cut to join the Bee Gees. I went from making huge money as a tour manager . . . to being on a straight wage of thirty pounds a week. But I was playing drums in one of my favorite bands of all time. I was playing drums with the Bee Gees.

MY FIRST GIG

It was January 1973. A brand-new year, a brand-new job, and a brand-new life. I was sorry to give up my work as a tour manager. I enjoyed the independence and freedom — and *especially* the money. I didn't need my Mercedes anymore, so I sold it to two guys who worked for The Cabin. Now I needed some transportation that was comfortable yet big enough to carry my drums. I found a brand-new white Volkswagen camper that was ideal. My drums fit perfectly in the space at the very back, over the engine. This left the living area behind the two front seats empty. There was a table in the back that had two bench seats at either side, a two-burner propane cooktop, a sink with running water, and a small built-in cooler. The roof of the camper elevated from one side, which made the inside feel huge.

My first work with the Bee Gees was a thirty-six day tour of North America. But before leaving we had one *little* show in London. Just a local gig . . . nothing really. It was merely at the *Royal Festival Hall* with the legendary ninety-two-piece *London Symphony Orchestra*, conducted by the famous *Stanley Black, OBE*. No pressure at all — especially knowing that the 2,500-seat concert hall was *completely* *sold out*!

It was my first time onstage in more than two years, and I was nervous as hell. We rehearsed for almost a month at Barry's house, and everything felt good, but I'd never played with an orchestra before — let alone one as famous as this. Finally, Monday, February 19, came around, and it was show time with the Bee Gees.

The Royal Festival Hall was big. I'd played most of the famous venues in London with Amen Corner — including the Royal Albert Hall, the Apollo, and Ronnie Scott's — but it was my first time in this historic place. The stage was wide and deep and my drums seemed to be lost. They were set up in the middle, about one-third of the way in from the front. Behind me, the back two-thirds of the stage towered up from the floor at an angle. This is where the ninety-two-piece orchestra would be seated. To my right was a full-size grand piano. Out front, there were countless rows of seats. They were covered in a red velvet material and looked very plush. Protruding from the walls on either side of the hall were at least a dozen boxes that stuck out like giant fingers above the seats below.

Behind the boxes, a balcony reached from side to side, leading all the way up to the ceiling at the back. It reminded me of the day, not so long ago, when I had seen The Beatles play in Cardiff. That day, I was at the back of a balcony just like this one. But today, here I was playing drums with the Bee Gees and the London Symphony Orchestra in London's very own Royal Festival Hall. *How did I get here?*

Backstage, before the show, there were a lot of nerves. There were people everywhere. Almost everybody from RSO was there, including the Bee Gees' manager Robert Stigwood. I think I was introduced to at least two dozen people that night, but all I wanted to do was to get onstage and set my butterflies free.

Before we performed, Barry introduced me to the conductor of the orchestra, Stanley Black. He was a tall man, proud, and immaculately dressed in a double-breasted black tuxedo.

"Have you ever played with an orchestra before, Dennis?" he asked.

"No, this is the first time."

"Well, hold on, you're in for the ride of your life." And he wasn't kidding.

The opening performer was another one of Robert Stigwood's acts. A fellow from Liverpool named Jimmy Stevens. Jimmy was a talented singer/songwriter who accompanied himself on acoustic guitar or piano. He always dressed very casually, wearing jeans, a T-shirt, and a denim jacket. His songs were raw and gritty.

Jimmy went down well, but before we took the stage, the LSO performed some classical pieces from their repertoire. I'd never seen an orchestra like this, and they were incredible. But the best was yet to come . . .

Alan and I were told to go out first, then the Bee Gees would take the stage after they were introduced. The hall was packed; every seat was taken and, as Alan and I walked out from the wings, a polite hush fell over the crowd.

"We love you, Den!" came from the balcony in a broad Welsh accent. It was Les and Annie, sitting up in the first row. The audience responded with subdued laughter. I looked up and waved, which got another chuckle. As I walked toward my drums, I could feel all ninety-two pairs of eyes looking down on me. The orchestra was massive. All the male players were wearing matching black tuxedos and white shirts with bow ties, while the women were dressed in chic black dresses.

I sat down on my drums and extracted two new pairs of sticks from my stick bag. I put one pair on my bass drum, just in case, and got the other pair ready to play. I reached down and pulled up on the strainer of my snare drum. Then I looked down and could clearly see the set list, taped to the floor next to my hi-hat. I was ready.

"Ladies and gentlemen, the Robert Stigwood Organization proudly presents . . . *the Bee Gees!*"

The Gibb brothers.

Barry, Robin, and Maurice confidently made their entrance. The audience clapped, whooped, and whistled. As I looked out, Barry was to my left, Robin was in the middle, and Maurice was in front of Alan, to my right. After Barry and Maurice plugged in, there was a brief silence. Barry looked out into the audience and flashed that huge smile. "Alright?" he shouted, and the audience responded with whistles and cries of "*Yeah!*"

The first song was "To Love Somebody," and Barry was to count it in. I had the tempo and the melody firmly fixed, running through my head. After all those rehearsals, I knew exactly what was coming next. Or at least I *thought* I knew, but I had no idea what was to come . . .

Barry counted, "One – two – three – four." The intro started, and from behind me the ninety-two-piece London Symphony Orchestra made themselves known. The effect was awe-inspiring; I'd never heard anything like it in my life. The sound of the strings was immense. Multiple violins mixed with a grouping of cellos and string basses. The sound came from everywhere, and I was right in the middle of it. Then I started playing the first verse, and I heard Barry singing in my monitor. This was getting scary; it was like breathing underwater in the middle of the most beautiful ocean on the planet. I'd never felt music like this before.

In rehearsals at Barry's house, I'd come to realize that with the Bee Gees, it was all about the chorus. All the verse melody, the beautiful harmony, and the words had only one direction — *the chorus.* I also figured out that if I *laid back* the groove in the chorus, it gave the song more emotion and more passion, and that's exactly what *they* wanted.

Laying back the groove is a tricky thing. You have to give the rhythm the appearance of slowing down, but the tempo must never change. I was playing the verse groove of "To Love Somebody," and I was trying my best to keep my playing tight and soulful. I could hear the different parts of the orchestra moving behind me. Then, as I did a big drum fill to take the song into the chorus, I heard different sections of the orchestra come to life: the percussion section had timpani drums and cymbals with tubular bells; the brass section had French horns, trumpets, trombones, and tubas; the woodwind section had flutes, oboes, clarinets, piccolos, and bassoons and, in the middle of it all, the most beautiful harp I'd ever heard. Then, just when I thought it couldn't get any better, the Bee Gees started singing in three-part harmony. This truly was one of the greatest moments of my life. I'll never forget the feeling of being inside something so beautiful, of touching something untouchable.

When the song was over, the audience went crazy, and every song after that got the same response. At the end of the night, the Bee Gees earned two standing ovations, finally ending the show with another one of their hits, "Lonely Days." Before walking off stage for the last time, every member of the London Symphony Orchestra stood and gave praise to such an outstanding performance.

Backstage after the show, everyone was elated. Even Robert Stigwood came over to me to introduce himself. He shook my hand and didn't let go as he thanked me for the night's great performance. He also told me the "boys" had been looking for the *right* drummer for some time, and now he thought they'd found him. My first show with the Bee Gees was a success. It looked like I was a drummer again.

CHAPTER 10

My First Bee Gees
Tour: North America

OH CANADA

After the show with the London Symphony Orchestra, I met Les and
Annie at a restaurant, as we'd prearranged, and we stayed out all night cel-
ebrating. I had a couple of days to get my things together, before leaving
for North America later that week.

My first time out with the Bee Gees was a thirty-eight-day, seven-
teen-city tour of Canada and the U.S. This was my first time in both
countries. The thought of visiting Canada didn't bother me, but I was
quite scared about being in America. I'd just seen the film *Easy Rider* star-
ring Peter Fonda, Dennis Hopper, and Jack Nicholson and, to be honest,
the film frightened the life out of me.

At nine o'clock sharp on the morning of Friday, February 23, 1973,
a large car pulled up outside our house on Fernhead Road. It was to
take Alan Kendall and me to Heathrow Airport. When we arrived, Tom
Kennedy and Dick Ashby were waiting for us in front of terminal three.
We gave our passports to Dick while Tom loaded our suitcases onto a
luggage cart, and then we followed Dick and Tom to the British Overseas

Airways Corporation counter. After Dick checked us in, he handed us our tickets and passports, before going back outside to wait for other members of the party. Tom led us to an escalator that went up to the BOAC first class lounge. As we walked in, I leaned over and whispered to Alan, "Are we traveling first class?"

"No, but they are. We just get to enjoy the free stuff before the flight."

In the lounge, I saw Barry and Linda Gibb sitting around a table with the Bee Gees' father, Hughie, and younger brother Andy.

"Here comes trouble," Barry said.

"Double trouble, if you ask me," Linda added.

We said hi to everyone, and Hughie got up from the table, turned his back to us, and walked over to the large window that looked out onto the airport. I felt a strange vibe coming from him. Hughie had managed the group when the Bee Gees were growing up in Australia. The brothers were born in the Isle of Man, a small island in the Irish Sea between England and Ireland, but the whole family had emigrated to Australia when they were just boys. Hughie was not interested in anyone but the brothers; he had shaped their careers from the beginning.

From behind me there was a slight commotion as Maurice arrived.

"Is this the Led Zeppelin tour? I'm the bass player!" he announced loudly. All the other passengers in the lounge looked around. Glyn Hale, the musical director, accompanied Maurice. In each city, we'd be playing with different local orchestras, and it was Glyn's job to rehearse and conduct the musicians. Then Robin arrived with Ray Washbourne, another tour assistant. Finally, Tom and Dick walked in with Jimmy Stephens, the opening act. I remember looking around and trying to take it all in. This was my new family, and we were about to get on a jet bound for North America!

It wasn't long before we heard the announcement to board the plane. Although most of our party was traveling coach, or *second class* as it was called it in those days, we were allowed to board at the same time as the first-class passengers. We said our goodbyes at the plane's entrance door as the Gibb family members headed for the front of the plane. It never bothered me flying coach while the Bee Gees party traveled first class. I was on the plane, and that's *all* that mattered.

This was the longest flight I'd ever been on. The eight hours in the air seemed to take forever. Finally, we touched down in Montreal, where we stayed on the ground for about half an hour before continuing to Toronto. As I looked down, the ground was covered with snow, but I had no idea just how cold the Canadian air really was. After we landed in Toronto and cleared customs, we were met by some of the Polydor record company staff, who drove us to the hotel.

We were staying at a brand new Holiday Inn, right in the heart of downtown Toronto, and I was about to find out what day-to-day life on the road with the Bee Gees was like.

At every hotel, Dick checked everybody in. He gave each of us a key and a list of all the room numbers. Tom and Ray handled the bags. They brought them from the airport to the hotel, and then delivered the appropriate bags to each person's room. The next day, or whenever we were leaving the hotel, I'd leave my packed suitcase in my room on the bed. Tom or Ray would pick it up and take it to the airport and check it in. The only time I ever saw my suitcase was in my hotel room. When we left the hotel, Dick paid the bill, and checked everybody out.

If the hotel was big enough, each brother had his own suite. Everyone else had their own double room. The Bee Gees paid for all my room service and any meals in the hotel restaurant. This even included my laundry, if we were at the hotel for more than one night.

Of course, Dick kept a thrifty eye on everybody's spending habits at the hotels. If he thought anyone was overcharging, or taking advantage, that person would get a firm talking-to on the plane the next day.

I was paid by the show. My retainer of thirty pounds a week was still being deposited into my bank account back in London. At the beginning of each week, Dick gave me a cash per diem for out-of-pocket expenses. It was easy to live well on the road with the Bee Gees. They were very generous. The only things that were no-nos were phone calls and bar bills. If you wanted to call home or long distance, that was down to the individual, and if you wanted to get *plastered* at the bar, you owned the bill.

I had a really nice room on the tenth floor of the Holiday Inn. It had two king-sized beds and a large bathroom with an oversized bath and shower. There was a desk, as well as a round table with four chairs, and I had my own television. The room had a beautiful view of the city. Everything was new.

I turned on the television and, almost before it had time to warm up, there was a knock on my door. I opened the door to see one of the hotel bell staff outside, with my suitcase on a large luggage trolley. Standing in the hallway supervising was Tom Kennedy, who instructed the bellman to put my suitcase on one of my beds.

"Alright, my son?" Tom said in his London accent.

"Yahh monn," I replied in my best fake Jamaican tongue.

"Hey, you wanna meet for dinner?" Tom asked. "There's a good restaurant here in the hotel."

The restaurant did turn out to be nice. Everything was brand new. Dick and Alan were sitting at a table with Tom, and they called me over. The food was good, and during dinner Dick explained some of the road rules. He told me that on occasion it was okay to have a bottle of wine with dinner, just not *every* night. And he requested I always get a separate check, so he could keep track of how much I was spending. He also told me the boys would pay for the tip in the hotel restaurant or room service, but never more than fifteen percent.

After dinner and a few glasses of wine, I was ready for bed. I got to my room and opened up my suitcase, which was on the spare bed. I looked underneath one of my shirts in the suitcase and found my tour itinerary from RSO. I had thought I'd lost it and was a little too embarrassed to ask Dick for another one. I opened the pages to today's date. There, on page three, written in longhand, were two messages: one from Annie, and one from Les. The first message read:

"Night-night, Den — from Annie and Les. We are thinking of you!"

Underneath, the other one read:

"Nos da, my flower!" (Good night, my flower!)

I laughed out loud, as I figured out Les and Annie had hijacked my itinerary. They wrote personal messages throughout the pages and hid it underneath my clothes in my suitcase. Today's message was the first of many.

I went to the window and looked out over Toronto. The downtown buildings were tall and brightly lit. Then it started to snow; the snow came down so hard that within seconds I could barely see the street below. As I gazed into the whiteout, everything I knew seemed so far away. It *was*.

I was in Canada at the beginning of a journey to who knows where.

The first show of the tour was on Sunday at Toronto's O'Keefe Centre on Front Street. Rehearsals were at one o'clock, with a thirty-piece orchestra led by our conductor Glyn Hale. Tom took Alan and me to the venue in a cab, as the roads were still nasty from all the snow. The O'Keefe Centre was another huge 3,000-seat auditorium. It wasn't quite as lavish as the Royal Festival Hall, but was just as grand in its own fashion.

The show was ninety minutes long — seventeen songs — with a break in the middle where the Bee Gees would sing an acoustic medley of five or six of their hits. At the end of the set, there were two encore songs.

We finished rehearsing most of the songs with the orchestra, when suddenly there was excitement everywhere. The Bee Gees had arrived. "Evening all!" Maurice shouted to the members of the orchestra as they walked in. "Evening all" was the catch phrase popularized by police constable George Dickson, the main character in a British television series about life in a London police station. It was nice to have a bit of London here in Canada.

The orchestra tapped their instruments and waved back. Glyn rushed through the rehearsal of the last few songs, not wanting to keep the brothers waiting. There was definitely a different atmosphere backstage, now that the Bee Gees were in the building.

Maurice put on his bass guitar, and Alan switched back to his Les Paul. Barry plugged in his electric/acoustic guitar and approached his microphone, while Robin stood at his mic between Barry and Maurice. Some of the people who worked for the O'Keefe Centre took seats in front of the stage, eager to watch as the Bee Gees rehearsed.

Each brother had his own monitor speakers in front of him, so he could have his very own personalized mix. Barry liked plenty of drums, while Robin wanted Barry's guitar loud, with lots of vocals and strings in echo. Maurice liked to hear his own voice louder than his two brothers', with a good amount of bass and electric guitar thrown in. The monitor man at the side of the stage was able to give each brother exactly what he wanted in his mix and he could make the speakers in front of them as loud or as soft as desired. Behind the seats at the back of the hall was another mixing console, manned by two more sound engineers. They controlled the mix that the audience heard.

We started the sound check with "To Love Somebody." This gave the sound mixer out front a good sampling of Barry's powerful vocal, the three-part harmony, the full orchestra, and soft and loud drums, along with Alan's powerhouse guitar. We played the song all the way through. Then we did "Massachusetts," letting the engineer focus in on Robin's solo voice. As we went through the song, Barry went out front to listen to what the audience would hear. Then he returned to the mixing console and gave the sound mixer a thumbs up.

When Barry came back onstage, we went through "I've Gotta Get a Message to You" and "Lonely Days." Then, that was it — our rehearsal was done. Glyn continued rehearsing the orchestra while we made ourselves comfortable in the dressing room.

Before I knew it, it was showtime, and Jimmy Stephens was warming up the audience. The place was packed, and Jimmy had created a great rapport with the crowd. He talked about how each song was written and what it meant to him. The crowd loved it.

As we had done in the London Festival Hall, Alan and I took the stage first. Again, this allowed a formal introduction. "Ladies and gentlemen, it is with great pleasure that Cimba Productions proudly presents . . . the Bee Gees."

As Barry, Robin, and Maurice came onstage, the audience applauded loudly. Barry quickly plugged in his guitar and started scratching out the tempo of the first song. He counted the song in, and the whole orchestra began playing the intro to "To Love Somebody." Immediately, the audience recognized the melody and began clapping and cheering wildly. This happened with every song. Even the songs that were less well known got the same cheers as the big hits. I could see how popular the group was with the Canadian audience.

This was my second appearance with the Bee Gees, and I wasn't quite as nervous as I'd been during the first one. I'd gotten away with playing the first show without a mistake, so I knew I could do it again. I was a little more relaxed this time, and I was able to look around a bit. At the front of the large balcony, there were three huge spotlights: one at each side and one in the middle. A lighting technician operated each light. Hughie had a headset with a built-in microphone and was giving directions to the three technicians. Every time Robin or Barry sang lead vocal, Hughie would instruct the other two operators to dim their lights, putting the emphasis on the solo voice. When all three brothers sang together they were all lit up. The effect worked really well and added another dimension to the show.

All too soon, we were at the end of "Spicks and Specks" and started playing "Lonely Days." They were our two encore songs. After the brothers left the stage for the third and final time, the house lights came on, and the audience finally stopped clapping and cheering. It was another great show, and everyone was happy. I felt good that the way I played fit in with musical direction of the group.

The next day we left for Montreal. It was a particularly busy day. Apart from the travel, we had to check into our hotel and get to rehearsals by three o'clock in the afternoon for the show that night. We were playing at the Forum Concert Bowl, a huge venue with a capacity of 8,000 people. The organizers had changed the seating format, as they weren't expecting any more than 2,000 people. Huge rolling walls were wheeled into place to cordon off most of the gigantic assembly hall. I'd never been in a place so big.

Rehearsals went well. It was the smallest orchestra so far, with just ten violins, four cellos, two violas, one harp, one trombone, one baritone sax (doubling on flute), two trumpets (doubling on flugelhorns), and a percussionist.

Again, the mood backstage changed when the Bee Gees arrived. But this time, the level of excitement doubled as the promoter made his entrance at the same time. Donald K. Donald was a great friend of the brothers and had promoted all of their previous Canadian tours. He was full of life, a real character bubbling over with enthusiasm. The first thing he did was take everybody in our party backstage to the dressing room. There, he showered us with gifts and mementos of the show.

Donald K. was also a huge fan of the Toronto Maple Leafs hockey team, and he had Maple Leafs jerseys for everyone. And they were the *real thing*; he had them made specially for our group. He shook my hand and welcomed me to Canada before proudly giving me my jersey. It was huge and blue, with the Maple Leafs logo stitched on the front. On each arm, below the logo, was the number five with two white rings stitched underneath. On the back of my jersey there was a huge number five sewn onto the fabric, and above it, in white lettering, it read "BRYON."

That wasn't all. He also gave everybody a couple of Donald K. Donald Promotions T-shirts and a trophy with their name, the date, and lettering that read "Bee Gees Live At The Forum Concert Bowl." This was a generous guy.

The cordoned-off part of the hall was packed. After Jimmy finished his opening set, we had another great show, with two huge encores. I rode back to the hotel with Barry and Linda in their limo, and Barry made a suggestion: "Why don't you come up to the room? Lin's got some wine. Come and hang out."

"Okay, great," I said. "Let me change, and I'll be right up." I went up to my room and got out of my stage clothes. After hanging them up to dry, I threw on some jeans and one of my new Donald K. T-shirts. When I got to Barry's suite, Hughie, Andy, Tom, and Alan were already there. The main room in the suite was enormous — you could have fit two of my double bedrooms in it, with room to spare. There were two large sofas, a couple of armchairs, and a large dining table with six chairs around it, along with, of course, the biggest television Barry could get.

On the table were half a dozen bottles of red wine, an ice-chest full of beer, and a metal flight case about two feet square by one foot high that was stenciled "Scientific Equipment." It was open and inside was an electric water kettle, a china teapot, some mugs, a packet of teabags, and some packets of sugar. All of these items were built into the strong Anvil case and protected by heavy-duty foam inside. It was Barry's on-the-road tea station.

Linda came over to the table where I was standing. "Beer or wine?"

"A glass of wine would be great, thanks," I answered.

Linda poured me a glass. "Just help yourself when you're done. No need to ask."

"L-i-n-d-a!" Barry shouted from the bedroom. Tom and Alan looked at each other and half smiled.

"What?!" she shouted back.

"Where's my shirt? You know, the one I really like?"

"Well, it wouldn't be in the suitcase, *would it*?!" she answered sarcastically.

"Which one?"

Linda threw her head back, sighed, and headed for the bedroom.

After a quick knock on the door, Robin let himself in. "Evening all," he mumbled, as he looked around. "Boy, this is a motley bunch . . . especially *you*," Robin said, looking at Alan. Then he focused on me. "I love Wales . . . Yes, Wales . . . where men are men and sheep are nervous."

"Especially when *he's* around," Maurice said, as he entered the room and pointed at Robin.

"Aye, aye," Barry said, emerging from his bedroom. He apparently hadn't found the shirt he was looking for; he was bare-chested.

Maurice just couldn't forsake the opportunity. "Den Den, come here a minute," he said. "I have to show you something." He called me over next to Barry, who was standing just outside his bedroom, and pointed to Barry's bare chest. When he was a small child, Barry had had a bad accident at his home involving a pot of scalding-hot tea sitting on a tablecloth he'd tugged on. Most of his chest was badly scarred.

"Right," Maurice continued. "This is where we're gonna start the world tour . . . India." Maurice pointed to the scar tissue on Barry's chest, which did somewhat resemble a map. "We're gonna start here, up to Russia, a sharp left through Moscow, then down to Germany, through Italy, then finish up in Africa." Barry stood there patiently, rolling his eyes.

Although everyone else in the room had been through Maurice's map routine many times, they still laughed. It was *funny*. When he was done, Maurice just stood face to face with Barry and stared into his eyes. After about five seconds of silence, Maurice said, "Okay, you can go now. We're done, thank you!"

Barry calmly walked over to the Scientific Equipment case. "Anyone for tea?" he asked.

"Lovely," Robin answered, rubbing his hands together. Barry poured tea for himself and Robin, then walked over to the sofa and sat down. He reached over and picked up an acoustic guitar sitting in a stand in front of the television and started tuning. Then the three brothers simply looked at each other and broke into The Everly Brothers' "Bye, Bye, Love."

Taken at the Castaways Restaurant on Miami Beach. Left to right: me, photographer Ed Caraeff, Tom Kennedy, Linda Gibb, Barry Gibb, Yvonne Gibb, and Maurice Gibb.

This was amazing. They were performing just as if they were in front of an audience. Even though they'd just finished at least an hour and a half onstage, they still felt the need for more. For the next two hours, they sang everything from The Beatles to Elvis to Ricky Nelson to Sinatra. Just the way they mimicked the original artists was astonishing, yet they somehow made all the songs sound as if they were Bee Gees originals. I was witnessing a side of the group few people had the privilege of seeing.

NEW YORK, NEW YORK

Finally, the day I was most apprehensive about had arrived. I was on my way to New York, on my way to America for the first time. It was a beautiful, sunny day as we took off from Montreal International Airport; the ground was still covered with snow. The city of Montreal looked beautiful as it shimmered in the frigid sunshine.

The flight time of only about an hour seemed to fly by. The plane was almost empty, so I was able to get a window seat that let me look down over the city as we came in. Suddenly, there it was . . . New York. We'd followed the Hudson down to New York Harbor, passing by the Bronx and Manhattan. The skyscrapers were huge, and there were so many of them. I'd never seen anything like it. They seemed to fill the sky, and were so near I felt like I could reach out and touch them. Then, at the end of Manhattan Island, standing fearlessly above all, were the twin towers of the World Trade Center. They took my breath away as we flew by. I pressed my forehead to the window and there, underneath, was Liberty Island and the Statue of Liberty.

I don't know why, but I felt inspired. I'd gotten used to, and taken for granted, all the wonderful architecture and history that London offered, but this was different. This was new, modern, brave. Something was calling to my emotions; something was pulling me in. This was not what I had expected.

We landed at JFK International and went through immigration without any problems. Dick had taken care of all the visas and permits necessary for us to work in America. Our bags arrived, and we all cleared customs without challenge.

Two stretch limos waited to take us from the airport to the hotel. Tom had a van with a driver to handle the bags. As we walked out of the terminal I took in the cold New York air.

"Den, come with me. I want to show you something," Robin said as he yanked on my arm. He led me toward a single hot-dog vendor standing by the curb. Robin stopped and said, "Pay attention, I'm gonna show you how to order a hot dog in New York." Then, with me by his side, Robin sauntered up to the vendor with the cart. In his best New York accent, Robin ordered, "Hey, bud . . . gimme a dawg."

"Sure ting, wat-ya-wonn on it?" the vendor replied.

"Gimme da woiks," Robin said.

"Ya got it, mac."

The vendor pulled out a bun and slapped a steaming-hot frankfurter on it. The frankfurter was twice as long as the bun. He slathered on mustard, ketchup, onions, and sauerkraut and handed it to Robin. Then he looked at me.

"Gimme a dawg, bud," I said, but it just didn't sound right. The vendor kept looking at me.

"Ya wan me ta load 'er up?"

I didn't know what the hell he was talking about, so I looked to Robin.

"Sure ting, give him the woiks," Robin said. The vendor made an identical dog and handed it to me.

"Three bucks," the vendor said.

Robin and I looked at each other. "You got any money?" Robin asked.

"Only Canadian."

Robin ran back toward the limos. "D-i-c-k!" he shouted. I stayed with the vendor; I didn't want him to think we were making a run for it.

"He's gone to get some dough," I said reassuringly.

"Say what?"

"Dough . . . you know, money . . . bucks . . . moolah."

"Ya guys sure do talk strange. Where ya from, anyway? Germany?"

Robin came back with a five-dollar bill. "Hey, keep the change, bud."

The vendor took the money and gave us both a suspicious look. "Yeah, man."

As we walked away, I looked back at the vendor and, in my best German accent, said, "Danke schön."

The vendor kept looking at me as he slowly nodded his head and said, "Whatevah!"

Our hotel was called the City Squire, and I decided I would stay in my room for the night. I wanted to watch the city get dark, and I wanted to watch some American television. I flipped through some literature on the table next to the window and came across the room-service menu. I paged through it until I found exactly what I was looking for: the American classic, hamburger with cheese and fries. I dialed the number on the menu and ordered a cheeseburger with da woiks, large fries, and two bottles of Heineken. This was my first time ordering room service in a hotel in America, and I was a little intimidated, but as I would find out, there was no need for me to worry.

About an hour later I was going through the channels on the television when there was a loud pounding on my door.

"*Room Service!*" a voice shouted. I cleared a space on the table for the tray and glanced at the television on my way to the door. I didn't realize it, but the last channel I had selected was a cartoon channel. I peeped through a tiny viewer in the door. Outside, a large black man in uniform was holding a tray. I opened the door.

"Hey, man. How ya doing?" the waiter said as he barged past me and headed toward the table. "Holy shit! *Road Runner!*" he noted as he passed the television. He put the tray down on the table and sat on the bed in front of the TV. "You seen this one? Watch this . . . he almost gets it!"

On the screen, Road Runner came to a screeching stop on a deserted desert highway; dust flew everywhere. On a cliff high above, Wile E. Coyote started to push a huge boulder toward the edge. The boulder began to fall. Below, the Road Runner nonchalantly looked around at the desert, moving his head in a jerking motion.

"*Look out, man! Above you!*" the waiter shouted, and at the last split-second Road Runner took half a step to the left. The boulder crashed through the desert floor right next to him. The bird's feathers ruffled in the turbulent air and dust.

"Motherfucker, that was close," the waiter said as he stood up to let me pass. I sat down at the table next to the television.

"M'beep beep," Road Runner cried out as he took off into the desert.

"You think that was close, watch what the little fucker does next," the room-service waiter sat back down on the bed.

I removed the cover from the plate and picked up the large cheeseburger. I took a big bite; it was juicy and good. Meanwhile, the waiter began telling me in precise detail what was going to happen next, and he was right every time. He was a *Road Runner* aficionado. By the time the episode was over, I'd finished the cheeseburger and fries and one of the beers, but more importantly, Road Runner had survived another run-in with Wile E. Coyote. I signed the check after adding a fifteen percent tip, and thought to myself, *I'm in New York.*

PASSAIC, NEW JERSEY

The first gig in America was in Passaic, New Jersey. Rehearsals for the show took place in a huge rehearsal hall on 41st Street, not far from the hotel. As usual Alan, Glyn, and I arrived early to get things started. I rehearsed on rented drums, as my real drum set, along with all the other road equipment, was being set up in Passaic.

Rehearsals went well. We had a thirty-piece orchestra who were mostly New Yorkers. They were fast, and in just under two hours we had gone through the whole show. Then Barry, Robin, and Maurice arrived and, as usual, things became perky. We went through the usual five or six songs without a problem. Everyone was happy, so after about an hour Glyn wrapped up the whole thing. We all piled into the two limos and went back to the hotel.

We were scheduled to do two shows that night, so I put an extra shirt into my suit bag, along with a towel from the hotel. On the way to the lobby, the elevator stopped at the nineteenth floor. Alan Kendall got in. He was carrying his guitar and wearing a small shoulder bag.

"All right, mate-tee?" Alan asked.

"Not bad. How ya doing?"

Even before the elevator stopped on the ground floor, we could hear the commotion outside. Alan and I looked at each other as the door opened.

"I'm not fucking going! I don't care what you say! I'm not doing it!" Robin yelled, before storming off. Ray Washbourne went after him.

"Fine. Then we'll do the show without you!" Barry yelled back.

Tom and Dick were standing by the elevator doors. "What's going on?" I asked Tom.

"They've had a death threat."

"What?" I replied. "How?"

"Somebody sent a letter to the venue saying, '*I'm gonna kill a Bee-Gee tonight!*' It's freaked Robin out; he's refusing to do the show."

"Let's go! Everybody . . . let's go . . . *now!*" Barry shouted as he took charge of the situation. He led the way to the cars parked outside the hotel. Everyone followed. I got into the first limo with Barry, Linda, Maurice, and Alan. Andy, Hughie, Glyn, Jimmy Stevens, and Tom got into the second limo parked behind.

Just before we pulled away, Dick came over and opened up the back door. "I'm going to stay to get Robin," he told Barry. "We'll be there as soon as I can calm him down."

Dick slammed the door, and we moved off. It wasn't a long journey from Midtown to Passaic, but because everyone was so edgy it seemed to go on and on. Finally, we pulled up at the back of the Capitol Theatre on Monroe Street. There were police cars everywhere. Our driver had a two-way radio and was in communication with his office. He turned and told us Robin was on his way in a third car. Then he got out and made sure the backstage door wasn't locked. He banged on the door and, when it opened, two police officers came out. We all got out of the car and headed for the door of the building.

As we walked in, I could hear the orchestra tuning up backstage. "This way, guys," the stage manager said as he led us to the dressing rooms. Barry led Linda into the first room. Maurice, Andy, and Hughie followed. My instinct led me to go to the second dressing room; Alan, Glyn, and Jimmy followed me. I felt this was a time for the Gibb family to be alone together, but I was wrong.

"Hey, guys . . . what are you doing?" Barry asked, peering into the room. "Come in with us. We all need to be together."

As we entered the big room, Robin, Dick, and Ray arrived. Robin looked pale. "They say it doesn't take very long," Maurice said in a serious voice.

"What doesn't take very long?" Robin asked.

"Death!"

"Mo, this is not the time for joking around," Barry said, but his brother's humor took the edge off everything.

"Well, Alan would know," Robin continued. "He's been dead for years." Everyone laughed, and no one more than Alan. Robin seemed a little less pale.

Dick led a man into the room. He was tall and wore a suit and tie.

"Hi, guys. I'm Detective Scott, Passaic PD. We think we know who this guy is. We've had threatening letters from him before. He always says someone's going to die, and it's always a musician or group. Seems a musician stole his girlfriend one time, and he never got over it.

"We've got people out looking for him right now," he continued. "An early look at the handwriting says it's him. We don't think this guy is much of a threat, but we do have to take him seriously. Go out there and have a great show; let us do the worrying."

Detective Scott started to walk away, and then he stopped and turned. "Who do I see about an autograph? My girls are big fans. In fact, they'll be in the audience tonight. That'll tell you how worried I am about all this."

Dick raised his hand. "I'll take care of it," he said. The detective walked out of the dressing room. "I hate to ask this, especially with everything that's going on, but do you feel like any visitors tonight?" Dick asked Barry.

"Not really," Barry said. "But yes, bring them in."

"These two young ladies shared first place in a 'Meet the Bee Gees' competition on local radio," Dick said as he brought two girls into the dressing room.

"'Ello, my darlings," Maurice said as the girls approached. The girls had their autograph books open and ready to go. Each brother signed the books and spent time talking with the girls. Then the door opened and a Vietnam veteran in a wheelchair was pushed into the dressing room. He was unshaven and wore a camouflage combat jacket that had two rows of shiny medals pinned to his front left side. The soldier had on his military beret; his company's insignia was stitched on the front. There were dozens of pins and metal tokens fastened all around. He looked tired as he proudly clutched the stars and stripes. His legs were missing.

"Hello, mate. You've been through it," Barry said softly. The soldier nodded.

"There are no words to thank you for your service," Robin said.

"But there *is* music," the soldier answered. "That's why I'm here tonight. I took you guys with me wherever I went when I was over there. I made it! And now I'm here with the Bee Gees."

Barry grabbed his guitar and started to sing: "In the event of something happening to me . . ." The dressing room was silent as the brothers soulfully paid their respects to a stranger who had given so much. My eyes filled up, too.

NEW YORK AND WASHINGTON, D.C.

The second and third shows in America were in New York at the Philharmonic Hall in the Lincoln Center. This place was grand, just like the Festival Hall in London. The shows weren't sold out, although they were very well attended. The New York crowd seemed a little harder to please, a little more discerning, I thought. The attendees looked older, and they appeared to be wiser. They weren't so much fans of music as they were *connoisseurs* of it. But how could they not love the well-crafted melodies, lyrics, and arrangements the Bee Gees had to offer — and, of course, a thirty-piece classical orchestra to boot? We didn't get the response we had in London, but we received standing ovations both nights.

The next day we left for Washington, D.C. As we flew over the city, two things stood out: the Washington Monument and the U.S. Capitol Building. These were two landmarks I recognized; I'd often seen them on the television news. There were so many other impressive buildings down there, too, but I didn't know their names.

We landed at Dulles International Airport, and it took almost an hour to drive to the hotel. We came in on the 267, Dulles Access Road, and went across the Potomac River. The driver took us around the Washington Circle, and the thing I remember the most was that the streets had numbers and letters, but they didn't have names. The next two shows were at the Constitution Hall, on D Street N.W. — very strange.

Barry asked the driver if he would go down Pennsylvania Avenue. He wanted to show me the White House. I couldn't believe how quiet everything was — not many cars were on the road, and just a few tourists. The White House was in the middle of the most beautiful gardens I'd ever seen; everything was immaculate. As the driver rolled slowly by, I remember thinking that I was looking at one of the most famous buildings on the planet. Everything was so normal: no police or security guards, just a couple of guys in a hut next to one of the huge gates and that was it. *How things would change!*

We were staying at another Holiday Inn, this one on Monroe Street near the Brookland District of D.C. It wasn't new like the one in Toronto, but as usual I had my double room. *Nice!* We didn't have any rehearsals that day, because we were using fifteen of the musicians from the New York and New Jersey orchestras. They were all bused in from "the city."

At about five o'clock I wanted to get something to eat, so I went down to the lobby and found the coffee shop. As I entered, I saw Barry and Linda in one of the booths. They were sitting next to each other, as always.

Barry waved me over. "Sit down, mate. How's it going? How do you like America?"

"Barry, I love it," I replied. "I love everything about it. One day I'm gonna live here, I swear."

Barry told me about *their* first time in America and how hard the group had to work to be accepted. The conversation threaded its way through my childhood in Wales, and about a ghost in our house. How I started playing the drums really fascinated them. Then I listened as Barry shared how the Bee Gees started in music, the *real* reason the Gibb family had to leave England for Australia (it was because they were always getting into trouble with the law), then of course, how Barry and Linda had met.

"I was already married," Barry told me, "but once I met Linda, I just couldn't live without her. It's as simple as that."

"Aye, he's *nothing* without me," Linda joked, and Barry didn't disagree.

As they looked at each other, I witnessed the promise in their eyes; their love was timeless. I felt the friendship amongst us for the first time.

Tom came into the coffee shop and sat down next to me. "Alright, me buckoes? Train leaves the station in thirty minutes," he said. Barry and Linda got up in a hurry; Barry had to get changed before leaving the hotel for the show. All I had to do was go up to my room and pick up my suit bag, so I had another cup of coffee with Tom.

Constitution Hall was only a fifteen-minute drive from the hotel. I was hoping to spot some of D.C.'s famous landmarks on the way, but it was dark outside, and I couldn't see much through the tinted windows of the limousine. As it turned out, it didn't matter because Constitution Hall was a landmark itself. As we drove by the front of the building, there were hundreds of people walking toward the entrance. Eight massive columns supported a stone overhang; the building was huge.

This auditorium held almost 4,000 people, and it was another example of American ingenuity. The seating area in front of the stage formed a large rectangle, reaching back. Individual boxes surrounded it. The mezzanine level circled the great hall, sloping up from the floor to the ceiling.

As the Bee Gees took the stage, the audience went wild. It was a full house, and the applause was deafening. After every song, the audience became more and more worked up. It took two encores — and the brothers walking back onto the stage for a third time — for the Washington audience to be satisfied. They didn't want to go home. The following night saw a new audience, but the response was exactly the same.

I'd never heard of Valley Forge, or even Pennsylvania for that matter. I wasn't good at geography at school, and I don't remember seeing either on any map. But the gig at Valley Forge was one thing I'll never forget.

My itinerary from Dick was marked "Valley Forge Music Fair: (In the Round)." *In the round? What's that?* I wondered. Were we playing in a circle, like in a circus? I was confused. After asking a few questions and not receiving any good answers, I guessed we would be performing on a stage that turned.

My only experience on a revolving stage went back to the old Amen Corner days. One of our biggest rivals was a group named Love Affair, and we often played on the same bill. A lot of the places we played had a round stage divided into two halves. The front half was exposed to the audience, while the back half was truly backstage. When it was time for the second band to go on, the stage would rotate, revealing the second band and taking the first band backstage. It worked well, giving the audience no time between acts.

When I got to rehearsals, I found out it was nothing like that. Yes, this stage was round, and it rotated, but the difference was *the audience*. The seats were arranged in a circle, all around the stage. They towered up at an angle, all the way from stage level to the back wall. I'd never seen anything like it.

The stage setup was different, too. The band and the orchestra were arranged in a circle, as well. I had to turn my head all the way to the left to even see Barry, Robin, and Mo. The theory was that, as the stage turned, everyone in the audience could have a front-row seat.

The place was sold out. There were people from the floor to the ceiling, and all the way around. After Jimmy finished his set, the orchestra, Glyn, Alan, and I took the stage to some polite applause. I couldn't believe how close the people in the audience were. There were only a couple of feet between my bass drum and the people in the first row. I sat down and picked up my sticks. Right in front of me was a very nice lady sitting between a man and two children.

"Hello," she said in a conversational tone, not needing to shout, we were so close. "You're new. This is my husband, John, and my children

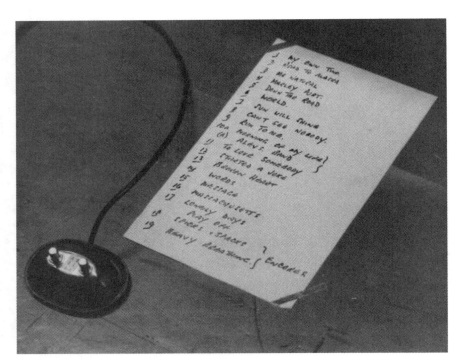

1974 set list taped to the stage floor.

Sarah and John Jr." I said "hello" back. Suddenly, from around the stage, the audience broke into cheers and applause as the Bee Gees took their places. All I could see were their backs.

Maurice started right off the bat, "God, you're an ugly crowd." All the people in front of him started to laugh. "Especially you." I could see Maurice pointing to a man in the fourth row. The crowd cracked up.

"Are we ready over there?" Barry shouted, as he looked around the stage. I shouted "*Yes!*" and so did Glyn. Barry started to count. As soon as we began playing the first song, the whole stage jerked and started rotating slowly to the left.

"Bye!" the woman in front of me said, as I got farther away. I couldn't believe this. I'd never experienced anything like it. I hadn't been so close to an audience in all my life. Every now and again I'd make eye contact with somebody and they'd smile or wave back. Next thing I knew we'd done a whole rotation and there was that lady with her husband and two kids again. They waved, and I smiled.

"Oh, bloody hell! Not you again!" Maurice shouted as he came to the man he'd insulted before. The stage did about six complete rotations before coming to a gentle pause. Then, after about ten seconds, my cymbal stands shifted to the left as the stage jerked into motion, this time in the opposite direction. As the night went on, I came to recognize people in the audience; we passed by so many times.

We returned to Valley Forge a few more times over the years. I always looked forward to playing *in the round.*

NASHVILLE, COUNTRY MUSIC CAPITAL

The tour continued and became a bit grueling, as we played night after night in Providence, Norfolk, Birmingham, Dayton, Detroit, New Haven, Chicago, and other cities. One of the places I was really excited about visiting was Nashville, Tennessee. It's the home of country music, which I loved, and we had a day off there. Maybe I'd get to see some bands . . . ?

We were playing at the Municipal Auditorium in downtown Nashville. This place was *big*, with seating for almost 9,000 people. But before we went to rehearsals in the afternoon we checked into our hotel. We were staying at the King of the Road, and, yes, it was built and owned by Roger Miller, who wrote and performed the sixties radio hit of the same name. It was a tall concrete building, about ten stories high. The lobby of the King of the Road Motor Inn was full of artwork showing exotic animals: elephants, tigers, giraffes, zebras, and more.

My room had two queen-sized beds covered by the brightest quilts I had ever seen. The TV was encased in a round cylinder made out of white Formica. The cylinder stood in the middle of the room and reached from the floor to the ceiling. It looked like a giant-sized segment of plumber's pipe. But the strangest thing of all were the walls. They were carpeted, and not just any carpet — *red shag carpet*. I thought I was on acid (which I've never done, by the way). That's just how much of an out-of-body experience it was!

Rehearsals were at four o'clock, and we had the thirty-piece Nashville Symphony Orchestra onstage with us. After rehearsals, there wasn't any time to go back to the hotel, so we hung around backstage. I was in the dressing room talking to Maurice when a gentle knock on the door got our attention.

"Come!" Maurice yelled, and the door opened. A tall man dressed in a black shirt and black trousers walked in. He had shiny black hair that swept up from the front, all the way to the back of his head. He was wearing thick-rimmed black sunglasses with red lenses. "Hello, mate," Maurice said as he stood up.

It was Roy Orbison. "How are you, Maurice? How's the tour going?"

"Great, mate. I'm doing great. And the tour couldn't be better. Roy, I'd like to introduce you to someone. This is our new drummer, Dennis Bryon. It's his first tour with us."

Roy looked at me and stuck out his hand. When I took hold of it, everything became still. *I am in Nashville, Tennessee, onstage with the Bee Gees and the Nashville Symphony Orchestra, and, if that isn't enough, I am in the room with, and shaking the hand of, one of my all-time heroes, Roy Orbison.* I savored the moment.

Then, like a tape recorder starting back up, the silence went away. "Hi, Dennis, nice to meet you. I'm looking forward to hearing you play," Roy said.

"I'm a huge fan. I've got all your records," I said. I wanted to reel off all the names of the hits that were burned into my soul, but I couldn't think of one of them. Then from the corridor outside, Barry and Linda walked in.

"Where is he? Where's he hiding?" Barry asked. "Hello, mate. How ya been?" Barry gave Roy a huge bear hug, which was rare for Barry to do. Then Robin came in, and the reunion was complete.

Linda looked at me and, when I was sure nobody was watching, I mouthed, *That's Roy Orbison!*

"Roy, have you met our drummer, Dennis?" Linda asked loudly.

"Yes, Linda. I've met Dennis, thank you." Roy returned to his conversation with the brothers. I looked at Linda and opened my mouth. *Wow.*

We had a great show in Nashville. The audience was filled with song-writers and musicians who appreciated the Bee Gees on a level beyond what we got from a regular audience.

The next day I woke up early. We had a day off, and I wanted to make the most of it. After I showered and shaved, I got dressed and was about to leave my room when there was a knock on my door. I looked through the peephole and saw a black woman in a white uniform standing next to a trolley full of towels, sheets, and pillowcases. I opened the door. She looked me in the eye, and then I heard this strange phrase for the very first time: "How *y'all* doing?" she asked.

"*Y'all*" echoed in my head. Maybe there was somebody else in the room I didn't know about? Maybe someone had snuck in when I was in the shower? I looked around, just in case.

"*We're* doing fine, thank you."

"Oh, I just love your accent. Where you from?"

I'd stopped doing the "Wales" answer a long time ago. It took too long to explain. "England."

"That's where the Queen's from, ain't it? Whooee, I'm gonna go there someday, sure enough, I'm a go'n."

She had the most lovely Southern accent. I could have listened to her talk all day. She sat on the edge of the bed and told me everything about her life. She wanted to travel and see the world. She was wonderful.

Later that day I walked along the streets of the famed Music Row, where all the important music businesses were located. On both sides of the street were the offices of recording labels, managers, booking agents, publicity firms, and publishing companies. There were recording studios everywhere.

Somebody told me to find Broadway, because that's where all the live music happened, so I took a cab from 16th Avenue South to Riverfront Park at the end of Broadway. As I gazed out over the Cumberland River, I imagined that someday I might live here, and then I began walking down the north side of Broadway. There were bars everywhere. It was eleven o'clock in the morning, and they were all packed with tourists. Every bar had a full band playing live music. Next to every bar there was a gift shop filled with brightly colored memorabilia. Everything from Johnny Cash T-shirts to Elvis sunglasses to mugs with the American flag printed on their sides. There were barbecue restaurants everywhere, too, with indoor fire pits where pitmasters cut up huge racks of smoked ribs. I *liked* this place. Broadway wasn't vast, but it wasn't limited either; it had a big-city feel about it — Broadway was *alive!*

We were getting to the end of the five-week tour, and the thought of going home was becoming more appealing. I'd never been out of the U.K. for that long, and, although America bowled me over, there's no place like home.

But first the Bee Gees were booked to host a television show at the NBC studios in Burbank, California. It was called *The Midnight Special*. I'd never heard of this show; it didn't air in the U.K.

After a long flight from Nashville, we landed at the Los Angeles International Airport. We would be staying at a hotel on Wilshire Boulevard, in the Beverly Hills district. As I walked out of the terminal at LAX, it was like stepping into yet another world. The air was warm and dry, and the sky was a deep blue. We took the San Diego Freeway to the hotel, getting off at Santa Monica Boulevard, then turning onto Wilshire. I'd never seen so many palm trees, and they were soaring high above most of the buildings.

Wilshire Boulevard was busy, with three lanes of traffic going each way. We were driving through a business district, with fancy showrooms and high-end jewelry shops on both sides of the road, and the wide sidewalks were filled with people shopping.

The hotel was another Holiday Inn, but this one wasn't your run-of-the-mill Holiday Inn. It was lavish, being in Beverly Hills. As we pulled up in front of its grand entrance, two doormen dressed in long, white embroidered coats with matching trousers and rimmed caps rushed to open the car doors. Inside the hotel, it looked like a chic designer with an unlimited budget had decorated the lobby. My room was bigger than normal, with two king-sized beds and a huge bathroom. Inside the bathroom, there was a Jacuzzi instead of a bath. And I had a balcony that stepped out over Wilshire Boulevard. I was *stylin'*.

The next day we drove to the NBC Studios, where we were to perform four songs: one acoustic and three "voice to track." This meant Alan and I would be miming on those three songs.

It was the first time I'd seen the Bee Gees host a television show. I couldn't believe how calm and at ease they were. And they were *funny*. As usual, Maurice had the audience in stitches. They were promoting their latest album, *Life in a Tin Can*, so they performed an acoustic version of one of the songs, "Living in Chicago." Then Alan and I took the stage for "To Love Somebody," "Massachusetts," and "Run to Me."

The last two shows of the tour were in Seattle and Portland, Oregon. Then we flew back to Los Angeles for that long ride home. I couldn't wait to be back in the U.K.

CHAPTER 11   Recording with
the Bee Gees

JAPANESE TOUR AND RECORDING *MR. NATURAL*

After a few weeks at home, following my North American debut, I had
a call from Maurice. He asked me if I did sessions. He said he produced
"adverts" for television and wanted me to play drums on a recording
session he had coming up. Of course I said yes. I wound up going into
the studio many times with Maurice; I became his studio drummer. I
also became friends with the other musicians Maurice used, and I started
getting calls from them to play. Soon I became very busy.

I spoke with Jenny every day, and we missed each other, and I missed
Babet. Although it didn't seem like it, we'd been apart for more than
a year. We both agreed that now that I had a steady job and a reliable
income it was time for us to get back together. I found us a nice apartment in Blackheath, in the South East district of London, and the three
of us moved in.

Being back with Jenny made me feel complete. Although we knew
everything about each other, it was like we were dating again. I took her
to nice restaurants. We went to movies. I tried to make up for lost time.

My first time in the studio with new producer Arif Mardin.

Babet loved the new apartment. We always had friends over who spoiled her and showered her with attention. Also, Greenwich Park was only a few miles away; I took her there every day.

Meanwhile, back in the music world, the Bee Gees hired a new producer, Arif Mardin of Atlantic Records in New York, to do the next album. The recording session was to start in London in November. Barry asked me if I would play on the new album.

Before the recording started, we had a tour lined up of Japan and the Far East. It started in Tokyo at the beginning of September and ended in Surabaya, Indonesia, at the end of the month. I thought America was wild, but this ride was ridiculous. We played all over Japan; we went to Kuala Lumpur in Malaysia, then on to Jakarta and Surabaya in Indonesia. It was eye-opening; I saw so many things I'd never seen before: tropical rainforests, volcanoes, spectacular mountain ranges. And I tasted food I'd never had, like fish steamed and served in huge banana leaves with an array of vegetables I'd never even heard of. It was quite a trip.

In November 1973, we went into IBC studios in London to start recording the *Mr. Natural* album with Arif Mardin. In addition to IBC, we also recorded at Command Studios in London and Atlantic Studios in New York.

Working with Arif was like a dream come true. Not only was he a genius composer, arranger, and producer, he also had the ability to bring out the very best in somebody. Not once in all the time that I worked with Arif did he ever tell me, or even try to tell me, what to play. He wanted to know what *I* thought the drum part should be; he wanted to know what was in *my* head.

Once I played him the part, we'd talk about it, and then he'd gently guide me in the direction of what he thought it could be, all the time letting *me* make the changes. He was always telling me my parts were "just right" and how good I was. When I was around Arif, my confidence soared.

BACK TO THE U.S.

My second American tour with the Bee Gees, in 1974, got off to a rough start at the Syria Mosque in Pittsburgh, Pennsylvania. Attendance was poor. The Bee Gees hadn't had a hit record for two years, and there was no radio airplay to generate ticket sales. All hopes were on the new single "Mr. Natural." It was a mild hit, disappointingly stopping at twenty-four on the Billboard charts. And that wasn't enough to attract box-office sales.

But I was in America again and having the time of my life. Every show was great. *If only there were more people.* Jimmy Stephens didn't come over with us this time; instead we had a vocal duo from Philadelphia open up for us. They were promoting songs from their upcoming album *Abandoned Luncheonette*, and they called themselves Hall & Oates. I loved watching these guys play. They had great songs and were very cool onstage — and they had a great drummer.

I don't remember which city we were in, but one evening in the dressing room before the show, somebody came in with a large cardboard bucket of something. Even before I'd seen it, the intense aroma made me stop whatever I was doing and turn around. "Hey, Denny, you want some?" Tom said as he offered me the bucket. It was full of Kentucky Fried Chicken. I'd never heard of it before. I reached in and grabbed a leg. I'd never tasted anything like it. This was worth eight hours on a plane any day of the week.

The tour also took us to Canada again, where we had more fantastic times with Canadian promoter Donald K. Donald. Then we returned to New York to record more tracks for *Mr. Natural*. We played Nanuet, New York; Boston, Massachusetts; Providence, Rhode Island; Passaic, New Jersey; New Haven, Connecticut; Baltimore, Maryland; Valley Forge, Pennsylvania; Westbury, Connecticut; Washington, D.C.; Norfolk, Virginia; Chicago, Illinois; Morehead, Kentucky; Chattanooga, Tennessee; Miami, Florida; and Nashville, Tennessee. I revisited old haunts and became acquainted with some new ones.

DEVASTATING NEWS BACK HOME

Everything was going really well. Jenny and I had a great relationship — and we had Babet, the wonder dog. We were living in a nice apartment in London, and I was traveling the world playing drums with the Bee Gees.

Then one day the phone rang. It was my sister, Carole, in Cardiff. Dad had been diagnosed with cancer, she told me, and I should come home.

We were in between things with the Bee Gees. *Mr. Natural* had just been released, and we had a world tour starting in August, so I had a couple of months off. Jenny and I put Babet in the back of the VW and drove to Cardiff.

Dad didn't look any different, he seemed to be fine; he was still the heavy, but not overweight, man he had always been. It was colon cancer — "nothing to worry about," according to Dad. Jenny and I were scared, but the worst news was yet to come.

Mum was acting strange. She had become very forgetful; she would stop talking mid-sentence, unable to remember her train of thought. Dad took her to the doctor, and she was admitted into hospital for some tests. The next day Dad called Jenny, Carole, and me into the kitchen; he had something to tell us. I'd never seen my dad cry before — he was always such a strong man — but what he said made us all cry.

He told us Mum had a condition that the doctors said was permanent. With his eyes streaming, Dad told us that Mum would never get better. We all hugged, trying to comfort each other.

I didn't know what to do. After I stopped crying, I told my dad I was moving back to Cardiff to be a part of the family. "You'll do no such thing!" Dad told me. "You've got a career in London and that's where you'll stay. It's only a matter of time before you'll be in the hit parade again. Your mother and I will be just fine; we've got Carole to help us."

He told me he was going sell the houses on Colum Road and give up the B&B business. He would buy a small bungalow where he and Mum could retire. I was devastated.

When Mum came out of hospital, she was different. She needed help with everything, not being able to remember where she had put things or what she was doing. In those days, Mum's condition was simply known as pre-senile decay. Today it has a name: early-onset Alzheimer's. Her illness was tragic; she was so young, she was only forty-nine when she was diagnosed. I felt guilty. I'd selfishly concentrated on my life as a musician, leaving home, not paying attention to my family when they needed me the most, and now look what I'd done.

Dad came over and put his arm around me. "It'll be okay, luv . . . It will all work out . . . It always does."

The entire time I was home, I was getting phone calls from Maurice and other producers in London. They wanted to know where I was and when was I coming back. They needed me in the studio.

Jenny and I stayed in Cardiff for a month, helping Mum and Dad pack things up and give stuff away. It was so sad, and leaving them was extremely difficult.

THE WORLD TOUR

I had to return to work, and the world tour was my biggest tour yet with the Bee Gees, and as it turned out, one of the most important for everybody. It was three months long, and we played fifty-two shows. We started off in Canada, and then played some dates in America including Hawaii, then we globe-trotted New Zealand, Australia, Malaysia, Thailand, the Philippines, China, Japan, and back to America.

The tour started on August 20, 1974, when the whole party left Heathrow Airport bound for Halifax, Nova Scotia. We had fifteen shows in Canada and, for the most part, they were well attended. We went everywhere from Halifax to Alberta in that huge country.

One night I was having dinner with Tom and Dick in a hotel restaurant. The conversation got on to how the tour was going and how *Mr. Natural* was selling, or more to the point, how it was *wasn't* selling. Dick told Tom and me that if the next album didn't have a big hit on it, Robert Stigwood was going to make some big changes. I almost choked on my water as my heart sank. I instantly knew what that meant: one of those changes was going to be me. If Robert was going to scale things back, I would lose my job. Something kicked in, and I immediately went on the defensive.

"That's easy," I told Dick.

"What do you mean?" Dick asked.

"They need to make some changes. We all know the songs are great, but they're out of date. Too many ballads and not enough rhythm and blues, not enough funk."

I had Dick's attention. "What do you suggest?"

"They need to get rid of the orchestra and put a band together. A real band, with two guitars, bass, Hammond organ and synthesizer, a five-piece horn section, drums, and even a percussion player." Dick looked at Tom. "And," I continued, "they need to write more up-tempo songs. Songs with a groove, songs people can dance to, that's what's happening."

"That would be a huge departure," Dick said.

"You want hit records, don't you? That's the way to do it."

Dick looked at Tom again and raised his eyebrows. "Why don't you talk to Barry about it? But when you do, try to be a little less forceful."

I didn't realize I had been forceful; I was just telling it like it was. Later in my room I thought about what I'd said. I *knew* I was right; I just had to find a way to convince Barry. But he was the leader, and he liked coming up with the ideas himself. He set the policy and always had both hands on the wheel. How would he react to me suggesting such changes? I had to find the right moment. The tour was three months long, so I had plenty of time, right?

From Canada, we went to Hawaii. This place was beautiful, with mountains and forests that fused with the sky. The beaches and ocean were breathtaking. From Hawaii we flew to Christchurch, New Zealand. I remember the air being dry, drier than I had ever experienced. There were lots of antique cars on the road, all in great condition. The people were great, too; they loved to talk and ask questions. They were very opinionated. It seemed to me New Zealand was twenty-five years behind the rest of the world, and that's exactly how the people there wanted it.

Australia came next, and it was the Bee Gees' second home — their *first home*, some people would say. Everywhere we went, it was like a homecoming. The brothers had family in every city. We played Brisbane, Sydney, Melbourne, Adelaide, and Perth.

From Australia we traveled to Malaysia, Thailand, the Philippines, and China. I didn't realize until then how exotic, diverse, and culturally fascinating our planet was. But across all those immeasurable miles, I just couldn't find the right moment to talk to Barry. Time was starting to run out; I could feel the end of the tour drawing closer. I knew if I couldn't find the courage to talk to Barry before the last show, I never would.

We were in Japan again, back at the Tokyo Hilton. It was the last two weeks of the tour and this big international hotel was our home base. The food was good, and everybody spoke English. Every time we came to Tokyo, this was where we stayed.

Eric Clapton and his band were also in town. He was playing one of the huge Tokyo stadiums. Robert Stigwood managed Eric too, so he and the Bee Gees were all good friends. Dick arranged for our whole party to see Eric and the band play. He was promoting his new album *461 Ocean Boulevard*.

After the show, we all went backstage to meet the band. I met a guy named George Terry who played guitar with Eric. We hit it off right away when we realized we both loved the same kind of music. He was from Miami and told me that Eric's new album was cut there, at a studio called Criteria.

"Dennis, you have to come and cut your next record at Criteria. It's magic. Everyone is coming to Miami. You have to come."

The next day we were back on the road, or to be more precise we were back on the tracks. Apart from anything local, everywhere we went in Japan we went by train — *bullet train!* I'd never ridden on anything like it before. The train looked like something out of a science-fiction novel. It reminded me of an enormous aerodynamic snake on steroids. It was white and had a pointed front end that cut through the air at 175 miles per hour. Inside there was a row of two seats and a row of three seats separated by an aisle. This thing could move! It was always full of people traveling from city to city.

On October 29, we were playing in a city called Shizuoka. It wasn't far from Tokyo, just over a hundred miles, and on a bullet train that's nothing. I still hadn't talked to Barry about the band, and there were only a handful of days left on the tour. It had been almost three months, but I hadn't found that magic moment. We were sitting around a table that was next to the bulkhead. I was facing Barry, and there was a large window to my left. All I could think about was that stupid idea I had for the band.

I looked out of the window, and there it was. I'd never seen anything like it: Mt. Fuji in all its magnificence. It gently rose up from its base to form a beautiful cone shape. The top of the mountain was snow-capped, and the snow was separated from the land below by a layer of white clouds that formed a perfect ring around the mountain. It looked like a giant smoke ring halfway up. It was glorious.

I looked over at Barry, who was staring at me. He looked as if he was waiting for me to say something. I looked back at the mountain. If right now wasn't the time, there wasn't going to be a time. I looked back at Barry.

"Barry, I've got an idea."

"Oh, this should be good," he quipped. Everybody around the table laughed, but I didn't care.

"Let's put a band together, a kick-ass R&B rhythm section, with two guitar players, keyboards and synths, a horn section, and somebody playing congas and percussion. It could be amazing; think of the records we could make." *Slow down, don't overdo it*, I thought to myself, *don't get ahead of yourself, remember what Dick said, not too forceful*. I didn't mention the orchestra or the songwriting; I just wanted to plant a seed.

I took a breath and looked out of the window. Mt. Fuji was gone.

Barry just stared at me, pouting his lips and nodding his head. "If you think it's such a good idea, you put it together," Barry said. Then he looked at Dick, who was sitting next to Tom on my side of the table. "Dick will help you; he'll give you anything you need."

"We don't need much, Barry," I said. "We've already got a great bass player and an incredible guitar player. All we really need is a good keyboard player with cool sounds and great ideas."

"If you think it's a good idea, you put it together," he repeated. "Let's see what you come up with." I looked at Linda, who was sitting next to Barry. I could see her smiling from deep within; she knew what was coming next.

For the remaining week of the tour, Barry and I did nothing but talk about the next album. I passed on what George Terry told me about Criteria Studios in Miami. He told me Eric had said the same thing.

Anchorage, Alaska, was the last stop on the tour and — wouldn't you know it — Northwest Airlines lost everyone's baggage in the flight from Tokyo. We arrived at the hotel, a brand-new Holiday Inn, at eight o'clock in the morning. It was *so* new the gift shop wasn't stocked yet, and there was nowhere to buy toiletries. I couldn't even brush my teeth. I met Alan and Tom in the new coffee shop for breakfast. We were back in U.S. territory so I ordered steak and three eggs over medium, with hashbrowns and white toast. That was the best steak and eggs I ever had. Then I went to bed.

BLUE'S AUDITION

Finally, I was back home in London. I had missed Jenny and Babet so much while I was away. When I walked in the door, the dog made a bigger fuss over me than Jenny did. That's always how it goes.

So much had happened while I was away, and things weren't good back home. Dad had sold the houses on Colum Road. He didn't even get close to what they were worth. The estate agent could see what dire straits Dad was in and practically stole them from him. Dad bought a two-bedroom bungalow in Radyr, a small suburb of Cardiff. While I was on tour he also had an operation to remove his colon.

After spending the night with Jenny and Babet in Blackheath, I drove down to Cardiff. I found the new house in Radyr without a problem. It was on a new housing estate. Dad loathed estate living; he was independent and liked living on his own terms. Now here he was surrounded by neighbors who watched every little thing he did.

The house was tiny, with two small bedrooms and a modest kitchen. It did have a comfortable living area where Mum and Dad could watch television, and Dad could play his records and tapes. He loved Mario Lanza and the Mantovani Orchestra. Dad had lost weight, but he wasn't skeletal. All in all, he was in good spirits. He still had his sense of humor and just laughed at the whole thing. *I wished I could.*

On the other hand, Mum had gone downhill fast. Her Alzheimer's was progressing. She kept asking me who I was and telling me my brother was coming home. I didn't have a brother, but Mum had lost four boys before my elder sister Carole was born. Mum was always very psychic, and I kept looking for the connection.

I got up the next morning and noticed the grass needed cutting. Dad had an electric mower in the garage, so I got at it. While I was mowing, the mailman arrived. I stopped cutting and introduced myself. He told me he was sorry for my family's situation. He said my sister had been marvelous, coming to the bungalow every day. I told him I worked out of the country, but I was home now for a few months. As I spoke with him, a new picture of the future was forming in my head.

I talked with Jenny every day and let her know everything that was going on. And one day when Mum and Dad were out shopping I told Jenny I was thinking about moving into the bungalow permanently. I couldn't tell Dad, or even discuss it with him; I was convinced he'd send me back to London, back to my career. He was too proud to accept any help from me. *Or was he?*

Apart from Jenny and Babet, I didn't need to be in London anyway. The work I did with the Bee Gees was out of the country. I could go up the day before the flight and stay in our apartment in Blackheath. That's what I'd do . . .

I also had to find a keyboard player, and quick. Now that I was based in Cardiff, the task of finding somebody would not be easy. I spent days wondering how I'd do it. I thought about putting an advert in the local paper: *Keyboard Player Wanted for Pro Band.* Naaah! I didn't know what kind of weirdos that would attract. *Keyboard players, that's who.* Then I thought about driving up to London and hanging out at some of the live music venues. Naaah! Too many wannabes.

Then, in a moment of genius — or it could have been a moment of *Duh!* — it came to me: Blue!

I hadn't seen my old friend and bandmate in years, so I had to do some serious searching. Finally I came across his telephone number in London. "Blue, it's Plent, how ya doing?"

"Hiya, Den. God I haven't heard from you in a while."

"Yeah, I just got back from a world tour with the Bee Gees. It was great."

"Yes, I heard you were playing with those guys. How are they to work with?"

"Fantastic, really great, in fact, that's one of the reasons I called you."

There was nothing but silence on the other end.

"We're doing a new album in January, I think we're gonna be cutting it in Miami, Florida, with Arif Mardin." More silence, then I popped the question: "We need a keyboard player — Hammond, synths — and I thought about you." I figured Blue would jump at the chance to record in America with the Bee Gees, but all I got was silence on the other end of the phone. "Blue, are you still there?"

"Oh, hi, Den, yes I'm still here . . . but I'm not sure I can do it right now."

"Why, what you got going on?"

"Nothing huge, but I'm starting to get back into the London music scene. I don't know if you know this or not, but after Fair Weather broke up, I went through a really hard time. I had to get a job driving a cab. I have a little girl and a wife to support, and it's taken me this long to get back on my feet. I've been working so hard to get back into music, and it's finally starting to pay off. I've been gigging with Mott the Hoople, Lou Reed, Strawbs. You know what it's like, Den, if you go out of town for a couple of weeks — when you get back, someone else has got your gig. I don't know about this, Den. I don't know."

"Blue, have you heard of Arif Mardin? He's producing the album. He produced the last Bee Gees album. To say he's amazing is such an understatement, the guy's a fucking genius. And he's a keyboard player, I know the two of you would hit it off, I just know it."

"I'm not sure, Den. Things are starting to get good for me . . ."

I was desperate. "Blue, how long have we known each other?"

"Aww, come on, Den, don't do that."

"Well, let me tell you, we played gigs together before Brother John and the Witnesses. When we were boys. We went through Brother John together, Amen Corner together, and Fair Weather together. You're practically my brother."

Silence.

"For all that we've been through, I'm just asking you for one favor."

Silence.

"Meet Barry. If after meeting Barry you don't want the gig, I'll never bother you again."

Silence.

"Blue, are you there?"

"Okay, I'll meet with Barry."

I called Dick straight away at his RSO office in London; I told him about Blue. Barry and Linda now lived on the Isle of Man. Dick suggested I take Blue to meet Barry at his house in the capital city of Douglas. I agreed, but I also insisted we take Alan Kendall with us — this would be the first coming together of the Bee Gees Band, and it was only right that all three be there.

Dick called Barry, and Barry invited the three of us to stay at his house the very next weekend. Dick booked the tickets, and I met Alan and Blue at Heathrow Airport on Friday afternoon. It was a cold November day, but the sun was shining brightly on a new beginning.

When we landed in Ronaldsway Airport, Linda's dad, George, was there to meet us. He was driving a Mercedes station wagon, so there was plenty of room for our small suitcases and Alan's electric guitar. He took us to Barry and Linda's house in Douglas, where Barry was waiting at the front door. Barry welcomed Blue with a warm handshake and big smile, and he invited us all inside. Barry and Blue instantly remembered each other from the Amen Corner days. They had a lot to talk about and hit it off right away. Linda came in with a tray of tea and biscuits; the house had a warm atmosphere.

Blue pulled out a board game he'd recently come across called backgammon. He explained the rules, and we started playing two by two. Everyone played except Alan, who noodled on his guitar.

Then Blue produced a large bottle of something I'd never heard of called Pernod. He suggested we try it with bitter lemon. Boy, did it have a kick to it. Not to be outdone, Linda produced some *cosmic cookies* she'd baked. After a cookie or two, the rules of backgammon didn't stand a chance. We all started telling stupid jokes and had tears rolling down our cheeks. I told the one about the guy who walks into the greengrocers and asks for a pound of kid-dil-lee beans. The greengrocer says, "Excuse me, sir, but did you mean kidney beans?" The guy says, "That's what I said, diddle I?" We howled. I didn't realize it at the time, but with all that I was going through in Cardiff, this was just what I needed.

The next morning, everybody came down from their bedrooms still laughing from the previous night. George and Linda made a huge breakfast, and we all sat around the big dining room table and scoffed the lot!

After breakfast, Barry was keen to show us around. With Linda at the wheel of the Mercedes, Barry sitting next to her, and Blue, Alan, and me piled in the back, off we went. We drove around the island on the Tourist Trophy motorcycle track that the Isle of Man is famous for, and then we drove along the Queens Promenade, the Central Promenade, and the Lock Promenade that wraps around the huge Baie de Douglas.

All along the oceanfront, tall hotels and B&B rooming houses loomed, waiting to welcome guests from all over the world. There were restaurants and pubs everywhere; I hadn't realized what a destination the Isle of Man was. We ended up parking the car and walking down the Victoria Pier on the southeast end of the waterfront. We looked out over the bay; the sun was directly overhead, and it seemed like I was a single thought in an impressionist's inspiration. *Hmm, Linda's cookies . . .*

"I've got a great idea," Barry said. "Why don't we come here tonight and do a bit of fishing? We've got plenty of rods, and when we're done, there's a great fish and chip shop right over there, the best one in Douglas."

We went back to the house and hung out. Barry and Linda had three dogs: a huge St. Bernard named Barnaby, a blond Afghan named Snoopy, and a wire-haired mutt called Kim. I spent most of the afternoon growling back at Kim, trying to get Snoopy's attention, and wiping the dribble from Barnaby's huge chops.

We passed the evening on the Victoria Pier. There were other people fishing too, but nobody caught anything. The highlight of the night out was the fish and chips. Barry was right on the money — the cod was some of the best I'd ever eaten. At about nine o'clock, we went back to the house. Blue got the backgammon out, and there was some Pernod left. Then Linda brought out her home-baked goodies. Oh-oh.

Late Sunday morning after breakfast we started talking about music. Blue told Barry about the new ARP 2500 electronic synthesizer that had just come out and about the Moog synthesizer that put out some very cool sounds. Blue had both. Then Blue mentioned the ARP Solina String Ensemble that was coming out any time. *An electronic string machine.* That definitely stirred Barry's imagination.

Barry was careful to tell Blue the new album was going to be all about great songs and great-sounding tracks. We weren't trying to make a record that sounded like ELP or Yes. Blue couldn't agree more. They were on the same page.

I watched, and tried not to get in the way as Barry and Blue sketched out the new album; they were inspiring each other. Things couldn't have worked out better. Blue had been the perfect choice.

Suddenly it was three o'clock and our flight back to London was only an hour away. George warmed up the car to take us to the airport, and the three of us said our goodbyes to Barry, Linda, and May, and of course the dogs. Just as we were getting into the car, Barry came rushing out of the front door. "Blue, Blue just a minute!" We all turned around. "I haven't heard you play . . . you can play, right?"

"Do you have a piano?" Blue asked.

"Yes, it's a bit out of tune," Barry answered.

The three of us walked back up the steps in front of the house and into the front room. Inside was an old upright piano that looked like it was from the dark ages. Blue sat down and played an out-of-tune chord; Barry was right.

I don't know where he got it from, but Blue produced a white paper cup. He put it over his nose, then broke into "I'm the guy who found the lost chord," by pianist and comedian Jimmy "The Schnoz" Durante.

"Sitting at my pianna the udder day. . ."

Then he went into another old sing-a-long pub song, then another one.

Barry looked horrified. "Okay, okay you got the job, just stop *please*, Blue, stop!"

The flight back to London was almost empty. I was sitting in an aisle seat next to Alan. Blue had the window seat a couple of rows down on the other side. After the seatbelt sign went off, I looked over at Blue. He was looking down at the ground; he had a huge smile on his face. I went over and sat next to him.

He looked at me. "Alright, Den?"

"So what do you think, Blue?"

"Yes."

CHAPTER 12 Interlude:
The Bee Gees
Handbook

SPOTLIGHT ON THE BEE GEES'
SONGWRITING AND CREATIVE PROCESS

One of the incredible benefits of being in the Bee Gees Band was that I observed firsthand how the Gibb brothers worked together as song-writers — the ways in which many of their classic songs were born. Their methods were unorthodox, but there is no denying the results: the Bee Gees ultimately wrote more than twenty number-one hits.

Here's how they did it: when we recorded in London, Barry, Robin, and Maurice would go into the men's bathroom and write in there, because the floors were tiled, the walls were tiled, it was big, and it had natural echo. They *loved* echo on their voices. Most people don't go into the bathroom to write classic songs, but they did! And the first time I saw it I thought, *Wow, that's unusual!* But that's just the way they did it.

Later in Miami, we would stay in these mansions that would always have big entrance halls, with grand staircases, high ceilings, and marble on the floor. They would go *there* to write, because of the natural echo.

I can still see it so clearly in my mind: Barry, Robin, and Maurice standing there, huddled together. Maurice would have his guitar, Barry would have his guitar, and Robin would be standing without an instrument. And then they would start communicating song ideas to each other. They were so close they barely even needed words. They could just laugh, and they were always laughing when they were writing. I would go somewhere out of sight, but I'd try to listen in. I could hear what was going on. It always amazed me that they'd be laughing and joking and cutting up. Then, from out of that laughter would come an incredible melody and sometimes bits of lyrics, too. From *nowhere*, it seemed! And Barry would say, "That's good! That's good! Sing it again!" So Robin or Maurice would sing it again, and Barry might embellish it, and from nowhere came this haunting melody. Later they would add the lyrics; they almost always wrote the entire melody before adding the lyrics.

Barry would lead the creative process, but it was an easy follow for Robin and Maurice, because they were blood brothers, fraternal twins. They all just had this chemistry that was built-in. And they could even write in front of other people.

Part of the brothers' personal and creative chemistry together involved their absolute willingness to defend each other. They had many arguments and squabbles among themselves over the years, but if someone attacked them they would defend each other viciously. One time, when we were recording at Atlantic Studios in New York, a reporter came in and started saying pretty nasty things about the Bee Gees to their faces. I thought, *Wow! What brought this on?* And then Barry said something to the guy and the guy answered back. Then Robin jumped in. And within twenty or thirty seconds they verbally destroyed this guy — just absolutely took him apart. And with great efficiency, too. I'd never seen the Bee Gees act like that before. They were nice people. And as the reporter was walking away, you could see they were physically shaken. But they had stood their ground against that jerk. And stood up for each other. I thought that was cool, and it showed me another side of them.

My creativity and drumming also had an impact on the Bee Gees' songwriting. I don't mean to overstate that in some self-serving way, but there were, in fact, times when percussive ideas I came up with ended up being the foundation for a Bee Gees song. The first time that happened was when we were recording *Main Course* in Miami. I was sitting at my drums and we were jamming or warming up. I started playing a country-ish drum part and, before I knew it, Barry was playing his acoustic guitar within the groove I'd established, just making up this song on the spot. The song became "Come On Over," which wound up on our multi-platinum album *Main Course*, and later was a smash hit for Olivia Newton-John. A lot of the lyrics in the finished song were ones Barry just sang off the cuff after hearing that drum groove.

Another time, when we were recording the *Spirits Having Flown* album, I had gone into the studio to practice. I'd just bought an album by Boz Scaggs, featuring a song called "Lowdown" that I loved. I was playing the "Lowdown" feel when Barry walked in and said, "Hey Den, what's that groove you're playing?"

"Nothing really, just something I'd heard."

"Well, play *nothing* again."

I started playing the groove and Barry took his acoustic guitar out of its case. He got down on one knee and started playing along with my drums. After a minute or so he shouted, "Got it." Later that day we started recording a new song, "Love You Inside Out." It would soon climb to number one on the Billboard charts.

The same thing happened to Blue Weaver. I was there a number of times when Barry and Blue were writing songs. Barry would come to a part in the song and say, "Give me your best chord." Then Blue would play something really nice and Barry would go "yeah" and start tapping his foot and singing to it, and then Blue would follow Barry. Or Blue might play a chord and Barry would say, "No, don't go there. Try down there." And Blue would play another chord and Barry would say, "Yeah, that's it." A lot of times Barry would follow Blue and they would come up with the melody together. So Barry and Blue wrote quite a few songs together.

BARRY GIBB'S GUITAR PLAYING

One unusual aspect of Barry's guitar playing and songwriting was that he never used standard tuning on his guitar. Instead, he tuned his guitar to an open D. So when he strummed open strings (not using any fingers on his left hand), it made a D major chord. Then he would bar his guitar to form other chords. And he had all these combinations of fingerings he would use to make minor chords, passing chords, and so forth.

It certainly worked for him. Barry Gibb is the greatest rhythm guitarist I ever played with. His right hand and my right hand played very well together. We could really lock in together on the groove.

WHEN BARRY MET JOHN . . . BUT JOHN DIDN'T MEET BARRY

I was talking to Barry one day, and I asked him, "Did you ever meet The Beatles?"

Barry responded, "I met John Lennon . . . but John Lennon didn't meet me."

I looked at him like he had three heads and said, "What?"

Barry smirked. "I was in a club in London, with Robert Stigwood. We were just sitting there chatting, and all of a sudden, there was this big commotion by the door. In walks John Lennon and Brian Epstein, along with a bunch of girls and guys — this big entourage around John. Robert and Brian knew each other, so Robert turned to me and said, 'Do you want to meet John Lennon? It will be good for you to meet him.'

"'Yeah, okay,' I said. So, we walked over into this crowd of people, and I was standing behind John Lennon. Robert said to Brian, 'This is Barry Gibb of the Bee Gees, he wants to meet John.' So Brian said, 'John . . . this Barry Gibb of the Bee Gees.'

"John didn't turn around, but he put his hand over his shoulder to shake my hand. And — like an idiot — I reached up and shook his hand! Then he walked away!

"So I met John Lennon, but John Lennon didn't meet me."

MAURICE GIBB: COMEDIAN AND BASS MASTER

As you've properly gathered by now, Maurice was the comedian in the group. All the Gibb brothers had a great sense of humor, but Maurice always took it to the next level. He was the jokester. He'd be onstage, playing and goofing around with the audience or making silly faces at his brothers. You could hear the audience pick up on it, and Barry would

Robin Gibb.

stand there, frowning and standing his ground — sometimes waving his finger at Maurice — but it was all part of the act.

Maurice was a fantastic bass player. He was a very melodic player, as well as *really* solid in the groove. As musicians, Maurice and I were very supportive of each other. That's always a key element of any great band. If the drummer and bass player can really lock in, you lay a great foundation for the song. On many of the records I cut with him, Maurice's bass lines are just incredible.

When you listen to the Bee Gees' records, you notice Maurice almost never sang lead. And he never sang *any* lead on the records I played on. When Barry and Robin sang lead, they were incredible. Their voices blended so well together. But when Maurice added his part, his harmony, it became the Bee Gees.

While Maurice was cutting up, Robin would try to take no notice of him. He was usually fairly serious, and he was *very* serious about his craft, about his music. Robin also had a very sharp wit, as all the brothers did. They could communicate on another level; everybody else was on the outside.

Robin pretty much kept himself to himself. He didn't socialize nearly as much as Maurice and Barry. While we were on tour in America or elsewhere, we would all congregate in Barry and Linda's room after each show, because they always had the biggest suite, and because Barry tended to be the center of things. Barry would always bring out his guitar, and Robin and Maurice would sing, but always other people's material, never their own. And Robin certainly participated and enjoyed those get-togethers as much as anyone, despite being a quieter person.

I didn't hang out or socialize much with Robin. I really only saw him when we worked together. I certainly liked him and considered him a friend, but we never were *best* friends. It was just harder to get to know him than it was Barry, Maurice, or even, later, Andy.

CHAPTER 13

Main Course
and the Bee Gees'
Comeback

I DIDN'T SHOOT THE SHERIFF

After we cleared customs at Miami International Airport, I went with Tom and Dick to the Hertz counter, where we rented two Chevrolet station wagons. Pete Wagner, a local limousine driver, picked up the boys, Linda, Alan, and Blue, and took them to our rental house on Miami Beach.

Dick went with Tom, and I followed them out of the airport. We got onto 95 north and made an exit at NE 163rd Street. When we reached Collins Avenue, we went north. I looked to the right, and there was the Atlantic Ocean. The sun was shining intensely and turned the ocean into dark sparkling blue. After two or three miles, we pulled into the driveway of a large house. The limo was already there.

The house was covered with white stucco and had a Cuban barrel-tile roof. A single palm tree in front of the house curved toward the sky. I had a strange feeling that I'd been to this place before. As I helped Tom and Dick carry the suitcases into the house, I looked at the number on the front door: 461.

No, this couldn't be . . .

"Den, you got to see this . . ." Barry shouted and led me through the kitchen to the backyard. I couldn't believe my eyes. I looked down; where the grass in the backyard stopped, the sand of the beach began. Fifty feet from the house, frothy, white circular waves came crashing down. As far as I could see to the left and to the right, there was nothing but ocean and sand. And, to top it all, there were girls in bikinis, walking both ways. Had I died and gone to heaven?

"Isn't this amazing," Barry said.

"Is this the place Eric stayed when he cut *the* album?" I asked Barry.

"Yes," Barry said. "This is 461 Ocean Boulevard. You didn't know?"

We had a few days off before recording began. Somebody had the bright idea that we might need a little time to get over jet lag. *Good thinking, whoever-you-are!* We became beach bums! I took whoever wanted to go to the local Walgreen's on Collins Ave., and we loaded up. We bought baseball bats, baseball gloves, and balls. We got kites, footballs, plastic waterbeds, Frisbees, fishing rods. Whatever could be used on the beach, we bought. Oh yes, and we bought suntan lotion, lots and lots of it.

There was a great atmosphere at the house. Everybody got along really well; we were like a big family. We played on the beach all day and at night we drank wine as we listened to the ocean's melody.

CRITERIA STUDIOS

Meanwhile, our equipment had arrived from London and was waiting for us at Criteria Studios. The day before we were due to start recording, Tom, Alan, Blue, and I drove to the studio, on NE 149th Street, not far from the rented house.

It was a long two-story building, with glass windows stretching all the way along the top floor. Tel-Air Films occupied the offices behind the glass. Next to the roof was a sign that read *Criteria Studios* in large red lettering. There was an entrance on the far left side of the building that led to the main Criteria reception area for Studio A and Studio B. On the far right side of the building was another reception area for Studio C. I parked the wagon in the large parking lot and the four of us walked into the closest entrance on the left. The ceiling was high, and the walls were decorated with an arrangement of what looked like driftwood. The wall behind the front desk, as well as the hallways that led to Studio A and B, were covered by dozens and dozens of gold and platinum albums.

Tom went up to the girl behind the desk. "Hello, we're here to set up for the Bee Gee sessions."

"Oh hi, you're in Studio C, the entrance is over there," she replied, pointing to the doors on the other side of the building. We walked out into the parking lot, over to the other side, and entered the Studio C reception area. This one, however, was not furnished as lavishly as the main reception area we'd just left.

The room was plain, with a hallway to the left running to Studio C and the corresponding control room. To the right, a staircase led up to the Tel-Air offices. On the back wall under the stairs was a large red pinball machine and beside that was a door leading to the bathroom. Just to the left of the glass entrance door was a low square table with long plastic bench seats all around it. Studio C was to be our home for the next six weeks.

I walked down the hallway, past the control room on the right, and into the studio. The room was large but not huge. It was square, with wide soundproof panels that went from the floor to the ceiling. The panels were different colors — one light, one dark, and so on. On the right-hand side of the back wall, I saw my drums in their flight cases next to a round soundproof baffle. It was semi-circular, about five feet high, and looked like a round bar as it protruded out from the corner. Above the baffle was a small round canopy that pointed toward the ceiling. The whole thing looked like a hat. Inside the canopy, a white sheet hung down like a giant handkerchief. This must be the drum booth, I surmised, but what the hell's the white thing?

In the middle of the room on the right-hand side, there was a full-sized black Steinway grand piano. As I walked over to my drums, I heard Blue playing it. It sounded beautiful. I looked past Blue and the piano: in the front wall, a giant double-glazed window looked into the control room. A guy with long hair was sitting at the desk.

I started opening up my drum cases, and the long-haired guy came out. "Hi, you must be the Bee Gees Band. I'm Karl Richardson. I'm engineering the record. Welcome to Criteria."

"Hey, Karl, what's this?" I asked as I pointed to the white fabric overhead.

"That's a real parachute made from pure silk. It absorbs and deflects certain frequencies we don't like. You must be the drummer, right?"

"Yeah, Dennis Bryon, how ya doing?"

We shook, and Karl pulled the circular baffle back, giving me plenty of room to set up. Only when I finished arranging my drums did Karl go to work. After he had placed his mics, my Gretsch drums looked like a million dollars.

On Monday, January 6, 1975, we started recording *Main Course*. When we got to Criteria that day, Arif was already there. He was in the control room talking with Karl. When we all met again, there were a lot of handshakes and hugging. As soon as Blue and Arif were introduced, I could see they were instant studio buddies. The first thing Arif did was ask Blue to show him the ARP and the Moog.

My drums were set up, mic'd, and ready to go — I had come in the day before and worked on drum sounds with Karl. After Arif finished talking with Blue, he came over to my drum booth. As I sat at my drums Arif asked me if I knew what a *click track* was. He told me it was an electronic metronome that had become very popular in recording. He said he wanted to experiment with one if I was willing.

"Some drummers take to it straight away, while others never get the hang of it. If you have trouble or feel uncomfortable playing to a click, we'll go back to recording the old-fashioned way." He said the benefits of playing with a click were huge. "If the tempo of the song is exact from beginning to the end, we can take, say, the first chorus vocals, copy them, and insert them when the second chorus comes around. It's the way everyone's recording today. If you feel confident, I'd like to give it a try."

If Arif wanted to give it a try, then so did I. "Yeah, man, I'm up for it."

Arif assembled everybody in the control room and told us how he had been looking forward to this record. He called the Bee Gees one of the best vocal groups in the world. "*Excuse me?*" Maurice interrupted. "*The* very best vocal group in the world." Arif continued that they should feel incredibly fortunate to have such a talented band. He also said how lucky we all were to have an engineer as great as Karl. Arif made everybody feel special.

Arif explained the benefits of the click track that we were going to experiment with. Playing with a click, he said, was very different, and we should be patient with each other. *Be patient with the drummer* — that's what he meant.

We started running through the first song without the click. Before the session, we'd rehearsed a song called "All This Making Love" in the house, where we had a duplicate set of the musical equipment to learn the new songs.

Karl began mixing the sound in our headphones. He had four different mixes he could go to, so anyone could have anything they wanted in their phones. It was all sounding great until Karl turned on the click. Then everybody stopped playing.

"Get that thing out of my phones!" Robin shouted, and Maurice, Blue, and Alan chimed in, too. The only person who was willing to tolerate it was Barry. But he only wanted a smidgen.

I have to admit, they were right; the click was obnoxious. The reason it's called a click track is because that's precisely what it is. It's an electronic beat generated by who knows what. The click was set to a fixed tempo and pumped through the phones. The only way I could hear it over my drums was to have it blasting in my headset.

Karl pulled it out of everybody's mix except for Barry's and mine, and we continued. Now, not only did I have to remember the feel and arrangement of the song, I had to keep up with this *damn thing*.

The click kept getting away from me, or I kept getting away from it, I didn't know which. There's no worse feeling in the world for a drummer than to hear the tempo of a song fall behind the rhythm of the click track. It was a nightmare; every time I fell behind, I had to speed up, then I'd overdo it and play faster than the click.

Arif called everybody into the control room for playback. I knew exactly where I'd gotten off with the click — going into the first chorus and during the second chorus — and I went off big-time. Arif told everybody how well we'd played and told me how great I was doing with the click.

We listened back without hearing the click. When the song got to the first place I was off, it didn't sound too bad. There was a bit of a change in the feel as I tried to catch up, but it sounded nowhere near as horrific as it did when we recorded it.

Arif said all the parts were good and we were going for a real take. He told me once the tempo and the feel of the song were established, he was going to fade out the click.

"'All This Making Love' take two," Karl announced on the talkback, and the red light went on. With the click pounding in my head, I counted the song in. "One . . . two . . . one-two —"

We all came in nicely; I was concentrating on the click and trying to keep a laid-back feel. I could hear instruments getting off tempo, but I just followed that click like my life depended on it. We got through the first verse and the turnaround; second verse I got a little off but managed to pull it back. Then on the third verse, I heard the click starting to fade away. By the time the instrumental came around it was gone. Freedom at last. We finished recording, and Arif called us in.

The first thing he did was mute everything except the drums. He played the whole track from beginning to end; he asked me if I was satisfied with the track, then gave me a nod of approval. Next, he wanted to replace Maurice's bass track. By the time we replaced the guitar, keyboards, and laid down some vocals it was ten o'clock. It was a good first day; everyone was satisfied.

Before we went home, Blue and Barry started fooling around at the piano. Blue was playing some beautiful chords, and Barry started singing along. Barry gave Blue some hints and direction, and Blue followed. Arif came into the studio carrying his briefcase; he was just about to leave. He went over to the piano and listened. "That's beautiful, guys . . . finish it, and we'll cut it tomorrow." The next day we recorded "Songbird."

"JIVE TALKIN'"

The first week flew by. After the sessions had finished early Friday afternoon, Arif flew back to New York to be with his family. He was returning Sunday; the session was scheduled to start at four o'clock in the afternoon. On Friday night and Saturday afternoon, we rehearsed at the house. The brothers had new songs they wanted to share with the band before going into the studio. One of the new songs was called "Nights on Broadway." I had a bit of trouble with it in rehearsal; it was a fast-double tempo groove, and I just couldn't get the feel right. Barry wanted to record it on Sunday afternoon, so I went to Criteria early to practice it.

I got to the studio at two o'clock, giving myself a couple of hours to rehearse. I had the arrangement written on a yellow pad, and the tempo was in my head, but no matter how hard I tried I just could not get the *feel* of the song right. I was a bit worried.

At about three-thirty, Alan and Blue came in with Tom. Then, just before four o'clock, Barry came rushing into the studio overwhelmed with excitement, and Rob and Mo followed.

"Aw, man, we've got a new song, it's called 'Jive Talkin'' — we wrote it in the car on the way to the studio." Barry could hardly contain himself. "As the car drove over a metal drawbridge over one of the canals, the tires hitting the iron supports underneath the bridge produced a strange rhythm, and we wrote a song to it."

Arif arrived and wanted to know what all the fuss was about. After Barry told him about the new song, Arif asked if the song was complete. "It's almost done," Barry said. "All we need to do is polish it up a bit." Arif could see the excitement in the brothers and didn't want to miss the opportunity to capture it. He told them to go upstairs into one of the empty Tel-Air offices and finish it. Then we'd record it while it was fresh.

After about an hour, Barry, Robin, and Maurice came downstairs with the song finished. Karl set up a click track, and the six of us started to rehearse the new song, but we had trouble finding the right feel and the right parts. I asked Karl to turn off the click while we ran it down. After a very frustrating half hour, Arif's voice came through the talkback into our phones.

"Everybody come into the control room now!"

Barry and I looked at each other like a couple of naughty schoolboys who didn't finish their assignment. In the control room, Arif was standing next to Karl, who was manipulating a quarter-inch tape recorder in front of him. Arif had instructed Karl to record the whole rehearsal. During the chaos, Arif heard something he liked.

"It's here. You had it, then you lost it. We'll find it," he said confidently. Karl kept playing the tape until he found what Arif was searching for. "That's it! Stop the tape, rewind, play." Karl rewound the tape back a little too far, and we had to wait for the magic bars to come around. "That's it, rewind the tape just a little and mark it," Arif said passionately.

Karl pressed an auto-locate button on the machine, ensuring the tape recorder went back to the same place every time. "Dennis, listen to what you're playing, listen to *how* you're playing, and listen to the feel. Barry, listen to the groove you're strumming on the guitar, hear how it's perfect with what Dennis is playing. And Alan and Blue and Maurice, listen to what you're playing, it's right on."

Karl played it again, and Arif was right. Just for a few seconds, everything locked together. It was the groove for "Jive Talkin'" and Arif had found it. "Locate and play," Arif ordered, and Karl played it again.

After listening to the parts we had played at least a dozen times, we went back into the studio to rehearse it. Arif had Karl patch it through to our headphones so we could learn the parts. After about ten minutes we had the groove down. Barry went through the arrangement with us, and we were ready to put one down.

We thought it would be a good idea to start off with just his guitar and my bass drum. Then the whole band came in on the downbeat of the first chorus, right where Barry starts singing "Jive talkin'" for the first time. We recorded it this way on the first take, then went into the control room to critique our performances. Arif made some adjustments to the arrangement and tempo. We went back out to record it.

"'Jive Talkin',' take two," Karl said just after the red light came on. Barry began scratching his guitar, and I started in with my bass drum. We got to the place where Barry changes rhythm in the intro and were about to come in on the first chorus when Barry added a vocal ad-lib. He sang, "It's-just-your" before the "jive talking" downbeat.

I stopped playing and signaled to Barry. "Are you going to do that pickup before the downbeat of the chorus?" I asked.

"What pickup?" Barry asked.

"It's-just-your," I said.

"Oh, that thing, yeah I'll do it," he said.

"Okay, then I'll catch it with you."

"Right, here we go," Barry said.

The red light came on and . . . "'Jive Talkin',' take three," Karl said.

Barry started scratching, and I came in with my bass drum. Then I played a snare fill that matched Barry's ad-lib perfectly. I made every drum fill on the record match the feel of Barry's vocal pickup. Arif loved it.

As well as "Jive Talkin'" had gone, I was not looking forward to recording "Nights on Broadway." Every time I tried to play the groove, my hands and my feet just wouldn't work. The irony was that the thing I hated the most about this new way of recording was the very thing that saved me: the click. Once we established the right tempo, and we had an arrangement, Karl set the speed of the click, and it became something I could depend on. It was always there for me to follow. The click was becoming my friend.

It took about five or six takes, but in the end the band nailed the track. After some repairs on guitar, bass, and piano, Arif started working on vocals. Barry, Robin, and Maurice were set up in the middle of the studio, where they all sang around a single microphone, as they liked to do.

Whenever they were together — especially around a mic — it was like comedy central. They were good at impersonations and could pretty much do *anybody*. As they were rehearsing the vocals on "Nights on Broadway," they broke into a *mad* five minutes. They started singing in strange voices and making strange faces. It was hilarious; everybody in the control room was in stitches.

Suddenly Arif stopped the tape. "Barry, I have an idea. Try singing the chorus in falsetto."

Karl rewound the tape and Barry started singing in that high voice: "Blaming it all." Robin and Maurice joined in, and we all had chills. Barry was reluctant to change his style of singing at first, but Arif encouraged him: "Experiment with your voice, take it places it's never been."

When we got home that night, we played the rough mix of "Nights on Broadway" into the early hours. *This was a hit.*

The next day Arif told Barry, Robin, and Maurice he thought something was missing: the song needed a bridge. The brothers sat down with Blue at the piano and in a short time they had it.

Karl fired up the click, and we recorded eight bars of groove before the new bridge, then the bridge, then eight bars of groove after it. When Arif was satisfied, Karl edited the new bridge into the master track, and it was done: "Nights on Broadway."

The Bee Gees Band.

MAIN COURSE COMPLETE

While we were in Miami, we lived and breathed the *Main Course* album. Of course, at that time there was no name for the record — that would come later. We recorded incredible new songs like "Fanny (Be Tender with My Love)," "Edge of the Universe," "All This Making Love." Blue proved himself, coming up with state of the art sounds and cool bass lines on his moog. His piano playing was inspiring. Alan played funky R&B rhythms on all the songs and soulful licks on pedal steel, and Maurice's bass playing was right in the pocket.

When the recording was complete, Arif took the tracks to New York to add real strings, brass, and percussion. *Main Course* was ready for the radio.

The *Main Course* album reached number fourteen on the Billboard 200 chart, while "Jive Talkin'" reached number one on the Billboard Hot

100 chart, "Nights on Broadway" reached number seven, and "Fanny (Be Tender with My Love)" reached number twelve. The Bee Gees were back.

One final, very important note about *Main Course*. It was during the making of that album that Arif Mardin first heard and expressed enthusiasm for Barry's helium-like falsetto. That sound, of course, would later become a huge trademark for the Bee Gees. So Arif, in addition to being a wonderful person and producer, could also be considered the creator of the "helium years."

CHAPTER 14 Back to Reality

OH, DAD

When I got back to London, I spent a couple of days at the apartment with Jenny and Babet before heading home to Cardiff. I'd been away for only two months, but things had deteriorated for Dad. The cancer had spread to his liver. He was thin and didn't have much energy. I was home for two months, and I was determined to spend as much time with him as possible. Mum was holding her own; she didn't seem any worse, but I could see her slipping further away through Dad's eyes. He'd lost his best friend. It was so sad to watch.

Carole came over every day to take care of Mum's personal needs. Most days I'd take Carole out for some pub-grub at lunchtime. We'd have a drink and try to laugh about everything. As kids, we'd hated each other; we were always fighting. One day she'd said, "Put your finger in the light socket, I'll turn it on, and we'll see if you light up." I had climbed on a chair, took the bulb out of the wall light, and put my finger in the socket. When Carole flicked the switch, I lit up. But now we became closer than we ever were.

March just flew by, and in the middle of April, we had a week of rehearsal in the Isle of Man for the upcoming American/Canadian tour. The tour was a big one; we were promoting the new album. It started with rehearsals in New York on May 22. No orchestra, just a very cool five-piece brass section. We had a sound company and a lighting company. This was going to be a great tour.

The day before I left for New York, Dad had a small exploratory operation scheduled at Llandough Hospital, just outside Cardiff. His doctors wanted a better look at what was going on. While Carole looked after Mum, I took Dad to the hospital. He had his own room, which was unusual; most of the time patients were in the ward. I sat next to Dad's bed.

"Dad, I don't have to go, the Bee Gees can get another drummer in a second. I think it's best if I stay here with you."

"You're their drummer and you're going. It's your job, and they need you. I don't even want to talk about it. But there is something I do want to talk about, luv . . . It's about your mother." I held Dad's hand. "You do know at some point she *will* have to go into hospital, and when that time comes, if I'm not around, you have to take her."

My eyes filled up. "I know that, Dad, but it's not going to be for a long time."

"Doesn't matter when it's going be. The fact is, that time *will* come, and when it does, if I'm not around, you have to be ready. You do understand, Den?"

"Yeah, Dad . . . I love you, Dad."

"I love you, Den."

The next day I got on a plane for New York. We landed at two-thirty-five at JFK. As usual we were staying at the City Squire. I didn't get to my room until about six o'clock in the evening. I was tired and only glanced at the city below as I drew the curtains. After my suitcase arrived, I got undressed, pulled back the sheets, and got into bed.

The next thing I remember, the phone was ringing. It was six o'clock in the morning. It was my brother-in-law, in Cardiff. There had been complications during surgery. Dad had died.

I called Dick's room and told him what had happened. Dick was fantastic; he told me he'd get me home as soon as possible, and then get me back before the first show. That was, of course, if I wanted to come back. I did.

My phone rang again; it was Linda. She told me how sorry she was and that she loved me, then she put Barry on the line. He said he was going to hire a drummer for rehearsals. He told me to go, and do what I had to do; he said everybody would be here for me when I got back.

It was a tough week; there was so much to do. We had to register Dad's passing and get the death certificate, organize the funeral service, choose a headstone, and plan the wake. But with the efforts of Carole and Jenny, we did it.

Dad had a good turnout. The service was full, and the minister did a nice tribute. All the men Dad worked with at the airport came with their wives. It was nice. I felt so sorry for my mother — she didn't know what had happened. She thought it was all a party for Dad, but she couldn't figure out why he wasn't there.

I didn't want to leave, but Carole and Jen made me. They said it's what Dad would have wanted. But I was worried about leaving Mum. Carole said, "Now that the old bugger's not around, we're going to spoil her. The first thing she gets is a new hair-do, then a manicure, pedicure, and some new clothes. You won't recognize her when you get back. Go on, Den, go back to work, she'll be okay."

There weren't many passengers on the flight back. I had a window seat and there wasn't anybody sitting in the two seats next to me. I cried for eight hours.

1975 AMERICAN/CANADIAN TOUR

On May 29, 1975, I landed in Dayton, Ohio. It was great to see so many happy people, just the opposite of what I'd left behind. Everybody was so kind; they went out of their way to make sure I knew I was part of this family. I don't know how I did it, but I got through the first show without any rehearsals. I tried not to think about what I'd just lost, and plugged myself into the road.

It was a long tour divided into two sections. The first half was America, starting in Dayton and ending eight weeks later in Detroit, Michigan. It was a tough one for me, but I kept the energy up as we were promoting our new album *Main Course*. Then, midway through the first half of the tour, we got the news that the first single "Jive Talkin'" had entered and was going up the charts. To say we were happy was an understatement. Another element had entered the equation: success. All our hard work was starting to pay off.

We had a five-week break before starting the second half of the tour in Los Angeles. While I was home, on August 9, 1975, "Jive Talkin'" reached number one on the Billboard Hot 100. I sighed a big sigh and thought back to what Dad had said when I was about to give up: "Go back to London. It's only a matter of time before you'll be in the hit parade again." Maybe Dad wasn't so far away; maybe he could still pull a few strings.

When we arrived back in Los Angeles, we did the *Tonight Show with Johnny Carson*, performing "Jive Talkin'" and the next single, "Nights on Broadway." When the boys sat down with Johnny, they talked about how well the tour was doing and promoted Canadian dates.

The next day we did *The Midnight Special* hosted by Helen Reddy, where we performed "Jive Talkin'," "Nights on Broadway," "Wind of Change" and "To Love Somebody." The television studio was full of energy as we performed in front of a live audience. The Bee Gees had a number one hit and the brothers were full of confidence again.

AN EVENING WITH BRUCE JOHNSTON

I met another hero of mine while on that tour: Bruce Johnston, who had been a key member of The Beach Boys since 1965. We were in Los Angeles for a big concert at the Santa Monica Civic Auditorium. After the show, I looked across the dressing room, and there he was. I'm a huge Beach Boys fan; I have all their records and had been a fan of Bruce for years. Linda knew how much I loved The Beach Boys, so I caught her eye and made a little gesture toward Bruce. Linda came over to me: "What ya babbling about?"

"That's Bruce Johnston of The Beach Boys."

"You wanna meet him?" Then across the crowded dressing room Linda shouted, "Hey, Bruce." Bruce turned around, and Linda called him over. "Bruce, I'd like you to meet our drummer, Dennis Bryon. He's a huge Beach Boys fan."

We shook hands, and Bruce complimented me on my playing. "You wanna go for dinner and see a band play?"

"Yes!"

Bruce was fantastic. We hit it off right away. The next thing I knew I was on the back of Bruce's Harley-Davidson, riding through the streets of L.A., relishing the warm night. We had dinner in a trendy restaurant on Sunset Boulevard, where Bruce knew everybody, then we went to a club called the Whisky a Go Go on the Sunset Strip.

After an hour at the Whisky, Bruce asked me if I wanted to hear a song he was writing. We went back to his house where he introduced me to his wife, Harriet, and took me into his music room. He sat down at a full-sized grand piano and started playing some chords.

"This is a new song I'm working on; it's about where the music comes from. It's about how a song is born." Then he started playing "I Write the Songs." The song wasn't finished yet, but I got the idea. I didn't know then, but I was one of the first people to hear an idea that would turn into a mega-hit for Barry Manilow, and win a Grammy for Song of the Year. I was — and still am — thrilled beyond words.

We started the next half of the tour in Victoria, B.C. Donald K. was the promoter, so I knew we were in for a good time. We did twenty-five shows in only four weeks. It was hard work. "Nights on Broadway" was going up the charts, and the 8,000-seat venues were full every night. Donald was happy. We wrapped things up in the first week of October and flew home.

THE MOVE TO CARDIFF

After the long tour, I was exhausted, but I drove down to Cardiff to be with Jenny, who was staying at my sister's house with Mum and Babet. We had an offer on the bungalow in Radyr, and Carole and I decided to take it. Jenny and I had a long talk and agreed to give up our apartment in London and buy a house in Cardiff. We would move there permanently, so we could look after Mum.

I'd been on a permanent wage from RSO for almost three years and had a good relationship with my bank manager at Barclays. With the cash I earned from my half of the sale of the bungalow, and my good income record at the bank, I easily qualified for a mortgage. We found the perfect house in Cyncoed, one of the oldest districts in Cardiff. It was at the top of Pen-Y-Lan hill, a steep road that led into town. From the house, we could see out over all of Cardiff. Beyond, and clearly visible, were the waters of the Bristol Channel. Wow, this is ours!

It was our first house, and we felt blessed. It was big enough for Mum to have her room upstairs next to our bedroom, and right next to the bathroom. That was important. After a few trips to London in the VW camper, all of our stuff was in the new house.

I had a couple of months off before starting the new album in January. We were going back to Criteria in Miami, and Arif was going to produce us again, with Karl Richardson engineering. I couldn't wait to get back in the studio and be a part of this incredible team.

CHAPTER 15

Children of the World . . . and Arif's Exit

OFF TO A BAD START

On January 6, 1976, we were on National Flight 1 at Heathrow bound for Miami. Everything was normal; the cabin crew was cleaning up after dinner. I was sitting next to Blue right by the galley. Suddenly all the galley curtains were violently pulled closed. I looked at Blue. Then as suddenly as they were closed, they were yanked open.

All of the cabin crew had a look of horror on their faces and started quickly packing everything away. Blue pulled the window shade up, and we looked out. Instead of being 35,000 feet high, where we had been, we were just above the clouds. The sun, which had been in front of us, was now behind us. Blue looked back to the wing and told me we were dumping fuel.

Then the captain came on and told us we had had a bomb threat. He said whoever called it in gave the right code word, and they were taking it seriously. We were returning to Shannon Airport in Ireland. It was the longest hour of my life, knowing a hidden bomb could explode at any second.

Finally, we landed and disembarked. The plane was searched, along with everybody's bags. They didn't find anything. We spent twelve hours at the airport and didn't leave until six the next morning. When we finally got to Miami we were exhausted. But that wasn't the worst of it. Barry, who had flown in the day before, was waiting for us at the rented house on Miami Beach — and he told us he had some bad news.

There had been a disagreement between Atlantic Records and RSO. Because Arif was affiliated with Atlantic, he wouldn't be able to work with us on the album. After a lot of head scratching and "Oh my God what are we going to dos," it was suggested we take the whole thing to Los Angeles and work with another producer, Richard Perry.

I don't know how Dick did it, but the next thing I knew we were all staying at an elite mansion in Beverly Hills. When we went into the studio with Richard, though, it was clear from the beginning it wasn't going to work. Personalities clashed; the chemistry just wasn't right. Somebody made a personal remark about Robin's voice, and he took it to heart — so he should. And the studio sucked. They put me in a room that was on a different floor than everybody else. In the room, there was a small window next to the ceiling. It looked up into the studio above; I had a great view of everybody's feet.

In the control room, I heard somebody on the phone, "Yeah man, I just dropped a couple, but they ain't kicked in yet. Parteeeee!" I told Barry what I'd heard, and that was the straw that did it.

At the house the next day we all gathered around a huge dining room table. We decided we would produce the album ourselves, at Criteria, with Karl. Dick made a few phone calls and told us that, unfortunately, the slot we had reserved at Criteria had been given to somebody else. The only time available was mid-March and April. Dick suggested we fly home, take February off, and fly to Miami in March. It sounded like a plan, so that's what we did.

THINK ABOUT THE PARTS
AND MAKE THE GROOVE YOURS

Once we were finally able to get back into Criteria Studios, three months had already passed. It was great to be back in Miami and even greater to

We needed Karl in the studio: he had great ears.

be back in Studio C. We were all set up and ready to go. The Bee Gees had new songs, and the band and Karl were fired up. I was sitting in the reception area with Robin, Maurice, Alan, and Blue when Barry called us all into the control room. "Arif's on the phone, and he wants to talk to you."

The seven of us formed a circle around the mixing console as Barry talked to Arif. After a few minutes, he handed the phone to Robin. "Hi, Arif, how are you?"

The room was silent as Robin listened while Arif did most of the talking. Eventually Robin said, "Yep, okay, we will, then. Thanks, Arif." Then Robin handed the phone to Maurice.

"Hello, mate, where the hell are you? Do you know how much trouble you caused us?" Then Mo calmed down. "Aww, mate, thanks, yeah, I know . . . Miss you too." Then Maurice handed the phone to me. "Arif wants to talk to you."

"Hi, Arif, how ya doing?"

He spoke softly in his Turkish accent. "I'm good, Dennis; I just want to let you know the reason I can't be there stems from business and politics. I'd give anything to record with you guys again, but because of circumstances beyond my control it's not going to happen. But what's going to happen is this . . . the six of you and Karl are going to make the most incredible album yet. You are a great drummer, Dennis, and you can do it without me. Do what you do best, think about the parts and make the groove yours. Always be true to the song. The song is your mistress and will guide you. You can do it, my friend. Let me speak to Alan."

After a few minutes with Arif, Alan passed the phone to Blue. When Blue was done, he passed the phone to Karl. Finally, Karl passed the phone back to Barry, who finished the conversation and hung up.

The control room was silent as we all took in what had just happened. The greatest coach in the music business had just given us the ball.

We started recording, and things were going well. The brothers had a half dozen new song ideas and they were all good. Barry and Robin were writing with Blue, and they had a new ballad called "The Way It Was." I was happy, because the click had now evolved into a nice cabasa sound that was much more tolerable. Around the third day, a guy with long wispy hair and an equally wispy goatee came to the studio. He wore a faded T-shirt with jeans that were too short, and he was barefoot. He looked like a hippy. Barry introduced him as Albhy and said he had studied with Arif in New York; he was to be an advisor on the record.

The first thing he did was sit down on my kit. He couldn't play, but he started hitting the individual drums with one of my sticks. I asked him what he was doing; he told me he wanted to hear what the drums sounded like up close. "Put your head in my bass drum, then you'll hear what it sounds like up close," I growled.

Karl sat at my drums a million times while he was mic'ing them, but he never once played them. It's something you just don't do. You don't touch somebody else's instrument — not unless you're a fucking moron, that is. I could see I was going to have trouble with this guy.

Nothing was good enough for Albhy, and it wasn't just me. As the recording continued, he criticized Blue's playing, Alan's playing. There were terrible verbal exchanges between Blue and Albhy in the control room, a no-no when you're recording. He asked me if I could play more like Jeff Porcaro, or Russ Kunkel, or Steve Gadd. He had a fixation on drum loops — a short section of recorded drums, usually four bars long, repeated over and over. He wanted all the songs to be looped.

Since I'd started playing, I was always trying to get better, learning about the different microphones and how they recorded and colored the sound. I was exploring dynamics, learning how to build emotion during recording, and now here comes this guy who wants to turn me into a loop.

We were recording a song called "You Should Be Dancing," and Albhy told everybody exactly what they should play, instead of letting us add our own ideas, as Arif always did. The next day we were still trying to get the track. In the end, Barry looked at me and said, "Come on, let's just do it."

Barry sat on a high stool in front of my drums, playing guitar and singing into his mic. We both had the click, and that's how we recorded the track, just Barry, me, and the click. Later, Blue, Alan, and Maurice overdubbed their parts. The plan was to add percussion next, then after the vocals were finished we'd add the Bonnaroo Horn Section led by Peter Graves.

STEPHEN STILLS AND "YOU SHOULD BE DANCING"

We used an incredible percussion player from Los Angeles named Joe Lala; he was in town recording with Stephen Stills. Joe had two sets of drums in the studio. To the right was his three-conga setup, and next to it was his percussion setup, which consisted of a set of timbales, an assortment of crash cymbals, cowbells, triangles, and lots of other percussion stuff that was set up all around. Karl had everything mic'd up and ready to start the next day.

It had been a long day in the studio and we had got a lot done. At about eight o'clock in the evening, we were just about to wrap things up. Suddenly, the control room door burst open and Joe and Stephen flowed in. They'd just got back from a local fish restaurant called Port of Call and were very *happy*, to say the least. All Joe wanted to do was play congas while Stephen played his timbales.

All everybody else wanted to do was to go home, but Joe and Stephen insisted. Barry was reluctant but said he'd give them one shot. If they didn't get it on the first take they could do it the next day. Joe and Stephen huddled in the corner for some Dutch courage, and then they were ready to go.

Karl went into the studio with them and made some final adjustments to the mics. Back in the control room, Barry shook his head; we all feared this would take all night. Finally, Karl put the machine into play and pulled everything up in the mix. By the time the song got to the fade, Joe and Stephen had figured out their parts.

Karl got on the talkback. "Good luck, guys, here we go." Then he put the MCI twenty-four track machine into record.

From the first note to the last, everybody in the control room was gobsmacked. Not only were their performances perfect, they were inspiring. They nailed it in one take. By the end of the song everyone in the control room was screaming wildly. I had no idea Stephen Stills was such a great drummer. Of course they wanted to do it again — every musician always wants another go — but we didn't want to touch what we had. That performance made the record. We didn't know it yet, but "You Should Be Dancing" would be released as a single in 1976 and shoot to number one on the charts.

As we neared the end of the sessions, Robert came to the studio to check on our progress. He had done this on all our records, and whenever Robert appeared it was special, but never as special as on *this* day.

We were all in the control room playing Robert the rough mixes. When he heard "You Should Be Dancing," he went crazy, slapping his hand on his leg and yelling, "It's a fucking smash, it's a fucking smash!" He did the same thing with "Love So Right" and "Boogie Child." His reaction was what we *all* lived for.

After the playback, as usual, Robert met with the Bee Gees to discuss the progress of the record. They were upstairs in one of the Tel-Air offices, and the meeting was taking longer than the usual hour.

I was sitting in the reception area with Blue when Barry came down the stairs with the biggest grin I'd ever seen on his face.

"You're not gonna believe what just happened."

Blue and I looked at each other.

"Where's Alan? He has to hear this, too."

We told Barry he was out somewhere.

"Robert just made the band junior partners in RSO. From now on, the three of you will be getting royalties on everything we sell."

I looked at Blue. "Is that good?"

"It's not good," Barry said, "it's fucking *great*. The more records we sell, the more money you guys make. We're a unit now; it's the six of us."

I wished somebody would tell Albhy.

There were some great songs on the album — "You Should Be Dancing," "Love So Right," "You Stepped into My Life," "The Way It Was," and, of course, "Children of the World."

The *Children of the World* album reached number eight on the Billboard 200 and sold 2.5 million copies. "You Should Be Dancing" reached number one on the Billboard Hot 100, while "Love So Right" reached the number three position and "Boogie Child" reached number twelve. We had done it again.

MUM GOES INTO HOSPITAL

I had almost five months off before the next U.S. tour. I loved living in our new house in Cardiff, but Mum was slipping further away. It seemed my life had turned into an ocean of waves, and the latest one was about to come crashing down. Mum's doctor came to the house every Friday afternoon for a checkup; this Friday he gave me the news I feared the most — she had reached a stage in her illness where she needed to be cared for by professionals. He said Carole, Jenny, and I had done an admirable job in our care for her, and not to feel any guilt or shame in letting her go. Easy for him to say.

The day to take her in came far too soon, but I'd lived with what Dad had told me, and I was ready, or at least as ready as any son could be when taking his mother to a place from where she'd never come home. Jenny packed a small suitcase for Mum, and at three o'clock in the afternoon, with Babet in the front seat of the VW and Mum in the backseat, we started our journey to the hospital.

Babet knew exactly what was going on. The front passenger window was open, but instead of sticking her head out into the wind like she loved to do, she was curled up on the front seat, very quiet.

We got to the hospital, and I led Mum in through the large front doors. It smelled and sounded like a hospital. There weren't many people around, just nurses dressed in white uniforms and a couple of doctors in suits. We checked in at the admittance desk; the woman there was lovely. She called Mum Iris and took her by the hand. They were expecting her. She led us to the room that would be Mum's, sat Mum down on the bed, and started unpacking her suitcase. "We start dinner in five minutes, luv, would you like to stay? You could help feed Mum; that would probably make her feel a bit more at home," she said.

After she had finished putting Mum's clothes away, she led us to a large open room with armchairs lined against the walls and tables in the middle. There were a lot of people in the room, and it was noisy. She sat us down at one of the tables, and I held Mum's hand, hoping she didn't know what was going on. She didn't seem like she did. The head nurse came over and welcomed Mum; she pinned an identification tag to her cardigan. It simply read *Iris*.

Soon the food came — beef stew with mashed potatoes and peas, orange jelly with fruit for desert. I sat next to Mum and started to feed her with a spoon as I always did. Throughout dinner, nurses kept coming up and introducing themselves to us. Everyone called her Iris; they were so nice. I felt they were really concerned about her.

After the trays had been taken away, the head nurse said I should go home now, they could take it from here. This was the part I had feared the most, leaving her. I got up and said, "I'll be back tomorrow, Mum, see you then." I kissed her on the top of her head and squeezed her hand. I turned and headed for the door. *Don't turn around,* I said to myself, *whatever you do, don't turn around.* But as I got to the door, of course, I turned around.

Mum was sitting at the table, her arm reaching out to me. She was saying no, no, no . . . I started to turn back, when I felt a hand grab my shoulder. It was the head nurse. She turned me around. "Come on, luv, best if you don't go back. It'll be easier on your mum if you don't go back. Please, luv, come on."

By the time I got to the camper I was a mess. I was crying uncontrollably. I sat and put my head down, over the steering wheel. Babet was crying, too; she got down from the front seat and stood on the floor between the seats. She rested her head on my leg, then looked up at me and licked my hand. "It's okay, girl, everything's gonna be okay," I said. Then Babet nudged my arm with her snout and let out a gentle whimper. As she looked me in the eyes, I tried to comfort her . . . then I realized it was Babet who was trying to comfort me, and the nurses in the hospital weren't so much concerned about Mum as they were about me.

Every day, without exception, I went to the hospital at exactly four o'clock. It became a ritual; I hoped my feeding Mum helped the nurses just a little bit. I always stayed for at least two hours, and on my way out, I always looked back and waved goodbye.

CHAPTER 16 The *Saturday Night Fever* Explosion

1976 U.S. TOUR AND RECORDING *HERE AT LAST*

After four months off, in early October we were back on the Isle of Man, rehearsing for the next tour of America. This one was a walk in the park compared to earlier tours; we only played thirteen shows, with a day off between each. The thing I loved about this tour more than any of the others was that I was able to take Jenny with me. She got to see most of the major cities in America, including New York, Chicago, New Orleans, Nashville, Denver, San Francisco, and Los Angeles; we even went to Toronto and Montreal.

On this tour Jenny and Linda became best friends, and Jenny almost became a surrogate mother to Barry and Linda's first son, Stephen. Jenny loved Stephen like he was her own child. She spent as much time with him as she could.

The last show on the tour was at the Los Angeles Forum, where we recorded a live album called *Here at Last . . . Bee Gees . . . Live*. It reached number eight on the Billboard album chart and sold 4.6 million copies.

In early January 1977, we had time booked at Château d'Hérouville, a recording studio in France. We were mixing the live album tracks we had just recorded in Los Angeles there, because our visas allowed only a certain number of workdays per year in the United States. We needed to save those days, as we had been so busy the prior year.

Before I left home for the studio, Barry called me at my house in Cardiff. "Hi, Den. Robert's making a film in New York. It's a low-budget project called *Tribal Rites of the New Saturday Night*; he wants us to put down a few songs for the film. After we finish mixing the live album, we're going to do some recording, so bring your drums."

I packed my drums into the back of my VW camper and on January 8, I set off for France. I boarded a hovercraft in Dover that would take me to Calais, then drove the 160 miles to the studio.

The studio was in a beautiful old French chateau in the village of Hérouville near Paris; it was picturesque. We lived in the main house on the property. After everyone had arrived at the studio and settled in, Karl loaded the two-inch, twenty-four-track tape onto the tape player, and we got to work on the live album. There wasn't much for me to do because the drums were the only things that couldn't be changed; we were stuck with my performance from the night of the show. Luckily, I hadn't made any major screw-ups, and I only recorded some tambourine parts in a few places that needed it.

After we did all the fixing and added some more vocal parts, we started the mixing itself. By the time we finished the last track, two and a half weeks had gone by, but *Here at Last . . . Bee Gees . . . Live* was finished. At last it was time to record the new material. I set up my drums and Karl mic'd them up.

The first song we recorded was a new one called "Night Fever." I'd been told that Robert's film was about a guy who loved to dance, so I tried to keep the drum parts simple and danceable. We got the track pretty quickly and started overdubbing more parts. The first thing we did was add an electric rhythm guitar. Alan played the guitar, and I operated the wah-wah pedal. This is something Alan and I had done with much success on the last studio album, where my credit read "Dennis Bryon, Drums and B-B-Wah-Wah."

The next track was another new song called "More Than a Woman," and after that, we recorded "If I Can't Have You." Things were going so well. All the songs were fabulous; the Bee Gees were writing better than ever before.

As we were playing back one of the tracks, Dick came into the control room and told me Jenny was on the phone. My heart skipped, because I knew Jenny wouldn't call me when I was in the studio unless it was an emergency. I went into the office to take the call. Jenny was at the hospital with Mum. She said Mum had suddenly developed pneumonia and was in a coma; the doctors didn't think she would last the day.

I told Dick the situation, and he booked me on the next flight to London. After clearing customs at Heathrow, I picked up a rental car and drove as fast as I could to Cardiff. By the time I got to the hospital it was nine-thirty at night. In the room with Mum were her sister Joan and Joan's husband, Doug, their daughter Christine, Carole and her new husband, Bob, Jenny, and one of the nurses.

Mum was lying in bed. She wasn't moving. Aunty Joan said, "Look who's here, 'I'" — our nickname for Iris — "it's Den." Mum opened her eyes, sat up a little, and turned her head toward me. Then she smiled.

The nurse, who was standing next to the bed, gasped. "She's been waiting for you, luv," the nurse said. I sat on the bed with Mum and held her hand as she went back to sleep.

We all sat in the room until about eleven-thirty. I knew Bob, Doug, and Carole had to work the next day, so I suggested everybody go home. Jenny and I would stay the night with Mum.

It was quiet in the hospital at night; all the other patients were asleep. Every now and again we'd hear somebody's faint cry or a little moan. In a whisper, Jenny asked me how it was going in France. As we held hands, I nodded back and whispered, "Everything's good."

Mum was in a deep, restful sleep, but at three o'clock in the morning she started to stir. Jenny wanted to get the nurse, but I told her not to. I got out of my chair and sat on the bed facing Mum, holding her hand. Jenny sat on the other side of the bed and held her other hand.

Mum took some deep, labored breaths, and then, with a faint, peaceful sigh she let out the last one. Finally, she was free.

The next day I returned to the hospital with Jenny, Carole, and Bob. We picked up Mum's belongings and the necessary paperwork to apply for a death certificate. By this time, we'd become friends with the nurses and staff at the hospital. We thanked them for all they had done for Mum.

I hadn't slept all night and on the way home from the hospital everything hit me at once. I burst out crying uncontrollably and almost crashed the rental car. My brother-in-law Bob took over driving, then took the rest of the week off from his job and helped me organize the funeral service and burial. Carole and I decided it would be nice to bury Mum with Dad in Cathays Cemetery.

At the service, a huge floral arrangement arrived from the Bee Gees.

BACK TO PARIS

The following Monday afternoon, Jenny and I boarded a plane for Paris. Dick had a limo waiting for us at the airport, and in no time flat, we were back at the studio. It was about six o'clock in the afternoon; the Bee Gees, the band, and the crew were taking a dinner break.

When we walked in everybody was so kind. After a round of embraces, Barry came over and put his arms around me. "I'm so, so sorry, Den," he said.

He was hugging me a little too long, and I had to push him away. "Alright, don't make a meal out of it," I said, stepping back.

"No, man, I just wanted to take a second to respect the memory of your mother and all you've been through."

Barry was different. Yes, he was respectful, but he had a buzz going on that he was trying to hide.

"Okay, what have you done?" I asked.

"Den, we got a new song. We wrote it while you were away, and instead of bringing in another drummer we made a drum loop from some of the bars from 'Night Fever.' We slowed them down a bit, then started recording to your drums. Den, you have to hear this thing. It's one of the best songs we've ever written, and it's perfect for the film. It's called 'Stayin' Alive.' Man, you've gotta hear it."

Everybody was waiting for my reaction.

Barry continued, "I know how much you hate drum loops. If you want to record the whole song again with the band, we can. Or, if you want to play a new drum track to what we've got, you can. Or, if you want to keep what we have and add some more drums to it, we can do that, too. Whatever you want to do, Den, it's up to you."

"I want to hear the song, that's what I want to do."

After dinner, we walked over to the other building and up to the studio.

"Give it some steam, Karl," Barry said. Karl turned up the volume and pressed play. Then I heard Alan's iconic guitar riff for the first time. Blue's piano parts were awesome, and the vocals were frightening. I normally had to listen to one of their songs two or three times before I heard the magic, but this thing was instant, it was breathtaking.

"Whaddya think?" Barry asked.

"Wow . . . Let's keep everything you've done and let me add some tom-fills and cymbals," I said.

"Fantastic." Barry was delighted. "We'll start adding drums first thing tomorrow." My response was just what Barry wanted to hear; he didn't want to lose the magic they'd created, and neither did I.

The next day I listened to "Stayin' Alive" again. It was as good as I remembered from the night before, but the drums had no dynamics. I wrote out the arrangement of the song and figured out where the hooks were. I added cymbal crashes and hi-hat parts before and after the strongest parts of the song. I tried to make the drum track feel like something I would have played.

I felt relieved to be in the studio again; it was great to be back in the creative flow. I was starting to feel good about everything once more. I was starting to look ahead. The recordings for the new film just sounded right, and the feedback we were getting from New York — where the cast was in rehearsal — was excellent. They told us the music was perfect. We had just created some wonderful music for a film, but unbeknownst to any of us, this wouldn't be just an *ordinary* film.

Apart from the music, what I remember most about living at the

Karl and Albhy mixing in Studio C at Criteria Studios Miami.

Château with everybody was the camaraderie. Jenny was falling more in love with little Stevie Gibb, and she and Linda were becoming the sisters they should have been. In the studio we were all on the same musical wavelength.

One day after a long session, Barry and I were sitting alone at the long dining-room table. "Barry, I've got an idea." He just looked at me. "Let's move to America. Let's move to Miami," I said.

He stared at me for the longest time, then: "You talk to Jenny, and I'll talk to Linda."

Later that night, after Linda put Stevie to bed, the four of us got together over a bottle of the local wine and a cuppa tea. We talked about the prospect of living in Miami. "*Shopping!*" the girls agreed, and our minds were made up.

The next day Barry sat down with me, Alan, and Blue, and discussed starting a production company together. "One where we'll all be involved," Barry said. "We can all work together on different projects. The brothers, the band, and Karl and Albhy, we'll be a big team. The eight of us can work together in different groups, helping each other.

We'll start a record label, just like Atlantic. We should even build our own recording studio."

In April 1977, everybody flew to Miami. We were there to finish the music for the *Tribal Rights* project, which was now called *Saturday Night Fever*. We were back in Studio C at Criteria, and everything sounded great. We recorded another beautiful track called "How Deep Is Your Love." The song was originally intended for Yvonne Elliman, another of Robert's artists, but once he heard it, Robert grabbed it for the film. As usual we used Joe Lala on percussion and the five-piece Bonnaroo Horn Section that had played with us on the last tour.

We stayed at a rental house on North Bay Road, one of the more prestigious roads that followed the contour of the peninsula all along the bay side of Miami Beach. The houses on the waterside are three times more expensive than the ones on the other side of the road. We were staying in a house on Biscayne Bay.

Jenny came with me on this trip, and I was able to share all the great places I knew in Miami. I wanted her to get a feel for the city; this was the place we would be moving to.

After the film music was completed, we flew back to the U.K., while the Bee Gees went on to Canada to work on another film for Robert: *Sgt. Pepper's Lonely Hearts Club Band*.

The *Saturday Night Fever* soundtrack reached number one on the Billboard Hot 100 chart in January 1978, and sat there for twenty-four weeks straight. It stayed on the Billboard chart for 120 weeks and sold 40 million copies.

MOVING TO AMERICA

Jenny and I put our house on the market, but very few people came to see it. I didn't know how I could move to America if I didn't have the money from the sale of the house, but I kept the faith. We started packing, selling furniture, and giving things away. My plan was to move in March 1978; that's when we were scheduled to record the new album in Miami. Barry, Linda, and Stevie had already moved, along with Dick, George, and May. As soon as Barry told Dick he wanted to live in America, Dick had taken care of everything. What I didn't know was Robin and Maurice had moved, too. Maurice took his wife, Yvonne, and her entire family.

I was trying to get rid of anything I didn't have to take with me. A friend of mine made me an offer on the VW Camper, an offer too good to refuse. Now I needed something to drive around in the last few months at home. I thought it would be a good idea to buy a car I could ship to Miami. I made some inquiries and decided to buy a BMW 320i that was made for the American market. I ordered the car, and when it arrived at the dealership I took the train to London.

The car was brand new, a beautiful beige color, and had a great sound system. I had to be extra careful over the next few months. The car was made to be driven in America so the steering wheel was on the wrong side for the U.K.

Time flew by and soon the day we'd been planning for almost a year was upon us. I'd driven to London the week before and put the BMW on a ship bound for Miami. On Tuesday, March 7, 1978 — with Babet in the backseat — Jenny and I left Cardiff in a rental car on our way to our new home in America.

We checked Babet into at a kennel near London Airport; she was to be sedated for the journey and shipped in a custom-made crate. The next day on the flight over, all we could think about was our lovely Babet down below. We asked the stewardess if she could go below and check on her. She told us Babet *was* on board and in a secure, air-conditioned space for live animals. That news made us feel better.

When we landed in Miami, we cleared immigration without a problem. Then we went to get our suitcases before going through customs. When we reached the carousel that held our bags we couldn't believe our eyes. There was Babet, in her crate, coming down the ramp. When she started going around the carousel, I lifted up the crate and put it on the ground. I was careful that she didn't see Jenny or me; I knew she would have gone ballistic.

I placed the crate on a dolly and wheeled her to one of the customs men. I asked him if there was any grass nearby where she could pee; she'd been in the crate for at least twelve hours. Luckily enough he was an animal lover and led me to a nearby door. He slid a plastic card through a security scanner on the door and pushed the door open. I put the crate on the floor and opened the door.

Babet looked at me, then at the grass outside. She ran right past me to the green stuff. She stopped, then began the longest pee she'd ever done. When she was finished, she sniffed her pee and started again. She really needed to go. The customs officer told me she would have to get back in the crate, as animals were not allowed to walk free in the customs area of the airport. I looked in the crate to see if I had to clean it. I didn't.

I thought I might have some trouble getting her back into the crate, but she went right in. She was Babet; I should have known better.

We cleared customs without a problem; all Babet's papers were in order. When we got outside, I opened the cage door and put Babet's leash around her neck. She walked out into freedom. Jenny and I kneeled down on the curb and got the full treatment from Babet's tongue; she gave us *the woiks*. Jenny and I held hands and laughed. Here we were in America with our best friend. *What's next?*

CHAPTER 17

Spirits Having Flown

HOW MUCH?

We were settled into our rental house on Biscayne Bay. Barry, Robin, and Maurice had been in Miami for about six months and were settled in their new houses. Everything was buzzing! The *Saturday Night Fever* film and soundtrack were a phenomenal success. The film was all over the television, radio, and press. Nobody had any idea it would be this big. All the songs we recorded in France were huge hits at the same time. Everything seemed out of control. It was just unbelievable — but not as unbelievable as what was going to happen next.

I had my first royalty statement from RSO. The white envelope it came in was big, thick, and heavy. I opened it up and just stared at it. I didn't understand anything about it, not until I looked at the last page summary and the check that was attached to it.

The check was made payable to Dennis Bryon, and the amount was for $200,000. *What?*

I showed it to Jenny, and we almost died. We'd been looking at houses on the beach and had found an incredible Spanish mansion on North

Bay Road. It was on the water, in the very best part of Biscayne Bay. The house looked out over four miles of the bay and on the other side was downtown Miami. It needed a lot of work but it was *location, location, location*, and it was beautiful. As soon as my check cleared, I paid cash for it. Would this journey never end?

Soon we were back in Studio C at Criteria recording the *Spirits Having Flown* album. Albhy was doing the usual drum loop thing, and I had to fight just to play anything live. I felt sorry for Barry; he was caught in the middle. He wanted the rock-solidness of a loop, but he also saw my argument about the feel of live drums. After we recorded "Tragedy" a few times, Albhy got his way.

We also recorded another great song called "Too Much Heaven." Blue's piano and Alan's guitar work made the track. It also became a number one hit on the Billboard chart, as did the single "Tragedy."

I was sitting at my drums one day when a guy walked into the control room. He was carrying something that looked like a large box of chocolates. He put it down on the desk, and everybody gathered around him. I got off my drums and joined the crowd.

His name was Roger Linn, and he was demonstrating his latest invention, the Linn LM-1 Drum Machine. It was about two feet long by one and a half feet wide by six inches high. It had a sloping front on one end where square buttons, knobs, and faders were arranged. Karl plugged it in and Roger started the pitch. He began by hitting pads on the front panel. The first pad was a bass drum, the one next to it was a snare drum, the next was a tom, and so on. He could even play all the percussion instruments, from a cowbell to orchestral timpani and everything in between. I do have to say this thing sounded wonderful.

Then he demonstrated the sequencer that was part of the machine, and showed us how to record incredible drum patterns that could be slowed down or speeded up. He told us this was the future.

"Hey, Den, what does it feel like to have your job taken by a box?" Robin sneered. Everybody sighed out loud, "Oooohhhhhhh"

"It'll never happen," I said in my defense. "Wanna bet?"

My next royalty statement was for $220,000, and when we finished the *Spirits* album, I was given a $50,000 advance. *Spirits Having Flown* reached number one on the Billboard charts and sold 16 million copies,

Alan, me, and Blue receiving platinum records for the Main Course *album.*

while "Tragedy," "Too Much Heaven," and "Love You Inside Out" all made number one on the Billboard Hot 100 chart.

Jen and I started renovating the house. When we were finished we had a permanent Jacuzzi in the courtyard and a brand-new pool that overlooked the bay. I had a twenty-four-foot fishing boat that hung from electric davits in my backyard. Inside the house, we had a new kitchen, and we bought a brand-new full-sized Baldwin grand piano. Holy SHIT!

OUR BEAUTIFUL BABET

Jenny and I were having the time of our lives living on Miami Beach. We had a beautiful home on the bay, a boat, hit records with the Bee Gees, an incredible amount of money pouring in, and our health was good. But as with any fairy tale, sooner or later something had to give. For us it was our German shepherd, Babet. She'd been getting weaker in her hind legs for almost a year. We had an incredible vet on Miami Beach named Dr. Nass, who diagnosed her with hip dysplasia, an abnormal formation of the hip socket. We were comfortable leaving Babet with Dr. Nass; he treated her as if she were his own dog. Every time we had to leave town we'd board her at the Miami Beach Animal Hospital on Alton Road, where we knew she'd be spoiled rotten. Mary — one of the girls who worked at the hospital — loved Babet so much she'd take her home every night we were away.

Sadly, Babet's hip was getting so bad I had to lift her back-end with a towel just so she could do her business. We even had a wheelchair made for her that supported her back legs, but it was getting to the point where nothing helped.

In February 1979, Jenny and I took a trip to San Francisco. We were both mentally exhausted from seeing Babet go through so much trauma. A few days away would charge our batteries. Coincidentally, it was the week of the Grammys, and the *Saturday Night Fever* soundtrack had been nominated for Album of the Year. After a long day of sightseeing and wandering around the city, we were back at our hotel watching the show. We waited with bated breath as the nominees were read out. Then, finally: "And the Grammy goes to . . . *Saturday Night Fever!*" Jenny and I screamed with joy as we realized I was part of a Grammy-winning album.

Barry, Robin, and Maurice accepted the award and Barry personally thanked Alan, Blue, and me for our contributions. It was one of the biggest moments of my life. I opened a bottle of wine, and Jen and I toasted to our success.

And just then, the phone rang. Dick had our travel and hotel information, so I felt sure it was Barry calling to share a moment of elation with me.

Jenny answered. "Hello . . . oh hi, Dr. Nass . . . oh no!"

Our beautiful Babet had passed away earlier that day. The doctor said she had died peacefully at the hospital, with Mary by her side. We put the wine away and cried all night. It was a long trip home.

1979 *SPIRITS* TOUR

On May 28, 1979, we started three weeks of rehearsals in the space where the new Middle Ear Studios eventually would be on Miami Beach. The band was frightening. This was the band I had in mind when I

1979 Spirits *Tour.* ED PERLSTEIN / REDFERNS / GETTY IMAGES

approached Barry with the idea so long ago at the base of Mt. Fuji. Apart from myself, Alan, and Blue, we had a second keyboard player named George Bitzer, a second guitar player named Joey Murcia, a bass player named Harold Cowart, the amazing percussion of Joe Lala, and the Bonnaroo Horn Section led by Peter Graves. The Bonnaroos were comprised of Peter, Bill Purse, Ken Faulk, Stan Webb, Whit Sidener, and Neil Bonsanti. Also onstage with us, and providing vocal backing for the Bee Gees, was the all-female group the Sweet Inspirations. At that time the group was made up of Myrna Smith, Sylvia Shemwell, and Gloria Brown. The Sweet Inspirations had been founded by Emily "Cissy" Houston (Whitney's mother and sister of Lee Warrick, mother of Dionne Warwick). Over the years they worked with superstars like Aretha Franklin, Van Morrison, Jimi Hendrix, and had a Top 20 hit of their own in the 1960s.

We had our own private Boeing 720 that was painted black with the *Spirits Having Flown* name and logo painted on the side. No commercial flights for us on this tour; this was the *big one*. The stage set was designed to replicate the famous dance-off stage in the *Saturday Night Fever* film. The tour had fifty-five shows spread over three months. The venues were all sold-out 25,000-seat stadiums, which included Dodger Stadium in L.A. and five shows at Madison Square Garden. This was the big time.

The tour didn't get off to a very good start, though. During rehearsals at Fort Worth there were new people on the road crew that treated the band like shit. They had no respect for any of us and no idea that this was the band and horn section and percussionist who played on all those hit records. Arguably, it could be said we were one of the main reasons *they* were employed. There was nobody there to stick up for us.

Before the first flight, everybody was put on a school bus and driven to the private plane, but we weren't allowed to get on until the Bee Gees boarded first. We sat on the school bus with no air-conditioning for an hour and a half. It was one of the hottest days of the year, reaching 100 degrees. Who knows what temperature it was inside the bus. We opened all the doors and windows, but it didn't help. Jenny and some of the other girls started to panic in the crippling heat, but the crew wouldn't let us off or move the bus into the shade.

When the Bee Gees finally arrived, the crew still wouldn't let us out of the bus — not until the brothers had a tour of the inside of the plane, which took another twenty minutes. When we were finally allowed to board, we saw that the front half of the plane was cordoned off for the Bee Gees and their guests. The band, the Bonnaroos, and the rest of the stage crew were in the back.

After all the work and the passion, *it wasn't supposed to be like this.* I told Barry how I felt, and he told me lawyers and investors had put the tour together and they were counting every penny. He offered me, Alan, and Blue a limousine to ride from the airport to the venues and back to the plane; he said he would pay for it personally. After talking it over, the three of us decided we'd stick with the rest of the crew on the bus.

In the beginning everything was a little tense, but as we got used to old worn-out buses without a bathroom, we accepted the situation. Riding on the bus became a joke and we looked forward to it. The tour's public relations man, Michael Sterling, who was also on the bus, put out a publication called *The Bus Gazette*. The *Gazette* was a gossip magazine, and nobody was spared. It humorously reported on everybody's shortcomings and fuck-ups and told of *the dark side* of the *Spirits* tour. None of us could wait for the next edition. When Michael passed it out, the bus became a clandestine asylum of gut-wrenching laughter. Michael was always totally respectful, never mentioning any of the Gibb family in the paper. *The Bus Gazette* brought everybody together; even onstage we'd look at each other and chuckle at some of the stories.

Every stadium on this tour was packed. I'd never looked out on so many people. All the shows at Madison Square Garden in New York were sold out. I wanted to bring my sister, Carole, her husband, Bob, and my best friend Neil (from Amen Corner) and his wife, Dellah, to see the Bee Gees on tour, so I thought Madison Square Garden would be the best place to do it.

I paid for the return flights for everybody and reserved a two-bedroom suite for them in the St. Regis Hotel, where we were staying. When they arrived at JFK, Jenny and I were waiting in a white stretch limo. They couldn't believe the size of the car; they'd never seen anything like it.

As we drove into New York I opened the roof in the car and popped the cork on a chilled bottle of Champagne. I asked the driver to tour us through the city. It was ten o'clock at night, and New York was ablaze with light and activity. We drove through Times Square and between the skyscrapers. Everybody was in silent awe as they looked up.

We got to the hotel and their suite was a beautiful two-bedroom layout with a great view of the city. It had a large lounge area with plush sofas, armchairs, and a six-person dining table with chairs. On the walls were beautiful paintings and there were elegant lamps all around. All three rooms had a television. They were speechless.

I handed the room service menu to Carole and said, "Go for it, this one's on me. You deserve it for everything you've been through."

The next day we walked around Midtown Manhattan, and while Jenny, Carole, and Dellah went shopping, I took Neil and Bob to the very shady 42nd St.

Before and after every show, all six of us went from the hotel to the show and back by stretch limousine. Also, I'd arranged for full access backstage passes for everyone. This meant they could freely wander anywhere they liked.

Backstage they rubbed shoulders with dozens of famous people

— Diana Ross, Al Pacino, Billy Joel, Jimmy Connors, and members of the band KISS, to name just a few. None of the celebrities impressed Carole; she just wanted to have her picture taken with a New York cop. Chaperoning everyone was a lot of work and stress for Jenny and me, but it was worth it. We were seeing New York again for the first time through their eyes.

The biggest show on the tour was Dodger Stadium in Los Angeles. I was told the crowd was 80,000 strong. Then, finally we were home in Miami for the last show at the Orange Bowl. Backstage I met a young performer named Michael Jackson. Michael was just then becoming a solo sensation after his departure from the Jackson Five.

Flash forward several years: I was at home working on music for a television advertising company in Miami. I heard that Michael Jackson and Diana Ross were in Miami, staying with Barry and Linda. They were all planning to go fishing on Barry's boat, along with Linda and Jenny. I couldn't go with them, because I was working to deadline. Jenny told me later that they had caught a fish, but Michael insisted they throw it back, so it wouldn't die.

Later that day, Barry called me and said, "Michael's here at the house. Why don't you come over, I want you to meet him." So much time had passed, I didn't think Michael would remember me from the *Spirits* tour, especially since this was after his record-smashing success with the *Thriller* album. So much had changed!

I went to the house and walked into the great-room area, where we all used to congregate, and, sure enough, there was Michael Jackson, standing with Barry.

"Michael," Barry said, "I want you to meet my best friend. This is Dennis Bryon."

Then Barry turned and walked out of the room, leaving me standing there, alone, with Michael Jackson!

I'm a pretty shy person anyway, but this was a particular challenge. *What am I going to say to Michael Jackson?*

Then Michael said to me, in his high, quiet voice, "It's always so special to me when somebody has a best friend. That's such a beautiful thing, when someone can say they have a best friend."

"Yeah," I nodded, "Barry and I have been great friends for years."

And then I asked him about where he lived, and he told me about the Neverland Ranch, near Los Angeles. Sometimes, as we were talking, there would be some silence, because he was shy and so was I. But we found camaraderie in that silence. We talked for about five minutes in all, and I really enjoyed being with him. Michael was just a beautiful spirit . . . a really, really nice man.

I DO

In January 1980, Jenny and I were taking a tour of Barry and Linda's new house on North Bay Road. The house was empty and hadn't been lived in for some time; it was a mess. As Linda was showing us around, suddenly she stopped and remarked, "What this house needs is a party, a celebration, something festive like . . . a wedding reception." Linda looked at us. "Come on, it's about bloody time you two did it, and we can have the reception here."

Jenny and I looked at each other.

"You want to?" I asked.

"Yes," she answered.

"Good, then it's settled," Linda said, and we started planning the wedding.

We didn't want to get married in a church, and we weren't hip enough to get married on a beach; we wanted something more personal. Our house on North Bay Road had an incredible Spanish courtyard. It was about forty square-feet and surrounded by arches. In the middle was a huge round Jacuzzi, and around the Jacuzzi were beds of tropical plants. It was the perfect place for a wedding ceremony.

Barry was my best man and Linda was Jenny's maid of honor. Linda's dad, George, had agreed to give Jenny away. I still needed to find somebody who had the authority to conduct the ceremony. Tom said, "Why don't you ask Pete Wagner to do it? He's a justice of the peace."

Pete had a limousine company in Miami and had been driving us for years. Jenny and I loved him. I asked Pete if he'd marry us, and he said yes.

Barry and Linda paid for the whole thing. Linda hired a cleaning company to come in and make their house look like new. She rented all the tables and chairs we needed. She paid for all the catered food and drink; she even hired a five-piece string section. Because of a Miami Beach ordinance, no fireworks were allowed, so she hired a troupe of professional cancan dancers.

For another one of our wedding presents, Barry and Linda paid the airfare for Carole and Bob, as well as Jenny's mother, sister, and brother-in-law, to fly in from the U.K. They even paid for my cousin Jennifer to fly in from Canada.

I invited all my friends from Criteria, everybody who worked at Ace Music (the store where we bought everything), all the Gibb clan, and I even invited Albhy. We invited everybody we knew, which totaled about 150 guests. I didn't know I knew that many people.

Bob Sherman, who was the Bee Gees' personal photographer in Miami, agreed to shoot the whole thing as a wedding present for Jenny and me.

We chose Saturday, March 22, so everybody who worked had the day off. It started at eleven o'clock in our house. Everybody sent us flowers; our courtyard looked like a flower shop!

I had built a podium over the Jacuzzi, with arches draped in flowers. I was wearing a silk suit and tie, and Jenny had on the most beautiful white silk wedding dress. She had never looked so gorgeous.

We were never engaged, so for a surprise I bought Jenny an engagement ring with a large diamond in the shape of a heart. During the ceremony Barry forgot which pocket he put the engagement ring in and couldn't find it. After a few awkward moments he located it, and everything went smoothly.

After Pete had pronounced us man and wife, we took the celebrations to our backyard, where Bob took our wedding pictures from our dock. With Biscayne Bay and a beautiful sunset in the background, Jenny and I enjoyed one of the most important days of our lives.

Later that night, the reception at Barry and Linda's house was packed as all our friends joined the festivities. And at the end of the night the cancan dancers performed a high-energy chorus line in their black stockings, with long skirts and petticoats flying.

The next day Jenny and I boarded a first-class flight to Hawaii for a three-week honeymoon. When we arrived at our hotel in Honolulu we were led to the penthouse suite. There was a balcony that had the most

Our wedding at home on Miami Beach.
Barry was my best man, Linda was Jenny's maid of honor.

incredible view of Honolulu and its beaches, and we had our own private butler who was on call twenty-four hours a day.

The room was filled with flowers and gifts from the hotel, and then a man arrived with a case of Jenny's favorite Champagne. We opened the case, which held six bottles of Louis Cristal, and read the card inside.

Love you always, Barry and Linda.

CHAPTER 18

Fired!

BLOOD ON MY DREAMS

At the end of October 1980, we started the new Bee Gees album at the new Middle Ear Studios on Miami Beach. The Bee Gees now had their very own studio, and all the plans for a joint production company and record label where we'd all be involved had been forgotten. Barry, Karl, and Albhy were a solid team.

From day one, the vibe in the studio was terrible. I was sitting next to Karl in front of the mixing console when Maurice came in and told me to get out of *his* chair. I couldn't believe it, I thought he was joking, but he was serious.

Blue and Albhy were at each other's throat all the time, disagreeing over everything. There was no flow or excitement about the music. Everybody just sat around reading magazines and comic books or played pool. Nothing was getting done. It was sad.

Beside the LinnDrum machine, Albhy had a Fairlight CMI (computer musical instrument) set up in the control room. We were working on a song called "Cornerstone." Albhy had programmed a bass line that he wanted me to play drums to. The bass line had a super-fast techno feel that was impossible for me to play along with. I remember trying to record it seventy or eighty times. I'd never been through anything like this before.

I played it so many times a huge blister emerged on my finger. Soon that blister burst and a second blister appeared. When the second one burst, the wound started to bleed everywhere.

When I saw blood on my dreams, I went home.

THE BOYS WANT TO USE ANOTHER BAND

It was the second weekend in January of '81. Linda was in the hospital giving birth to their third child. I was working in my house with two carpenters; we were building a new self-contained apartment over the garage. The phone rang.

"Hi, Denny, it's Dick. I'm afraid I have some bad news . . . the boys want to use another band."

I just stood there in shock as the carpenters hammered away. "Oh," I said.

Then there was silence.

"Sorry, Denny. I guess we'll be talking over the next couple of days."

"Yeah, okay, Dick . . . Thanks, bye."

I walked past the carpenters and down the stairs to find Jenny, who was sitting watching television in the great room. She could see the look on my face and asked me what was wrong.

"That was Dick on the phone. I've been fired; the three of us have been fired . . . He said they want to use another band."

Jenny was speechless.

I knew things hadn't been going well in the studio, but I had never expected this. I thought we were going through one of the usual *bumps* that Albhy had created.

Then the phone rang again. It was Blue. He asked me if I'd heard from Dick. He suggested that the three of us should stick together, get a lawyer and sue the shit out of them. He said we could get millions.

My head was spinning. I couldn't think straight.

How could they do this to us after all the success and everything we'd achieved together? How could Barry do this to me? I thought we were best friends. We could sell the house and go back to Cardiff . . . No, that wasn't possible. I had a sick sinking feeling in my stomach. Jenny and I were halfway through our applications to get green cards to stay in America permanently. I wondered how that process could go through now that I didn't have a permanent job in America. What was I going to do?

The phone rang yet again. It was Clive, my old bandmate from Amen Corner. Clive had moved to America, too. He had put his bass guitar aside and was now a successful sound engineer at the Record Plant, one of the biggest studios in L.A.; he really had his finger on the L.A. music scene.

"Hey, Plent, it's Clive, just thought I'd give you a call and see what's shaking, man."

I didn't want to say anything to Clive; maybe it was all a mistake, just a cruel joke. "Not a lot, Will, just doing some building in the house, and working on the new album."

"Are you sure, Plent? Come on, man, it's me, Will. Tell me what's going on, Den."

It was as if he already knew, but that wasn't possible. "Will, I've been fired, I just found out about it thirty minutes ago."

"Those fucking bastards, after all you and Blue and Alan have done for them. How the fuck could they do this to you? When I found out this morning, I couldn't fucking believe it."

"Wait a minute . . . you knew before me? How's that possible? I only just found out."

"L.A.'s buzzing with the news. Jeff Porcaro's been asked to be in the new band."

My heart sank even further. As usual, Albhy had finally got his way.

"What was Barry like when he told you? I know how close you guys are," Clive asked.

"He didn't tell me, Will. Dick told me."

"What? Aww, Den, that's just wrong, man . . . *He* should have told you himself. You have to go to his house and see him face to face and ask him what the fuck this is all about."

"I can't do it right now, Will, I'm still in shock. I just didn't see this thing coming. Besides, Linda's in labor at the hospital, it's not a good time for him."

"What do you mean it's not a good time for him . . . what about you, man? Why the fuck are you thinking about him when you should be thinking about yourself? You're too nice, man. You've always been too fucking nice. Plent, go to his house right now and get in his face. You can't let him treat you like this."

"Maybe I'll go over there tomorrow."

My call-waiting beeped. "Clive, I've got another call coming in, I'll call you later tonight."

I pressed the call-waiting button. "Hello?"

"Hi, Dennis, it's Albhy."

I could feel my blood starting to boil, what the fuck did this guy want . . . did he call to gloat?

Albhy continued, "I just wanted to call and tell you how sorry I am about how this thing went down. I know you probably think it was all *my* decision, but I'm calling to say it wasn't. Yes, I was part of the decision, but I only agreed with what was already decided."

"Come on, man, don't try to weasel your way out of it. You never liked the way I played, or Blue or Alan; we were never good enough for you. You always wanted the top session guys from New York and L.A. In a short amount of time, you managed to destroy what a whole team of people worked to create over many years. Well, now you've got your wish; I just hope you don't put Porcaro what you put me through."

"I don't know if they want to use Porcaro; nothing's been decided yet."

"Albhy, I just got off the phone with one of the top engineers at the Record Plant. Porcaro's been booked for the sessions; you're the producer and you didn't know that? Come on, man."

There was a silence I'll never forget on the other end of the phone . . . then, "I wanted to keep you on the project but Barry said, if one goes, all three have to go. I'm really sorry."

"Albhy, fuck off and don't call this number again." I slammed the phone down so hard I almost broke it.

Jenny came into the kitchen. "What was all that about?"

"That was Albhy; he tried to tell me it wasn't him who made the decision. He said it was Barry."

I sat at the kitchen table, my head in my hands. I was in total disbelief. Then the phone rang again. Jenny answered it this time.

"Hello . . . oh hi, Dick . . . Yes, we're fine . . . Oh great . . . A boy, that's fantastic news. How's Linda doing? . . . That's great, thanks, bye. Linda just had a boy. They think they're going to name him Travis."

The next morning at about eleven o'clock I went to have a talk with Barry. I let myself in through the electric gates and parked in the driveway. I got out of my car and started walking toward the front door. As I looked in through some of the windows, I could see people moving quickly. I got to the door and tried to let myself in. For the first time *ever,* the front door was locked. I knocked loudly.

After longer than it should have taken, Dick opened the door.

"Denny, we don't want any trouble."

"Dick, I'm not here to cause any trouble, I just want to speak to Barry. I'm not drunk or high, and I don't have a gun . . . I just want to talk to Barry."

"Come on in." Dick led me to his office, then got on the house telephone system. He dialed Barry's room. "Dennis is here to see you . . . Okay, I'll tell him. Barry says he's too tired to talk right now; he had a late night at the hospital."

"Right, if he won't come down, I'm going up." I walked out of Dick's office and ran up the stairs toward Barry and Linda's bedroom. I banged on the door. "Barry, it's me, I have to talk to you."

"I can't talk right now, Den; I'm too tired, I've been up all night."

"Me too, Barry, I've been up all night as well. I have to talk to you, Barry. Please open the door."

"Can't we do this later?"

"No, I have to talk to you *now.*"

I heard the door unlock. Then it opened and revealed Barry standing in his bathrobe. I was going to scream and yell and remind him of the promises he never kept, the things like: the band being part of the production team, the record label we were all going to form, the recording studio they built without us, and how, when the success we all planned went through the roof, the band was completely forgotten.

But Barry looked worse than I felt, so I said, "Listen, man, *you're* the Bee Gees, you can do anything you want. You can work with anybody you want. I know that . . . It's not the decision I'm pissed about; it's how it was done. You got Dick to call me, and Alan and Blue. After all we've been through together, the three of you couldn't sit down with the three of us and tell us face to face? I would have understood, Barry, I really would have. All you had to say is 'Listen, guys, it's been a good ride, we made some great records together, but now we want to try something else.' You're the Bee Gees; you can do anything you want."

"I wanted to, Den, but I was too embarrassed to face you."

We both just stood there looking at each other.

I let out a big sigh . . . "Congratulations on your new son."

"Thanks."

"I would have understood . . . Later, Barry . . . Later."

As I headed down the stairs, I heard the bedroom door gently close behind me. When I got to the bottom, George walked up. "Aye, laddie, ya won-some tea?"

"No thanks, George, I've got to get back, I've got the builders in, today's the only day they can work."

"A hot cuppa tea always fixes things, ya-noo."

"Not this time, George."

ALL IS FORGIVEN

Over the next few days, I met with Alan and Blue — Blue still wanted us to get a lawyer and take legal action. I said no and so did Alan, so Blue started negotiating by himself with the Bee Gees via Dick. Both Blue and Alan owned property in Miami. Alan was married to his British wife, Astrid, and had two children. He wanted to stay in America. Blue was married to his British wife, Ann; she lived in London with her two children and only came to America for vacations in their Miami home. Blue would end up going back to England and become a very successful songwriter and producer.

Everything really came home when Beanie, one of the employees at Middle Ear, showed up at my house with my drums and all my belongings from the studio. That was a gut-wrenching day. I started drinking way too much. I wasn't a violent drunk or an angry drunk; I just drank to make it all go away.

Jenny and Linda talked daily on the phone for hours. Linda and May brought Travis to the house almost every day, but no sign of Barry. Finally after about three weeks, the phone rang late one Friday night. Jenny answered it. It was Linda. Linda said Barry wanted to come over and asked if it would be okay. Jenny asked me, and I said of course.

Five minutes later the large front doors to the courtyard opened; in walked Linda, followed by Barry. Jenny and I walked out to meet them. Barry was carrying two bottles of wine. He handed them to me and gave me a hug.

"I come with peace offerings," Barry said sheepishly. Then he looked at me and said, "I wasn't afraid of seeing you, mate, it was her I was afraid of," as he looked at Jenny.

"So you bloody well should be," Jenny shot back. "I haven't forgiven you yet."

I lifted the bottles of wine to show Jenny. "Jen, it's Château Lafite, *all is forgiven.*" Barry hugged Jenny.

We went into the house, and Barry and I sat down in the great room. Jenny and Linda went into the kitchen to open the wine.

"How's it going at the studio?" I asked.

"Okay, I suppose. It's different without you guys."

"Well, you knew it would be . . . It's gonna be good, Barry . . . Different . . . That's what you wanted, a change; it's gonna be great."

Barry nodded.

"Barry, I don't hold grudges, it's what I was trying to tell you outside your bedroom. We've been through too much together for me to be angry. I was mad, because you didn't sit down with me, just like this."

"Den, I know you think it was all Albhy's fault, but it wasn't. The three of us made that decision, and Albhy and Karl agreed."

"Yeah, that's what he told me on the phone. I was really rude to him — I told him to fuck off. I've been wanting to do that for years." We laughed. "Barry, do me a favor, the next time you see him, tell him I'm sorry for what I said . . . tell him what I really wanted to say was FUCK THE FUCK OFF!"

We had a good laugh as the girls came in from the kitchen with the wine. I made a toast to absent friends, the old days, and the new days yet to come. Cheers.

The next time I saw Blue, he told me he'd made a settlement with the boys. They'd agreed to give him a one-time $150,000 severance payment. The next time Barry came to my house I brought it up. Barry told me whatever one of us got; the other two should get the same. He told me he would talk to Dick. I did get the same check as Blue, but I didn't realize at the time, it was a non-refundable but recoupable advance on future earnings. My next royalty check would come *eighteen years later* in the fall of 1999.

LIVING ON SWEETZER

I'd gotten into a fabulous rut of lying by the pool in the daytime and having my friends over for barbeques and "beer-identifying" games on the weekend. Most nights Linda came to our house to sit with Jenny. I don't know what they found to talk about for so long, but they always had a good laugh. And after a long day at the studio, Barry would call in for a glass of wine (which he never drank) on his way home and we'd laugh some more. Every Saturday night without fail, Barry and Linda would come over for a curry. I'd make breast of chicken curry, beef curry with sautéed vegetables, baked saffron basmati rice, homemade hot onion chutney, mango chutney, raita, and plenty of papadums. Linda always brought wine. *It was a hard life.*

When anyone was in town visiting, they came over on Saturday night for one of my famous curry feasts. I loved to cook. One day Andy Gibb was in town, and he showed up for a curry. He had just had a payment from RSO, and he showed me his royalty check for one million dollars. Whoa. Jenny and I were living high on the hog, but without any new money coming in, I knew I had to find a way of making some.

I spoke with Clive every week, and he always told me to "get the fuck out of Miami and come to L.A. and get back into music." But I'd had my heart broken on the music front and was scared of having it broken again. I'd lost the urge to play drums, and I'd stopped listening to music altogether. Besides, where do you go from the Bee Gees?

Clive and his wife, Maddo, invited us to stay with them in L.A. for a few weeks. We really enjoyed ourselves. So many great Indian restaurants and so little time.

We liked it so much that we decided to move to L.A. for a while. We answered an ad in one of the local papers and found a modern, unfurnished, two-bedroom apartment on North Sweetzer Avenue in West Hollywood.

We flew back to Miami, rented a U-Haul van and flatbed trailer for the BMW, and started on a new adventure, driving across America to our new home. We weren't in a hurry and had the luxury of taking as much time as we liked to get there. *Smokey and the Bandit* had been a huge success at the box office and made the CB radio craze huge. I bought a CB for the journey, and we tuned in to the truckers on channel nineteen.

"Break-a one-nine for an eastbound?"

"Go ahead, westbound."

"What you got over your shoulder, buddy?"

"You got one in the bushes at 24, and a plain wrapper, flip-flopping around 65. How's your back door?"

"You got it clean, all the way back to the scales."

"That's a 4 westbound, keep it between the ditches."

"Cheers, mate, westbound gone."

Jenny and I just looked at each other and cracked up. Who'da thought I'd ever be talking with truck drivers in their own language?

I loved my CB radio. In the beginning, the truckers had a hard time understanding my accent, but that CB radio made the drive from Miami to Los Angeles in a U-Haul van bearable.

We settled into our apartment and had a great time zipping around L.A. in the Beemer. While we were there I took an audio engineering class with Clive, we both did well on the test. Maybe it would be useful for something later.

We didn't know it at the time, but our whole building was gay. It didn't matter to us; all the other tenants were always very nice to us. That is except for the tattooed, 300-pound biker dude in the next apartment. I don't think I was his type.

We had some minor earthquakes, but nothing scary. Also, while we were there, Air Florida Flight 90 crashed into the Potomac River. Jenny and I watched in horror as the live CNN broadcast showed rescuers pulling a few survivors from the icy waters.

One of the highlights of our stay in L.A. was the Royal Wedding.

Charles and Diana were finally doing it. We got up really early to watch the whole thing on TV. Jenny decorated the apartment with anything British and we flew the Union Jack from our balcony that overlooked Sweetzer. I think the locals thought we were crazy.

At that time in the early eighties there was so much cocaine going around it wasn't funny. It seemed like every day somebody was trying to get me to try it. I'd seen the results of cocaine, and I was scared of it.

Besides Clive and Maddo, we had some great friends in Los Angeles. I hooked up with some of the RSO people I knew when I had been with the Bee Gees. One of those people was Michael Sterling, the publicist on the *Spirits* tour. Michael also worked as maître d' in one of the best restaurants in L.A. We ate there at least once a week. We drank the best wine and dined on some of the best food in the city.

We lived in L.A. for just over a year — without finding any work — before moving back to Miami in August 1982. It was good to be home.

HOW OLD ARE YOU

Jenny and I settled back into the *good life* again — not that we weren't living it in Los Angeles. But being back in our Spanish home on Biscayne Bay was marvelous. The only thing that was missing was our beautiful Babet.

I'd heard through the grapevine that Robin was recording a solo album, and Maurice was producing it with him in his home studio. Next thing I know the phone rang. It was Maurice.

"Hi, Den Den, it's Mo. Where the hell have you been?"

"Hey, Mo, I just got back from a short stay in L.A. How ya doing?"

"I'm great mate. Listen, I'm in the studio with Rob and we had this crazy idea. As you probably know I'm working on a solo album for Rob. Most of the tracks are already done, but we thought it might be great to have the band play on a few songs. Are you up for it?"

"Yeah, man, I'd love to. Where, when?"

"Next week at the studio."

"Okay, great, count me in."

"Fantastic, I'll call Alan and Blue," Maurice said.

This was just what I needed; I was excited, and I felt like I had a purpose in life again. I went to the music store and bought some new sticks and fresh drumheads. When I got home, I unpacked my drums, gave them the *once over*, and tuned them up.

The next Wednesday I drove to Middle Ear Studios on Miami Beach and set up. The engineers on the project were a former Criteria employee named Samii Taylor and one of the Middle Ear engineers, Dale Peterson. It was good to see my kit under an array of expensive microphones again. It took a couple of hours of tweaking to get the drums sounding right, and then Blue arrived with a bunch of synthesizers. Alan walked in with his guitar and amplifier and set up behind a baffle next to Blue.

Finally, Maurice and Robin arrived, and we all congregated in the control room. Everybody was so happy to be together again; it was almost a reunion. There was a warm atmosphere in the room. Maurice played a demo he'd made at his home studio, a song called "Kathy's Gone." We all made some notes and went out into the studio to run it down. Soon, Samii got a headphone mix to everybody's liking, and we were off. It felt right to be playing with the band again, and to have Maurice on bass. We got the song on take three. (Phew!) Everything sounded wonderful. Samii was a really good engineer; she made my drums sound huge. Next thing we did was add more keyboards and guitar, then some cymbal swells, before calling it a day.

Next morning we all met at the studio at eleven. Maurice played the demo of "In and Out of Love." These were such great songs, and the band was in the studio again. I was *elated*. After we got the track, Robin went out and sang a guide vocal. We added keyboards and more guitars. At about five o'clock, we called it quits for the day.

When I got home, I was surprised to find out we had a guest for the night. One of our friends from L.A. was in town; she had called Jenny and asked if she could stay with us for the night. Of course, Jenny said yes.

This unnamed person was one of the people who was always trying to get me to try coke. Sure enough, after dinner and a couple bottles of wine, and while Jenny was in the kitchen talking to Linda on the phone, she pulled it out again. She offered it to me, and for the very first time in my life, I thought about saying yes.

I'm thirty-four years old . . . I'm mature enough to make a stupid decision about trying something. It's not like I'm gonna get hooked on the damn stuff.

Just one go . . . after all this time I just want to see what all the fuss is about! Just one hit, that's all I'll do.

I nodded yes, and she handed me a rolled-up dollar bill. She made some lines on the glass table and in I went. I'd seen so many people do this stuff over the years; the snorting came naturally to me. I did two of the six lines. She told me to take it easy, but it was too late. Within seconds, it hit me like a slap across the face. I became euphoric. Any timidness and apprehension instantly vanished. As for my shyness, what was that?

"Shit, this shit's great. I can't fucking believe it. Why didn't you tell me this shit was this good? Fuck, I can do anything. *Jenny, you got to try this shit!*" I shouted. I became obnoxious.

"I'm on the phone," Jenny shouted back.

"I want to do another line, okay?" I said to our guest.

I thought about the talk I'd had with myself just a few minutes ago, *just one hit, I promised myself.* Fuck that!

I went in for lines three and four. Nothing could stop me now. I couldn't believe how dumb I'd been, missing out on this shit for all those years, idiot.

Finally, Jenny got off the phone with Linda and joined us.

"Babe, you gotta try this stuff, it's amazing." I said.

"I don't like it; I tried it in L.A. It gives me a headache."

"You tried it in L.A., you little devil you." I felt so good I would have forgiven anything.

"Den, take it easy. Remember, you're in the studio tomorrow. Take it easy, luv, please."

The studio, that's right. I forgot all about the studio tomorrow. If only I were in the studio right now, the way I'm feeling I could play the shit out of anything. If only I were in the studio now. Damn it!

Jenny went to bed, but I stayed up with our guest until 4 a.m. We drank another two bottles of wine, countless beers, and smoked a few joints. I did most of the coke.

As I lay on the bed next to Jen, I could feel my heart racing a million miles an hour. I was so tired, but I couldn't sleep. The feeling of euphoria was fading fast; withdrawals and the hangover from hell were fast approaching.

There was nothing I could do to make myself feel better. The more time went by, the worse I felt. I went downstairs and drank some orange juice, but I immediately threw it up. At eight o'clock I thought a hot shower might help; I stood there for an hour. Finally at ten o'clock I started to feel tired, but it was too late. I had to be in the studio in an hour. I lay on our bed and closed my eyes. Suddenly, I felt Jenny shaking me violently. "Den, wake up, you have to be in the studio in half an hour, wake up."

I threw on some clothes, got in my car, and headed for the studio. I'd never felt this bad in my life. I felt so nauseated, the thought of death was better than this. As I was driving in, I said a prayer.

"Oh God, it's me again, and yes I want something else. Please let me feel better; please let me get through this day at the studio. I was so wrong last night; I just wanted to see what it felt like. If you help me get through today, I promise, promise, promise, I'll never ever do coke again. Amen, thank you, God."

I walked into the studio, and everybody looked at me. "You all right, Den Den?" Maurice asked. "You look rough."

"No, man, I think I'm coming down with something. I think it's the flu."

I looked past Maurice to see Samii and Dale pushing the huge MCI twenty-four track tape machine out of the control room.

"Sorry, guys, the session's off, one of the motors seized up. We'll have it running by Monday.

"Go home, Den Den, and get some rest. Feel better, mate," Mo said.

On the way home, I said another prayer and thanked God. To this day, I have never touched that evil white stuff again, and I never will.

THE THIRD HARMONY

The next Monday at eleven o'clock we started recording again. We cut two more tracks that day: "How Old Are You" and "Another Lonely Night in New York." After the session was over, Alan and Blue packed up their instruments. I was about to pack up my drums when Maurice asked me if I would play some drum fills and cymbals on some of the other tracks. Of course, I agreed.

The next day I came in as usual at eleven in the morning to do some drum parts, but instead Maurice asked me if I would help him record Robin's vocal track. Robin came in and sang one of the songs for about an hour. He recorded multiple takes, and then went home. Then Maurice and I started going through the different performances, choosing what we thought were the best parts.

After the session was over for the day, Maurice asked me if I would come in the next day to help him again. This happened every day, until it reached the stage where at the end of the day Maurice would just say, "See you tomorrow, Den Den."

I absolutely loved working with Robin and Mo, but something even more incredible was about to happen. Maurice and Robin were around the mic singing harmony-backing vocals for "In and Out of Love," and I was supervising the recording with Samii. They were cutting up as usual between takes when Robin said, "We need a third harmony. Dennis, come and sing with us." I looked at Samii; she raised her eyebrows and opened her mouth.

"Go," she said, "you'll never get an opportunity like *this* again." I went out into the studio, and Robin told me to stand between him and Maurice. Dale came out and plugged in a third set of headphones. I knew the melody to the song quite well by now, and the lower third harmony came naturally to me. When we were rehearsing it a cappella, I suddenly realized where I was. I was standing between Robin and Maurice Gibb, singing harmony on a Bee Gees song. I remembered all those years ago in my front room on Colum Road, singing third harmony with my Everly Brothers records, and now here I was in the studio, singing third harmony on a Gibb brothers record. *Unreal.*

We double tracked the part about three times, and when we were done, we went into the control room for a listen through the speakers. It sounded perfect — *it sounded like the Bee Gees.*

"Um, Samii luv," Maurice said, "get Barry on the phone and tell him he's fired. Think of the money we'll save."

"Come on," Robin said, "let's go and get the other choruses."

Boy, did I have a story for Jenny that night.

About six weeks had gone by, and still nobody had mentioned

Maurice Gibb.

anything about me getting paid for the work I was doing. I didn't even know whether I was officially part of the project or just "hanging out" at the studio.

The next time Barry came to the house, I talked to him about it. He told me I should discuss it with Maurice. He said that for the amount of time I was putting in, he thought I should at least be co-producer. I talked to Maurice, and he agreed.

The *How Old Are You* album was released in May 1983. It didn't do very well in America but went to number six in Germany. I was disappointed the record wasn't a bigger hit in the U.S. — I was hoping to get my name out there as a record producer.

CHAPTER 19 My Days with Andy Gibb

HAVE YOU THOUGHT ABOUT IT?

I haven't spoken much about Andy Gibb except to say he was there at the start of my very first tour, when we all met at the airport back in 1973. But Andy was always present in the background, studying how things worked and generally being a kid. He had the same sense of humor as his three brothers, and he could certainly hold his own.

Andy was only fifteen years old when I met him, but I knew he was someone very special. Barry's little shadow, he followed and mirrored every move his elder brother made. He even copied Barry's guitar technique, tuning to an open D chord. Andy was fearless, too. When he lived on the Isle of Man he bought a Kawasaki dirt bike and rode against riders a lot older; he wasn't afraid of anything. But it was music that Andy had a passion for; it was in his blood.

Andy accompanied his brothers on most of my early tours but was never a part of the act. Although he was young, Andy had the confidence of a seasoned performer. It was just a matter of time before he would take his place as a headliner. He was slim, good-looking, and always dressed immaculately. Backstage he would grab one of Barry's guitars and sing anything that came into his head; he was always playing, singing, and dancing around. It was obvious to everybody that one day Andy would shine.

While on tour in the early seventies, Andy spent a lot of time in my room. I had a beautiful Martin D-28 acoustic guitar he loved to play; we'd just hang out. I don't know how, or when, or why this odd thing started, but one day Andy said to me, "Have you thought about it?"

I didn't know what the hell he was talking about, so I answered back, "Of course I've thought about it. How about you, have you thought about it?"

"I've been thinking about it all day, but I just can't make up my mind."

"Well, let me know when you make up your mind. Think about it!"

"Okay," Andy said as he walked off. Every time we saw each other after that we'd go into our *Have you thought about it* routine.

Years later, in 1976, after Robert Stigwood heard some of Andy's demo recordings, he signed him to RSO Records. Barry took Andy under his wing and began working on his first record, *Flowing Rivers*. The album was recorded at Criteria Studios and was produced by Barry, Carl, and Albhy. The album produced two number one singles on the Billboard Hot 100 and got to number nineteen on the album chart. Andy was on his way. I played drums on two of Andy's biggest hits: "Desire" and "Don't Throw It All Away." Both of these songs were originally recorded for the Bee Gees but were given to Andy for release.

Apart from music, Andy loved the water. The first boat he bought was a thirty-one-foot Bertram sports fishing vessel. He went everywhere on it. He was a natural mariner; cruising to Nassau or the Bahamas was nothing for Andy. Sometimes he'd even go by himself. After the enormous success of his records, and the huge income that came with it, Andy was able to step up from the Bertram to a sixty-four-foot luxury Hatteras yacht. He had no trouble skippering this sizable vessel either; his confidence was abounding.

He moored the Hatteras at a very trendy, expensive marina right next to downtown Miami. Whenever Andy was in town, he lived on his boat and enjoyed the good life. He adopted a full-blooded lion cub that lived on the boat with him. The cub was cuddly and cute at first, but soon grew into a small lion that playfully clawed and bit everyone aboard. It broke Andy's heart when he had to give up the lion, but it was literally chewing up the luxury yacht and had grown too big not to be caged.

As Andy's success snowballed, so did his extravagance and his dependence on alcohol and drugs. He stopped using regular airlines and leased a Learjet for all his travels. He rented a mansion in the hills that overlooked Los Angeles and spent his money like it was melting snow.

Because of his addiction, Andy lost his role in *Joseph and the Amazing Technicolor Dreamcoat* in New York and his job as the host of *Solid Gold*, a successful syndicated music variety show in Los Angeles. When the love of his life, Victoria Principal, asked Andy to choose between her or his lifestyle, he chose alcohol and cocaine.

In the early eighties, Andy really did try to pull his life back together, spending time at the Betty Ford Center in Rancho Mirage, California. For a while, he was living a clean and sober life. In 1985, Andy's personal manager Marc Hulett called me and told me Andy wanted me to be his drummer. He was forming a new band in L.A. and wanted Jenny and me to move into his house in the Los Angeles hills; when we were ready, we'd all go on tour together. Andy loved Jenny, and Marc thought the presence of the two of us at the house might be a positive, sobering influence. I told Marc yes.

When we arrived at the house, Andy was there to meet us. He looked great; he was happy, sober, and full of energy. He gave me a serious look and said, "Den, have you thought about it?"

"Oh no, here we go again," Jenny said.

"No, I haven't thought about it, but now you've got me thinking about it. How about you, you thought about it?"

Andy and I played tennis every day, sometimes twice a day; we both loved it. We started rehearsing with the band for a two-week engagement at the MGM Grand casino in Las Vegas, then after that we were booked at a casino in Lake Tahoe for three weeks.

Andy had made regular guest appearances with his brothers on the *Spirits* tour of 1979, so I knew his energy level onstage. But this was different, this was his show and he was performing his hits. *He was the star.*

His presence and animation under the lights was awesome. He owned the stage as soon as he set foot on it. Andy had the ability to transform himself from a nice, modest, somewhat-shy kid into a full-blown, bona

Andy and me going head to head.

fide superstar, yet somehow he made every individual audience member feel as if he was performing just for him or her. Andy was full of energy. His performances at the casinos drew standing ovations every night.

Soon, Andy started to work his way back into television. He made a special guest appearance on a very popular sitcom called *Gimme a Break!*, where he was booked to perform two songs with the whole band. The producers sent Andy a couple of two-inch-thick scripts. Andy started reading the story.

The plot had Andy recording in a studio near the home where the *Gimme a Break!* family lived. One of the young girl characters was a huge Andy Gibb fan; when she found out Andy was recording locally, she sneaked out after dark to get a glimpse of him. Then came the twist. While she was waiting for Andy outside his hotel room, she fell asleep. Hours later, in the early morning after we'd finished recording, we were all walking back to the hotel.

While Andy was going through the script downstairs in his bedroom, I was watching television with Jenny and Marc upstairs. Suddenly, Andy came rushing up with the second script. He threw it down on the sofa next to me.

"Den, they've written you into the story. You have a speaking part," Andy said with excitement. "Go to page 124."

I picked up the script and thumbed to the right page. Sure enough, there it was in black and white. The script had me heading up the group as we came across the girl sleeping outside the hotel.

Drummer, who is at the front of the group, puts his hand up and stops the group in front of the sleeping girl.

DRUMMER
(speaking softly in a British accent)
Shhhhhhhh, there's a bird who's fallen asleep!

"What?! I'm not doing it," I declared. "I'm not an actor."

Jenny and Marc broke out into laughter.

"You have to do it," Andy insisted. "You're the only one with a British accent."

"What kind of line is it anyway? 'There's a *bird* who's fallen asleep.' The word 'bird' went out in the sixties. No, I'm not doing it."

"Aw, come on, Den, it'll be fun," Andy said.

The next Tuesday, Andy and I went for the first reading of the script. There had to be at least fifty people sitting around a gigantic table. Everyone was there: the regular cast, producers, writers, and all the production heads. But the people who paid most attention were the network censors. They were listening for the slightest little thing that might be inappropriate.

At exactly nine o'clock, we started the read. At certain intervals, the program director would stop the flow and explain a camera shot or give some production details. All the while, my line was getting closer. I'd rehearsed it a thousand times in the shower and at Jenny, who was sick of hearing it. But I wasn't an actor, dammit, and I had to get my lines — *line* — just right.

Before I knew it, we were at the hotel, and there she was asleep. I took a deep breath and out it came.

"Shhhhhhh, there's a bird who's fallen asleep."

I got a good laugh from my fellow actors around the table. Then Andy continued on . . .

"Aw look, poor little thing, she'll catch her death of cold. Shall I wake her up?"

And in a flash it was over. I'd successfully completed my first rehearsal as an *actor*. The next day we rehearsed the whole thing over. We taped the show in front of a live audience later in the week, and everything went without a hitch.

I had to join the Screen Actors Guild – American Federation of Television and Radio Artists for my speaking role. I was already a full-time member of the American Federation of Musicians, which covered my drumming legality as part of the strict television union code. I enjoyed my brief role as an actor, but the best was yet to come.

About four months later I received my mail that had been forwarded from my address in Miami. There was an envelope from Alan Landsburg Productions; inside was a statement and a check. The statement was addressed to Dennis Bryon (actor) for *Gimme a Break!* episode "The Groupie." The check was for $5,000. Soon after, I received an identical statement and another check for $5,000. The next statement was close to $4,000. The checks kept coming; they were getting smaller each time, but they kept coming. Over the years, I had to have made at least $25,000 for my one line on television. *Maybe I'm in the wrong business.*

SLIPPING BACK INTO IT

Jenny and I stayed with Andy until 1987. We loved him dearly and wanted to spend as much time together as we could. But as time went by, he started to get more remote, spending more and more time alone in his room. One time we had a show in a theater in Las Vegas. Everybody was meeting at LAX for the short flight, but Andy wouldn't come out of his room. No matter how hard we banged on the door or shouted, he would not respond. Marc called Barbara and Hughie to the house, but he still wouldn't open the door. Hughie told us to go to the airport and get on the flight; he'd make sure Andy made the show.

Jenny and I got a cab to the airport; it was strange boarding a plane with the band but without the star of the show. When we got to the theater, everything was set up and ready to go. We even did a sound check without Andy. I felt sure he wouldn't make the show, but fifteen minutes before show time he stormed in ahead of Marc, Barbara, and Hughie. He had left it so late he had to rent a Learjet.

I'd never seen Andy look this rough. He must have been up for days. When Jenny saw him, she got really upset. Andy pushed past everybody and slammed the door of his dressing room behind him. The way he looked, I didn't think he could perform. Hughie told the band to get ready to play and at exactly eight o'clock I counted in the first song, with Andy nowhere to be seen.

The first song was one of Andy's biggest hits, "I Just Want to Be Your Everything." We started to play the instrumental beginning to the song, and then, miraculously, Andy walked out from behind the side-stage curtain and into a spotlight that was waiting for him.

He was full of energy; he looked immaculate in his stage clothes and didn't miss a beat. I was amazed. He went on to give one of the best performances I'd ever been a part of. The audience was sitting at each side of the center aisle that rose up to the back of the hall. As he sang, he walked up and down the aisle, touching the hands of as many people as he could. Then about halfway through the show he singled out his mother, who was sitting in an aisle seat. Andy introduced Barbara to the audience.

"Now, I know you all have a mom, and I know each one of yours is special, but I want to introduce you to somebody who I think is the most special mother in the world . . . this is my mom. Stand up, Mom." Barbara shyly stood up, turned, and waved to the audience. As she did, the house lights came up a little and the whole audience gave Barbara a huge round of applause. Andy held Barbara's hand and continued to the audience . . .

Jenny and Andy.

"Now I know I can be difficult sometimes, Mom, and like all mothers do, I know sometimes you worry about me. But I just want to tell you that I'm okay and that I love you more than anything in this world." The audience became emotional and let out a collective *awwwww.* "So I'm going to sing a little song for you, Mom. It's a little song made famous by some group called the Bee Gees, whoever they are . . . It's called 'Words.'"

Barbara sat down, and Andy got down on one knee next to his mom. We started playing the intro, and as Andy held Barbara's hand and gazed into her eyes, he began to sing. By the time the song was over, there wasn't a dry eye in the house, or onstage for that matter. I know my eyes were streaming. The audience stood up and wouldn't stop cheering. Andy hugged Barbara and came back onstage.

"And I'd like to thank my wonderful band for believing in me. And to Marc and Jenny and Dad, I love you."

This was Andy's way of apologizing. Backstage, after the show, Andy hugged everybody. It was all very emotional, but for me, unfortunately, it was the beginning of the end.

Some very unsavory characters started showing up at the house. They always ended up in Andy's room downstairs, but we never saw them leave. After midnight most nights, different women would sneak in and out through the basement entrance.

Twice in one month, Andy was rushed to emergency. He was complaining of chest pains and convinced himself he was having a heart attack. After a few days of detoxing in the hospital he would come home and go at it again.

The shows became sparser as Andy spent more and more time downstairs by himself. One time we didn't see him for five days, and I wondered why I was even in Los Angeles. He only came upstairs when he thought nobody was home. When we did bump into him, he'd grab some milk from the fridge and run back downstairs. He couldn't face anyone; he just stayed behind that locked bedroom door.

Finally, I had to do something. I decided I had to talk to him, to find out what was going on. One evening, at about seven o'clock, I knocked on his bedroom door. There was no answer, so I knocked a bit harder, then a lot harder. I shouted, "Andy, I have to talk with you."

"Leave me alone" was all the reply I got.

I was so frustrated I kicked at the door. When I kicked it a second time, I broke the lock and the door opened.

I didn't believe what I was seeing. Andy was sitting on his bed in his robe playing with a real Uzi. There was an almost empty bottle of vodka on the side table and rotting leftover food all over the place. His clothes were strewn everywhere; the room was a complete disaster.

"Get out of my room!" Andy yelled, and stood up. He put down the machine gun and came at me. He pushed me back through the open door, and I pushed him back into the room. He tried to close the door, but I kept pushing back on it. We shoved each other back and forth, but that's as far as it went. Andy wasn't a hitter, thank God, and neither was I. He rushed past me and climbed the stairs as he shouted for Marc.

The next thing I heard was the screeching sound of tires as a car pulled away from the house. Andy didn't come back that night. The next day Marc returned from Barbara and Hughie's house. He told me Andy had fired me, and he wanted me out of the house right away. The next day Jenny and I left for Miami.

About six months later we were over at Barry and Linda's house. As we were leaving, Andy was arriving. He rushed up to Jenny and hugged her tightly. "Hello, my darling," he said. "I've missed you so much." Then he turned to me and reached out his hand. We shook. "No hard feelings, mate?" he asked.

"Never, Andy," I replied, and we hugged. Then Andy looked at me and in a serious voice said, "Den, have you thought about it?"

Not many years later, in 1988, Andy passed away in London as a result of myocarditis, an inflammation of the heart muscle caused by a viral infection, evidently made worse by his years of alcohol and cocaine abuse. The ironic thing is, before he passed he had been through rehab and, I heard, had not had a drink in something like nine months. But he evidently relapsed right before his death. It was a very, very sad day when I got the call saying Andy was gone. All he *ever* wanted was to be the fourth Bee Gee. He had it all — great looks, talent, and singing and songwriting ability. I loved him and still miss him.

CHAPTER 20

The Move
to Nashville

A BIG CHANGE

Over the years, Jenny and I had many incredible times living in Miami. Of course, we had some not-so-great times, too. By 1987, my friendship with Barry had dwindled to almost nothing. I hardly ever saw him or Robin or Maurice. Living on Miami Beach was now super expensive, and I didn't have the income to justify it. Even in those days my property taxes were $12,000 a year, and the upkeep and monthly utilities were just as outrageous. It was a hard decision, but Jenny and I knew it was time for a big change.

In 1988, we put the house on the market; we hoped all the money and hard work we'd put into it would pay off. And it did — we found a buyer, and after commissions, taxes, and paying off all my bills, we walked away with $400,000.

But where to now?

Jenny and I were happy living in America. We both had permanent resident status and didn't even think about moving back to the U.K. We'd always loved Nashville, having been there many times on tour. We'd even spent a week in Nashville on a short vacation. We decided this would be a good place to live. A good friend told us, "If you're thinking of moving to Nashville, go to Franklin first." Franklin is a small town fifteen miles south of Nashville, and we loved it so much we never made it to the city. With the money we had from the sale of our house in Miami, Jenny and I bought a twelve-acre farm just outside the city for $250,000.

It took years, but we renovated the house, and I built a really nice recording studio in the basement. I became a pretty good recording engineer and the plan was to rent my studio out, with me as the engineer. With all my experience in the big studios, I hoped I could make a decent income. It didn't really work out that way. By then, the home studio craze was in, and all the songwriters in Nashville (my target clients) had their own studios at home.

A Canadian production company doing business in Nashville offered me a job as an engineer in their studio. I did that for a few years, but the company folded and I moved back into my home studio. I had a few regular clients whose business helped, but for the most part I was spending more than I was making.

Everybody told me to start playing drums again, but I was too afraid. Music had given me so much, but it took its toll, too. My drums were my dreams, and those dreams had been shattered time and again. I wasn't willing to risk my emotions anymore.

Soon my savings were gone, and I had to get a mortgage on the house to pay the bills. My severance advance from the Bee Gees had been recouped, and I started getting a little money from record sales. It helped, but it wasn't enough to keep us afloat. I built up a huge amount of credit-card debt. Now I had no money for the mortgage payments, so I got more credit cards. I was aware of my financial downward spiral, but there was nothing I could do about it; at least I knew the house was worth more than the debt I was in.

My relationship with Jenny started to suffer. I moved into a separate bedroom, and we argued about money every day. Every night I'd lie in bed worried sick, not knowing where the next mortgage and credit card payments would come from.

Around that time, I recorded a salsa album for a famous producer named Al De Lory. During the sessions, Al brought a singer he was producing into the studio. Her name was Kayte Strong, and she had a fabulous voice. Kayte was also an independent artist; she wrote and recorded much of her music by herself. Kayte sold her CDs at live street shows and open-air festivals, mostly in Florida. She was out on the road more than she was home. And at home, she had a studio almost identical to mine, so we had a lot in common. When Kayte heard some of the drum tracks I'd recorded, she asked me to play and to program drums on all her albums; she always paid me well and in cash. I wound up recording a lot with Kayte, and we had a great time.

One time, I had a big session coming up at my studio and needed to borrow some mics from her. She had given me the keys to her duplex with the understanding that I could use anything in her studio while she was out on the road. So I drove into Nashville and went to Kayte's apartment. I was shocked to see her van parked outside. I thought for sure she'd be on her way to a show.

I knocked on the door but got no reply. I quietly let myself in and saw Kayte completely under the covers of her bed. She wasn't moving. Worried, I gently shook her, and she woke up. She was moaning, and I couldn't understand anything she said. Something was very wrong.

It turned out Kayte was really sick — she had developed pneumonia. In spite of that, she managed to climb out of bed and started getting ready for the 750-mile drive to New York for her next show. I told her she couldn't go and to get back into bed, and we had a big argument, because she didn't want to disappoint the people who ran the show. To make matters worse, it was only two weeks after 9/11. The promoter didn't believe she was truly sick — he thought she was making an excuse not to come to New York City.

I had no right to be so forceful. After all, we were only friends. But I bullied her into staying home and getting well. I drove into Nashville every day from Franklin to bring Kayte food and plenty of liquids. After a week in bed, she still wasn't completely over it — but she was a lot better.

Her next show was a huge three-day festival in Letchworth State Park, in upstate New York, near Buffalo. Kayte had never played this venue before. I was worried about her driving by herself more than 700 miles to do the show. She said if I were willing, she'd fly me up, and I could help her set up her tent and sell her CDs — and she'd pay me $500 cash. I desperately needed the money, so I said yes.

When I arrived at the park the day before the show, Kayte had already set up her tent and tables that displayed her collection of CDs. She also had a keyboard and a microphone connected to a full PA system. This was a complicated setup, and I had no idea this was what she did on the weekends. It was a lot of work for one person.

The next day, the festival was packed. People had come from miles around. This show was held every year on the same weekend and attracted thousands and thousands of music fans. As soon as Kayte started singing, the people started buying. For three days, there were always at least fifty people in front of our tent. They had cash in their hands and were clamoring to buy Kayte's music.

In the end, we sold $7,000 worth of CDs, nearly all in cash. Kayte told me this had been her biggest show ever and asked if I'd like to come out with her again. I'd had a great time, and we really needed the money, so I said yes. I went out with Kayte every weekend for the next three months. I was only making $2,000 a month, but it was enough to pay most of the bills at the house.

Kayte hadn't had a new album out for a while, and most of her fans had all the CDs she had to offer. For a while, income at the shows wasn't good, but Kayte always paid me before she paid her bills.

We did a show in Kissimmee, Florida, just below Orlando. It was well attended, but hardly anybody bought Kayte's music. I think we sold about fifteen CDs all day. We didn't have the money to eat at a restaurant that night so we had a snack at the motel. Kayte was having financial problems, too, and the diminished CD sales weren't helping. She became very upset and started to cry, and I put my arms around her to comfort her. I'd hugged Kayte a thousand times without having a single, romantic thought, but something was different this time. We stayed locked in each other's arms, and I kissed her tears away. I had no control over what happened next and neither did Kayte. We started to kiss and before very long we made a very big mistake.

The next day at the show, all I could do was apologize, and all Kayte could do was cry. On the drive back to Nashville that night we hardly said a word to each other. When we arrived at my house, Kayte dropped me off as usual, and when I walked in the front door, the first thing Jenny said was, "What's happened, are you all right? Something's wrong." How did she know?

The next weekend Kayte and I had a two-day drive to Phoenix, Arizona. Over the miles we tried to fathom why we did what we did, in an intellectual way. But something had changed. We were growing closer — but on another level.

At the hotel in Phoenix, we couldn't stay out of each other's arms; it happened again. I'd never felt anything as powerful as this before; I had no control over my emotions whatsoever. Again, we were both crushed. Kayte thought it would be a good idea for me to fly back to Nashville and leave her behind, so I agreed.

When I got home, Jenny wanted to know why I'd returned so soon. I told her there were no people at the show, and Kayte couldn't justify paying me. I don't know how, but somehow Jenny knew exactly what was going on. She asked me if I had any other feelings for Kayte besides friendship. Like a fool, I said I did.

Later that day, when I came back from the supermarket, Jenny was waiting for me with two of my suitcases packed full. She had a pile of unopened bills in her hand and threw the envelopes right in my face. "Now fuck off and don't come back, you bastard!"

I didn't know what to do; I drove into Nashville. I don't know how, but I ended up at Riverfront Park at the end of Broadway. I stood there gazing out over the Cumberland River and remembered dreaming of living here back in March of '73. I had never felt so far from home.

I went to the McDonald's on Broadway and sat down with a cup of coffee. I was a long way from being homeless, but *my God*, this was close to what it must feel like. I called my friend Cathryn in Nashville and told her what had happened. She told me to come right over, I could stay with her until I found somewhere, or until Jenny took me back. *Fat chance of that happening.*

After a brief time at Cathryn's, I wound up staying with my friend Sina in Goodlettsville for four months, until I was able to find an apartment of my own. Kayte and I resumed our friendship, and I started working for her again. Jenny wouldn't answer the phone when I called, but every week I went to the house to pick up the bills and leave $200 in cash on the kitchen table.

We put the house on the market and when it sold I was able to pay off the mortgage and all the credit cards. Jenny and I divided the remaining $400,000 equally. She moved into her own house in Hillsboro Village near downtown Nashville, while I stayed in my newly rented apartment in Green Hills.

For the first year apart, Jenny was very aggressive and screamed about lawyers and divorce. She said it was entirely my fault, and she was going to sue me for millions. *I was guilty, and yes, it was all my fault.* I don't know where she thought I would get the millions from, though. I tried to go to her house at least once a week for a chat and a glass of wine. After a couple of years she had mellowed and we started to laugh again. By 2003, we'd go for a curry lunch every Tuesday — without fail — with Jenny's new friends and some of our old ones.

One of our old friends from Franklin was a Canadian lady named Shirley King. Jenny and Shirley had become best friends, and Jenny had leaned on her heavily during the time of our breakup. One day Jenny called me on the phone and told me Shirley had been diagnosed with ALS.

Amyotrophic Lateral Sclerosis is a lethal neurodegenerative disease that destroys the nerve cells in the brain and muscles throughout the body. In time, Shirley would become totally paralyzed. There was nothing anybody could do. Shirley had a caretaker who moved into her house to give her the help she so desperately needed. Jenny and I visited her at least once a week to offer love and moral support; it was heartbreaking to watch her body deteriorate.

Jenny and I began to hang out more and more. I took her shopping and out for dinner at least five times a week. I was still working with Kayte but only in the studio; now we just wrote and recorded together. Kayte's business was never part of any conversation I had with Jenny, but whenever Kayte paid me, I always gave half to Jen.

In December of 2008, I was writing with Kayte at her apartment in Green Hills, when my cell phone rang. I saw it was Jenny. "Hi, Jen . . ."

Nothing on the other end.

"Hi, Jen . . ."

Nothing again.

"Jenny, is everything all right?"

"I've got a lump."

I told Kayte about the terror I heard in Jenny's voice as she uttered those four words. I dropped what I was doing and rushed to Jenny's side. She asked me to take her to a local walk-in medical center that we both used. I called my doctor; he told me to bring Jenny in straight away.

After an examination and some x-rays he told us the news wasn't good. He thought Jenny had breast cancer. He made some phone calls and made an appointment with — in his opinion — the very best oncologist in Nashville. The appointment was for nine o'clock the next morning. I took Jenny home and spent the night in her spare bedroom.

The next morning we went to Baptist Hospital Cancer Center in Nashville. The waiting room was filled with people who looked as scared as we felt. After signing in and waiting an agonizing forty-five minutes, Jenny's name was finally called. We were led down a corridor to a large square reception area; in the middle of the workplace were at least eight to ten medical assistants and nurses sitting at desks in front of computers.

The huge back wall was made of glass, and behind the glass were rows of people hooked up to large medical drip bags hanging from stands next to them. Most of the women had colorful bandanas covering their heads. I'd never been in a place that felt so dark.

Jenny and I were led down another corridor and into a small waiting room. We sat in this tiny space for another hour until, finally, Jenny's doctor entered the room, carrying Jenny's x-rays. She introduced herself as Dr. Nancy Peacock. She had a very nice manner, but she was all business — *that,* I liked. She said that, from examining the x-rays, it looked like advanced level two, or low level three, breast cancer. She told us this was just a guess at this point; she would have to do a lot more tests. She said if her assumption was correct she would like to start Jenny on a continuous infusion of chemotherapy treatment right away.

Later that day I went to Kayte's apartment and told her the bad news. We hugged, and at Kayte's suggestion, we agreed that the best thing to do was to give up any feelings we had for each other, so I could be with Jenny. We both thought we should go our own separate ways. And so Kayte and I parted.

I asked Jenny if she wanted me to move in with her. She said yes and with that I gave up my apartment in Green Hills.

The next thing I knew we were on a plane to Miami. Barry and Linda had paid for the flights. Linda wanted to be with Jenny before she began chemotherapy the following week. We had a nice time in Miami, and it was good to see Barry and Linda again. Barry was performing at the Love and Hope Ball, a diabetes research fundraiser that he sponsored every year.

Jenny and Linda had a lot to catch up on. It was great to see them together again. Olivia Newton-John was in town and came to see Barry and Linda, and Olivia and Jenny went off to have a private talk. Olivia is a breast cancer survivor, and her empathy meant so much to Jenny. They spent a lot of time together. We also met T.G. Sheppard and his wife, Kelly Lang, from Nashville, who were also very supportive.

On Friday, March 6, 2009, at 6 a.m., we left Jenny's house in Nashville for Baptist Hospital; she was about to begin chemotherapy treatment. Before we drove off, we had a moment of silence in the car outside the house. When we were done, we looked at each other and slapped a high-five: *Let's do it!*

The chemotherapy room was bigger than it looked from the reception area. It could hold more than twenty patients, and most of the chairs were occupied. A nurse placed a needle into Jenny's arm and connected it to a tube. Then she connected the tube to an intravenous drip. The treatment lasted for about two hours.

We knew Jenny would lose her hair. She had already had it cut from waist-length to just above her shoulders in anticipation of it falling out. The nurse told us with this type of chemotherapy her hair would start to fall in eleven days. On Tuesday, March 17, at 8 a.m., Jenny came into my bedroom. She was clutching a handful of her hair and crying.

I started to cry, too. I didn't know what to do . . . Then, as if a guardian angel had touched me, I had it. "Come on, luv, let's go into the bathroom."

I picked up a pair of sharp scissors and took Jenny into the shower. As the warm water ran over us, I cut off all of her beautiful hair. A lot of it came out by itself, but when I was finished, it was all gone. I dried her off in a big white fluffy towel and sat her down in front of the television. I went into the kitchen and made a lovely pot of tea for us. I remembered what George told me so long ago: "*A hot cuppa tea always fixes things, ya-noo.*" When it was ready, I served Jen tea and biscuits in front of the television. She told me she was afraid to look into the mirror. She looked beautiful, and I told her so. She didn't believe me, so I told her a couple of Yul Brynner jokes. She slapped my hand and threw the biscuits at me. She was starting to feel better. I went back into the bathroom and made sure I cleaned up every single strand of Jenny's hair.

Jenny had an eight-week course of chemotherapy; I sat by her side at every one. One day, while she was getting chemo, Jenny had a visit from Kelly Lang and T.G. Sheppard. It meant so much to her. A local cancer survivor group had given her an assortment of wigs, but she didn't feel comfortable in any of them. The skin on her head was beautiful, not a bump or blemish. She started wearing headscarves and didn't care what anybody thought.

Over the next few months, her hair started growing back, and the fire was back in her attitude. Sadly, our friend Shirley wasn't doing as well. Jenny made sure she went to every doctor's appointment with Shirley, who was now in an electric wheelchair permanently.

Shirley never got along with her caretaker; they were always fighting. One Wednesday afternoon in July, when we drove to Franklin to spend some time with Shirley, her caretaker was walking out as we were walking in. She was carrying her suitcase and had somebody waiting in a car outside. The caretaker slammed the door behind her, and Shirley was left sitting in her wheelchair crying. They'd had a big fight, and the caretaker had had enough.

Shirley didn't know what she was going to do now that she didn't have anybody to take care of her. She had no family in America, and because of the ALS, she had no close friends except for Wayne and Lesa, a couple of her neighbors, and Jenny. Jenny held her hand and tried to comfort her. "What am I going to do?" Shirley cried.

"Don't worry, Shirley. Dennis will take care of you," Jenny said. *What!?*

"It'll only be for a little while, Den, just until I can get somebody," Shirley said.

Shirley was in a desperate situation, and Jenny was getting better. I said, "You'll have to show me everything; I've never done anything like this before . . . Okay, I'll do my best."

I drove Jenny into Nashville, picked up some clothes, and drove back to Shirley's house. We drank beer and watched television until it was time for Shirley to go bed. She had a big double bed in her bedroom, but because she couldn't stand, she slept in her wheelchair.

The chair was an electric model made in Europe. It cost $53,000 and had been donated by the ALS foundation. It could do anything. Shirley controlled it with a small joystick on the left-hand armrest.

Shirley steered the way into her bedroom, and I followed. She told me her nightgown was in the bottom drawer of a chest next to the television. I opened the drawer and pulled out a clean nightgown. Now came the part I wasn't sure about.

"You're gonna have to tell me what to do, Shirley."

"Take my blouse off and put the nightgown over my head."

I started to undo the buttons on Shirley's blouse. When the buttons were all unfastened, I opened up her top. To say we were both embarrassed would be the understatement of the century. I didn't know where to look or what to say and neither did Shirley. As quickly as I could, I slipped her blouse off and dropped the nightgown over her head and covered her up.

The bedroom was filled with an awkward silence. Then it came to me.

"Nice tits, Shirley." We both started to laugh.

"Keep your eyes to yourself," she replied. And with that, the awkwardness was broken.

Now it was time to take Shirley to the bathroom for the first time. I'm not going into any details about this side of my care for Shirley. Anybody who takes care of a person with ALS or looks after somebody with a debilitating disease will know how hard this was for us.

Afterwards, Shirley was able to wash her hands and clean her teeth before bed. I gave her her medication and sleeping pills before covering her in a blanket. I turned on the television in the bedroom and made sure she had the remote and a good pile of tissues.

"Goodnight, Shirley."

"Goodnight, Den. Thank you."

After a month of my caring for Shirley, she called Jenny and me together for a meeting. She told us that in her life, she had only one wish left: she wanted to die at home. She didn't want to pass in a hospital bed. She told us if we could make that happen, she would leave the house to Jenny.

I was sure Jenny was going to beat the cancer, and this would be a good place for her to live, so I agreed to care for Shirley for as long as it took.

As the months rolled by, Shirley's ALS got worse, and Jenny's cancer wasn't in the kind of remission we'd hoped for. Jenny was now undergoing a course of radiation therapy. I wasn't allowed to go with her while she had the treatment; I had to stay in the waiting room. She handled it well and didn't experience nausea.

I was making all the medical appointments with both Jenny and Shirley. Some days I'd drive into Nashville and back two times, a forty-five-minute trip each way, and longer during rush hour. I wanted Jenny to move into the house with Shirley and me, but she was adamant about retaining her independence and keeping her home in Nashville.

The first few months of 2010 were not good, as Jenny's and Shirley's conditions both worsened. Shirley had now lost all movement in her arms, and could hardly hold her head up. I was feeding her with a spoon, and hospice was coming to the house twice a week to bathe her in her wheelchair.

Meanwhile, Jenny's cancer had spread to her lymph nodes, to her other breast, and was now in her bones. She looked like a skeleton.

On May 3, 2010, at her home in Franklin, Shirley died of complications from ALS. Jenny and I were with her as she passed. I held one of her hands; Jenny held the other. Shirley got her wish.

By this time Jenny couldn't eat at all; I had to feed her by tube twice a day, but that wasn't helping. She was admitted into the hospital at the end of May. Her sister and brother-in-law flew in from England. Linda came to the hospital with Maurice's wife, Yvonne, Jenny's friend Noeleen, and Barry and Linda's daughter-in-law, Therese. It really gave her a boost to see everybody, especially Linda.

I spent the last week of Jenny's life by her bedside, holding her hand; she was in an induced coma, on the sixth floor at Baptist Hospital. Her last wishes were simple: she wanted to be cremated, and she wanted me to take her ashes home to England.

On Friday, June 11, 2010, at 5:45 p.m., with me and her friend Chrissie Wold holding her hands, Jenny slipped away.

EPILOGUE

I was in a state of depression. It seemed I'd lost everything worthwhile in my life, and now here I was alone. I did have three friends: Shirley's dog Natchez (an Australian Shepherd mix), her cat George (a large tabby), and Jenny's cat Doody, a nineteen-year-old tortoiseshell. I adopted all three and tried to keep busy. I started moving everything out of Jenny's house in Nashville. I didn't know how one person could have so much stuff. I boxed everything up and brought it to the house in Franklin. Now I had all of Shirley's belongings, all of Jenny's belongings, and my stuff too. The house was stuffed, but at least it was all in one place.

I didn't think I would stay in Shirley's old house; it held so many bad memories. But the more time I spent with the animals, the more it felt like home. I was drained. When I made up my mind to stay, I transferred Shirley's mortgage into my name. I started to paint the inside of the house and soon it felt like my own place. I still get a little wistful about the way everything worked out. This house had been meant for Jenny.

Four months later I called Kayte and invited her to the house for dinner. I cleaned for a week and filled the place with flickering candles. She loved it. I persuaded her to move out of her duplex in Green Hills

Me and Kayte. BEV MOSER

and move in with me. I told her she could have all the space upstairs: two bedrooms, a bathroom, and a huge bonus room that was big enough for her studio and someday a full-sized grand piano. Now she has that piano of her dreams.

I asked Kayte to marry me as we were packing up all of her things in front of her duplex. She said yes. But when? *That* was the big question. How much time has to pass after losing one's spouse before it's respectful to remarry? A year? Two years? Five years? That question would be answered for me in October 2011, when I was diagnosed with an aggressive form of prostate cancer.

A few months later — on December 23 — Kayte and I drove down to

Vero Beach, Florida. We stayed with our best friends Rick Monday and his wife, Barbaralee. Rick is a legendary baseball player. He played for the Dodgers and became a national hero when he saved the American flag as somebody tried to burn it during a game.

Kayte and I couldn't be prouder that Rick was my best man and Barbaralee was her maid of honor. We got married on the beach at sunset with people waving from their balconies in the hotels behind us. So much for a private ceremony!

In March 2012, I had an operation to remove my prostate. A wonderful doctor named Joseph A. Smith, Jr., at Vanderbilt University Hospital in Nashville supervised the operation, but a very friendly robot computer I named Hal performed it. *"Thank you, Hal."*

I've been asked over the years: what happened to the Bee Gees after the *Spirits Having Flown* album — was my absence a factor? That's really not for me to say. But the truth is, I was fortunate enough to have played on the biggest records of their career.

I pretty much gave up the drums after playing on Kayte's last studio album in 2010. Although, once a drummer, always a drummer. I'm just waiting for the right band to come along.

Just a last mention of the other two band members: after I left Miami for Nashville in 1988, Alan Kendall went back on tour with the brothers, before moving on; Blue sold his house in Miami, moved back to London, then Spain.

As for Arthur Dakin, the boarder at my parents' B&B who'd been responsible for my becoming a drummer . . . One day in 2002, after a huge storm, Arthur was driving on a flooded road near his home in London. His car was washed away and he drowned. I was saddened to hear of his death, for it meant I would never be able to tell him how much he had inspired me and how my life became magical because of him.

R.I.P. Arthur Dakin.

On July 26, 2013, I received my Certificate of Naturalization and proudly took my place as an American citizen.

What's next? *Maybe it's time to pull out those dreams again . . .*

ACKNOWLEDGMENTS Special
thanks to:

MY WIFE
Kayte Bryon: for your encouragement, inspiration, energy, and love.

MY BUSINESS MANAGER
Alice Sells: for your wisdom, vision, guidance, and friendship.

MY AGENT
Anne Devlin: for believing in my life story, and in me as an author.

MY DEVELOPMENTAL EDITOR
Dave Carew: for your talent, mentoring, patience, and commitment.

Published by ECW Press
665 Gerrard Street East
Toronto, ON M4M 1Y2
416-694-3348 / info@ecwpress.com

To the best of his abilities, the author has related
experiences, places, people, and organizations
from his memories of them. In order to protect
the privacy of others, he has, in some instances,
changed the names of certain people and
details of events and places.

LIBRARY AND ARCHIVES CANADA
CATALOGUING IN PUBLICATION

Bryon, Dennis, author
You should be dancing : my life with
the Bee Gees / written by Dennis Bryon.

Issued in print and electronic format.
ISBN 978-1-77041-242-2 (pbk)
978-1-77090-766-9 (pdf)
978-1-77090-767-6 (epub)

1. Bryon, Dennis. 2. Drummers (Musicians)
—United States—Biography. 3. Bee Gees.
4. Rock musicians—Biography.

I. Title.

ML421.B43B92 2015   782.42166092'2
C2015-902817-5   C2015-902818-3

Cover design: David Gee
Cover image: Bob Sherman
Author photo: Bev Moser

Unless otherwise stated, interior images are from the author's personal collection. Every reasonable
effort has been made to locate the copyright holders of materials reprinted in this book. In the event
of an error or omission, please notify the publisher.

Printed and bound in Canada   Printing: Marquis   1   2   3   4   5